THE CULTURAL ORIGINS

OF THE FRENCH REVOLUTION

A BOOK IN THE SERIES

BICENTENNIAL REFLECTIONS ON THE FRENCH REVOLUTION

General Editors: Keith Michael Baker, Stanford University
Steven Laurence Kaplan, Cornell University

Soldiers of the French Revolution, Alan Forrest
Revolutionary News: The Press in France 1789–1799, Jeremy Popkin

THE CULTURAL ORIGINS
OF THE FRENCH REVOLUTION

Roger Chartier

Translated by Lydia G. Cochrane

DUKE UNIVERSITY PRESS

Durham and London

1991

© 1991 Duke University Press
All rights reserved
Printed in the United States of America
on acid-free paper ∞
Library of Congress Cataloging-in-Publication Data
appear on the last printed page of this book.
This translation has been made possible in part by a
grant from the Wheatland Foundation, New York.

For Isabelle

CONTENTS

ACKNOWLEDGMENTS

THE REFLECTIONS OFFERED IN THIS VOLUME HAVE much benefited from the criticisms and suggestions of the participants in my seminar at the Ecole des Hautes Etudes en Sciences Sociales. This is thus their book as well as mine.

I would also like to thank the students at Cornell University who were the first to hear and discuss the drafts of these chapters during a seminar held at Cornell between January and May 1988, where I was invited to be the first Luigi Einaudi Professor in European and International Studies.

My gratitude goes to all those, on both sides of the Atlantic, who encouraged me, after my lectures or after reading my articles, with observations on certain of the ideas that appear in this book today.

Finally, I express my thanks to the first readers of this manuscript—my friends Keith M. Baker and Steven L. Kaplan—and acknowledge my debt to Robert Darnton, who has been a close companion in work and debate for twenty years.

EDITORS' INTRODUCTION

I N PARIS, IN THIS SYMBOLIC NIGHT OF 14 JULY, NIGHT of fervor and of joy, at the foot of the timeless obelisk, in this Place de la Concorde that has never been more worthy of the name, [a] great and immense voice . . . will cast to the four winds of history the song expressing the ideal of the five hundred Marseillais of 1792." The words, so redolent in language and tone of the instructions for the great public festivals of the French Revolution, are those of Jack Lang, French Minister of Culture, Communications, Great Public Works, and the Bicentennial. The text is that of the program for the grandiose opera-parade presenting "a Marseillaise for the World," the internationally televised spectacle from Paris crowning the official celebration of the bicentennial of the French Revolution.

The minister's language was aptly fashioned to the occasion. It was well chosen to celebrate Paris as world-historical city—joyous birthplace of the modern principles of democracy and human rights—and the Revolution of 1789 as the momentous assertion of those universal human aspirations to freedom and dignity that have transformed, and are still transforming, an entire world. It was no less well chosen to leap over the events of the Revolution from its beginning to its end, affirming that the political passions engendered by its momentous struggles had finally ceased to divide the French one from another.

The spectacle on the Place de la Concorde exemplified the unavowed motto of the official bicentennial celebration: "The Revolution is over." Opting for a celebration consonant with the predomi-

xii   Editors' Introduction

nantly centrist, consensualist mood of the French in the late 1980s, the presidential mission charged with the organization of the bicentennial celebrations focused on the values which the vast majority of French citizens of all political persuasions underwrite—the ideals exalted in the Declaration of the Rights of Man. It offered the nation—and the world—the image of a France finally at peace with itself: a people secure in the tranquil enjoyment of the human rights that constitute France's true revolutionary patrimony, confident in the maturity of French institutions and their readiness to meet the challenges and opportunities of a new European order, firm in the country's dedication to securing universal respect for the democratic creed it claims as its most fundamental contribution to the world of nations. No hint of subsequent radicalization, no echo of social conflict, no shadow of the Terror could mar this season of commemoration. It followed that the traditional protagonists and proxies in the great debate over the Revolution's character and purposes, Danton and Robespierre, were to be set aside. The hero for 1989 was Condorcet: savant, philosopher, reformer, "moderate" revolutionary, victim of the Revolution he failed to perfect and control.

But the Revolution—ambiguous, complex, subversive as it remains, even after two hundred years—still proved refractory to domestication. Not even the solemn bicentennial spectacle on the night of 14 July was sheltered from certain treacherous counterpoints. Spectators watching the stirring parade unfold down the Champs-Élysées toward the Place de la Concorde already knew that this same route would shortly be followed by participants in a counterrevolutionary commemoration returning a simulacrum of the guillotine to its most notorious revolutionary site. These spectators were moved by the poignant march of Chinese youths pushing their bicycles in evocation of the recent massacre in Tienanmen Square, even as this brutal silencing of demands for human rights was being justified in Beijing as reluctant defense of the Revolution against dangerous counterrevolutionary elements. The spectators were stirred by Jessye Norman's heroic rendition of the *Marseillaise,* even as it reminded all who cared to attend to its words that this now universal chant of liberation was also a ferocious war song calling for the letting of the "impure blood" of the enemy. On the very day of the parade a politely exasperated Margaret Thatcher, publicly contesting the French claim to the paternity of the Rights of Man and insisting on the identity of Revolution with Terror, reminded the world of the jolting equation, $1789 = 1793$. For their part, the performers sent by the USSR to march in the parade, garbed in dress more Russian than Soviet, raised questions about the socialist axiom that the Russian Revolution was the necessary conclusion to the French. As men and women throughout the communist world rallied for human rights, was it any longer possible to see 1917 as the authentic future of 1789?

The tensions and contradictions of commemoration have their own political and cultural dynamic, but they are nourished by the tensions and contradictions of historical interpretation. If the Revolution has been declared over in France, its history is far from terminated—either there or elsewhere. Indeed, the bicentennial of the French Revolution has reopened passionate historiographical debates over its meaning that began with the Revolution itself. As early as September 1789, readers of the *Révolutions de Paris*—one of the earliest and most widely read of the newspapers that were to play so powerful a role in shaping the revolutionary consciousness—were demanding "a historical and political picture of everything that has happened in France since the first Assembly of Notables," to be offered as a means of explaining the nature of "the astonishing revolution that has just taken place." Observers and participants alike sought from the outset to grasp the causes, nature, and effects of these remarkable events. And if they concurred on the momentous character of the Revolution, they differed vehemently on its necessity, its means, its fundamental mission. Burke and Paine, Barnave and de Maistre, Condorcet and Hegel were only among the first in a dazzling succession of thinkers who have responded to the need to plumb the historical identity and significance of a phenomenon that has seemed from its very beginning to demand, yet defy, historical comprehension.

This rich tradition of political-philosophical history of the Revolution, which resounded throughout the nineteenth century, was muted and profoundly modified in the wake of the centennial celebrations. In France, 1889 inaugurated a new age in revolutionary historiography dedicated to that marriage between republicanism and positivism that underlay the very creation of the Third Republic.

This marriage gave birth, within the university, to the new Chair in the History of the French Revolution at the Sorbonne to which Alphonse Aulard was elected in 1891. From this position, occupied for more than thirty years, Aulard directed the first scholarly journal devoted to the study of the Revolution, presided over the preparation and publication of the great official collections of revolutionary documents, and formed students to spread the republican-positivist gospel. He established and institutionalized within the university system an official, putatively scientific history: a history dedicated to discovering and justifying, in the history of the Revolution, the creation of those republican, parliamentary institutions whose promise was now finally being secured in more felicitous circumstances. Danton, the patriot determined in 1793 to institute the emergency government of the Terror to save the Republic in danger, but opposed in 1794 to continuing it once that danger had eased, became the hero of Aulard's French Revolution.

Given his institutional authority, his posture as scientific historian, and his engaged republicanism, Aulard was able to marginalize conservative interpretations of the Revolution, ridiculing the amateurism of Hippolyte Taine's frightened account of its origins in the philosophic spirit and culmination in the horrors of mass violence, and dismissing, as little more than reactionary ideology, Augustin Cochin's analysis of the genesis and implications of Jacobin sociability. Within the university, the revolutionary heritage became a patrimony to be managed, rather than merely a creed to be inculcated. But this did not preclude bitter divisions over the manner in which that patrimony was to be managed, or its now sacred resources deployed. Aulard's most talented student, Albert Mathiez, became his most virulent critic. The rift was more than an oedipal conflict over the republican mother, Marianne. Mathiez questioned Aulard's scientific methods; but above all, he detested his mentor's Dantonist moderation. As an alternative to an opportunistic, demagogic, and traitorous Danton, he offered an Incorruptible, Robespierre, around whom he crafted a popular, socialist, and Leninist reading of the Revolution. The Bolshevik experience reinforced his Robespierrism, investing it with a millennial hue, and stimulated him to undertake his most original work on the "social movement" of the Terror. Thereafter the relationship between the Russian Revolution and the

French Revolution, between 1917 and 1793, haunted the Marxian-ized republican interpretation to which Mathiez devoted his career.

Although Mathiez was denied Aulard's coveted chair, he taught in the same university until his early death. His exact contemporary, Georges Lefebvre, shared much of his political sensibility and his interest in history from below, and succeeded him as president of the Society for Robespierrist Studies. Lefebvre's election to the Sorbonne chair in 1937 proved decisive for the consolidation, and indeed the triumph, of a social interpretation of the French Revolution based on the principles of historical materialism. More sociological than Mathiez in his approach, and more nuanced in his judgments, he broke fresh ground with his monumental work on the peasants (whose autonomy and individuality he restituted) and his subsequent studies of social structure; and he rescued important issues from vain po-lemics. His rigor, his pedagogical talent, and the muted quality of his Marxism—most effectively embodied in the celebrated study of 1789 he published for the sesquicentennial of the French Revolution in 1939—earned him, his chair, and the interpretation he promoted worldwide prestige. After 1945, and until his death in 1959, he presided over international research in the field as director of his Institute for the History of the French Revolution at the Sorbonne. Under Lefebvre's aegis, the Marxianized republican interpretation of the French Revolution became the dominant paradigm of revolution-ary historiography in France following the Second World War; and it was largely adopted, from the French leaders in the field, by the growing number of historians specializing in the subject who became so striking a feature of postwar academic expansion, particularly in English-speaking countries.

Lefebvre conveyed his mantle of leadership to his student, Albert Soboul, who succeeded to the Sorbonne chair in 1967. Soboul owed his scholarly fame above all to his pioneering thesis on the Parisian sansculottes, a work recently subjected to severe criticism of its sociological and ideological analyses, its understanding of the world of work, and its often teleological and tautological methods. But his influence far transcended this acclaimed monograph. A highly placed member of the French Communist party as well as director of the In-stitute for the History of the French Revolution, Soboul saw himself as both a "scientific" and a "communist-revolutionary" historian.

Tireless, ubiquitous, and prolific, he tenaciously rehearsed the Marxist account of the French Revolution as a bourgeois revolution inscribed in the logic of the necessary transition from feudalism to capitalism. But his relish for confrontation, and his assertive defense of an increasingly rigid orthodoxy, eventually invited—and made him the chief target of—the revisionist assault on the dominant interpretation of the Revolution as mechanistic, reductive, and erroneous.

Challenges to the hegemony of the Sorbonne version of the history of the French Revolution were offered in the late 1950s and early 1960s by Robert Palmer's attempt to shift attention toward the democratic politics of an Atlantic Revolution and, more fundamentally, by Alfred Cobban's frontal assault on the methodological and political assumptions of the Marxist interpretation. But such was the power of the scholarly consensus that, condemned more or less blithely in Paris, these works drew relatively little immediate support. Not until the late 1960s and early 1970s did the revisionist current acquire an indigenous French base, both intellectual and institutional. The charge was led by François Furet, who left the Communist party in 1956 and has subsequently gravitated toward the liberal political center. One of the first French historians to become intimately familiar with Anglo-American scholarship (and with American life more generally), Furet served as the third president of the École des Hautes Études en Sciences Sociales, accelerating its development into one of Europe's leading centers for research in the social sciences and humanities—and a formidable institutional rival to the Sorbonne. Disenchanted with Marxism, he also turned away from the *Annales* tradition of quantitative social and cultural history vigorously espoused in his earlier work. For the past fifteen years he has sustained a devastating critique of the Jacobin-Leninist "catechism," redirecting scholarly attention to the dynamics of the Revolution as an essentially political and cultural phenomenon; to the logic, contradictions, and pathos of its invention of democratic sociability; to its fecundity as a problem for the political and philosophical inquiries of the nineteenth century upon whose inspiration he insists historians must draw.

It is one of the great ironies of revolutionary historiography, then, that whereas the centennial of the Revolution inaugurated the consolidation of the official republican exegesis, so the bicentennial has marked the distintegration of its Marxist descendant. The field of inquiry is now more open, more fluid, more exciting than it has been for many decades. By the same token, it is also shaped by concerns and sensibilities deriving from recent changes and experiences. These latter are many and varied. Any comprehensive list would have to include the eclipse of Marxism as an intellectual and political force; the dramatic decline in the fortunes of communism, especially in France; the resurgence of liberalism in the West, with its rehabilitation of the market as model and morality, asserting the intrinsic connection between political liberty and laissez-faire; the dramatic shifts in the East from Gulag to glasnost and perestroika, from Maoism to Westernization, with their oblique and overt avowals of communist failure and ignominy extending from Warsaw to Moscow to Beijing. But such a list could not omit the memory of the Holocaust and the traumas of decolonization among colonized and colonizers alike, from the Algerian War to the sanguinary horrors of Polpotism. It would have to include the stunning triumph and the subsequent exhaustion of the *Annales* paradigm, with its metaphor of levels of determination privileging a long-run perspective and quantitative techniques; the emergence of a new cultural history, pluralistic and aggressive, fueled by diverse disciplinary and counter-disciplinary energies; the striking development of the École des Hautes Études en Sciences Sociales as counterweight to the traditional French university; and the efflorescence of a tradition of French historical studies outside France whose challenge to Parisian hegemony in the field can no longer be ignored. Neither could it neglect the dramatic eruption of the revolutionary imagination in the events of 1968, and the new radical politics of race, sex, and gender that have become so profound a preoccupation in subsequent decades.

The implications of this new situation for the study of the French Revolution are profound. Many fundamental assumptions, not only about the Revolution itself but about how to study it, have been called into question. Though the Revolution is better known today than ever before, the collapse of the hegemonic structure of learning and interpretation has revealed egregious blind spots in what has hitherto counted for knowledge and understanding. While the republican-Marxist view innovated in certain areas, it sterilized research in many others. Today it is no longer possible to evoke complaisantly the bourgeois character of the Revolution, either in terms of causes or effects; the roles, indeed the very definition, of other social actors need to be reexamined. A rehabilitated political approach is avidly reoccupying the ground of a social interpretation in serious need of reformulation. Questions of ideology, discourse, gender, and cultural practices have surged to the forefront in fresh ways. Fewer and fewer historians are willing to accept or reject the Revolution "en bloc," while more and more are concerned with the need to fathom and connect its multiple and contradictory components. The Terror has lost the benefit of its relative immunity and isolation. And despite extravagant and often pathetic hyperbole, the Right has won its point that the Vendée in particular—and the counterrevolutionary experience in general—require more probing and balanced treatment, as do the post-Thermidorian terrors. Finally, there is a widespread sense that the narrow periodization of Revolutionary studies must be substantially broadened.

When the bicentennial dust settles, there will therefore be much for historians of the French Revolution to do. Many questions will require genuinely critical research and discussion, searching reassessment, vigorous and original synthesis. Our ambition in editing these Bicentennial Reflections on the French Revolution is to contribute to this endeavor. In organizing the series, which will comprise twelve volumes, we have sought to identify fundamental issues and problems—problems that have hitherto been treated in fragmentary fashion; issues around which conventional wisdom has disintegrated in the course of current debates—which will be crucial to any new account of the French Revolution. And we have turned to some of the finest historians in what has become an increasingly international field of study, asking them to reassess their own understanding of these matters in the light of their personal research and that of others, and to present the results of their reflections to a wider audience in relatively short, synthetic works that will also offer a critical point of departure for further work in the field. The authors share with us the belief that the time is ripe for a fundamental rethinking. They will of course proceed with this rethinking in their own particular fashion.

The events that began to unfold in France in 1789 have, for two hundred years, occupied a privileged historical site. The bicentennial has served as a dramatic reminder that not only our modern notions of revolution and human rights, but the entire range of our political discourse derives from them. The French Revolution has been to the modern world what Greece and Rome were to the Renaissance and its heirs: a condensed world of acts and events, passions and struggles, meanings and symbols, constantly reconsidered and reimagined in the attempt to frame—and implement—an understanding of the nature, conditions, and possibilities of human action in their relation to politics, culture, and social process. To those who would change the world, the Revolution still offers a script continuously elaborated and extended—in parliaments and prisons; in newspapers and manifestoes; in revolutions and repressions; in families, armies, and encounter groups. . . . To those who would interpret the world, it still presents the inexhaustible challenge of comprehending the nature of the extraordinary mutation that gave birth to the modern world.

"Great year! You will be the *regenerating year,* and you will be known by that name. History will extol your great deeds," wrote Louis-Sébastien Mercier, literary anatomist of eighteenth-century Paris, in a rhapsodic *Farewell to the Year 1789.* "You have changed *my Paris,* it is true. It is completely different today. . . . For thirty years I have had a secret presentiment that I would not die without witnessing a great political event. I nourished my spirit on it: there is *something new* for my pen. If *my Tableau* must be *redone,* at least it will be said one day: In this year Parisians . . . stirred, and this impulse has been communicated to France and the rest of Europe." Historians of the French Revolution may not bid farewell to the bicentennial year in Mercier's rapturous tones. But they will echo at least one of his sentiments. Our tableau must be redone; there is something new for our pens.

Keith Michael Baker and Steven Laurence Kaplan
26 August 1989

THE CULTURAL ORIGINS

OF THE FRENCH REVOLUTION

INTRODUCTION: THE CULTURAL ORIGINS

OF THE FRENCH REVOLUTION

OR WHY WRITE A BOOK THAT ALREADY EXISTS?

W HEN HE PUBLISHED *LES ORIGINES INTELLEC-tuelles de la Révolution française* in 1933, more than fifty years ago, did Daniel Mornet not formulate the question and state all possible answers, once and for all? Like Borges's Pierre Menard, who rewrote *Don Quixote* word for word and line for line, are historians inexorably condemned to restate Mornet's observations and recapitulate his conclusions?

There are two possible ways to counter this objection. First, our knowledge is no longer (or is no longer exclusively) what it was fifty years ago, and there are now a number of solid monographs capable of backing up an analysis of the subject as a whole. Second, even if we suppose that neither the question nor the responses have changed, our relation to the problem of the origins of the Revolution would have to be cast in different terms from those familiar to Mornet and his contemporaries, just as Menard's *Quixote* was no longer Cervantes's work because four centuries separated their identical texts. History has become more circumspect in the designation of causality, and historians have learned prudence and skepticism from the difficult task of subjecting the brutal emergence of the revolutionary event to rational categories, as well as from their inability to conceive of historical development as necessitated and commanded by one discernible thread.

Do we think that by substituting the word *cultural* for the term *intellectual* we can escape the perils of a kind of retrospective prediction that offers foresight after the fact? Such a switch would, of course, permit us to echo the course of historiography in the last twenty or thirty years, which has stressed research in cultural sociology over the traditional history of ideas. It is also a way to assert that even the most powerful and most original conceptual innovations are inscribed in the collective decisions that regulate and command intellectual constructions before they achieve expression in clear thoughts. Above all, however, it would indicate a shift in the investigation itself. It is now less important to know whether the event was already present in the ideas that announced it, prefigured it, or demanded it than it is to recognize changes in belief and sensibility that would render such a rapid and profound destruction of the old political and social order decipherable and acceptable. In this sense, attributing "cultural origins" to the French Revolution does not by any means establish the Revolution's causes; rather, it pinpoints certain of the conditions that made it possible because it was conceivable.

One last word. This slim volume is neither a synopsis nor a précis. It was conceived and written as an essay. Its intention is not to summarize what we know on the topic but, perhaps quite to the contrary, to suggest doubts and queries concerning some of the most broadly accepted working hypotheses and principles of intelligibility. My method privileges commentary on individual texts, old and new, and it owes much to the work of historians who, in recent years, have turned our understanding of the practices and thoughts of the French during the eighteenth century upside down. I hope only to clarify some new perspectives on a well-worn problem.

Thus my intention is not to rewrite Mornet, but only—more modestly or rashly, as the reader prefers—to raise some questions that would not have occurred to him.

1

ENLIGHTENMENT AND REVOLUTION;

REVOLUTION AND ENLIGHTENMENT

ANY REFLECTION ON THE CULTURAL ORIGINS OF THE French Revolution leads ineluctably back to a classic, Daniel Mornet's *Les Origines intellectuelles de la Révolution française 1715–1787*.[1] Mornet's work seems to dictate the only possible perspective for further work, a perspective that postulates an evident and obligatory connection between the progress of new ideas throughout the eighteenth century and the emergence of the Revolution as an event. For Mornet, three laws governed the penetration of the new ideas that he identified with the Enlightenment into general public opinion. First, ideas descended the social scale from "the highly cultivated classes toward the bourgeoisie, the petty bourgeoisie, and the people."[2] Second, this penetration spread from the center (Paris) toward the periphery (the provinces). Finally, the process accelerated during the course of the century, beginning with minorities who anticipated the new ideas before 1750 and continuing in the decisive and mobilizing conflicts of the mid-century to arrive, after 1770, at a universal diffusion of the new principles. This led Mornet to the book's underlying thesis, that "it was, in part, ideas that determined the French Revolution."[3] Even if he did not deny the importance— indeed, the primacy—of political causes, Mornet set up Enlightenment thought, in both its critical and its reforming aspects, as a necessary precondition for the final crisis of the old monarchy as it moved toward revolution: "Political causes would doubtless not have been sufficient to determine the Revolution, at least not as rapidly. It was intelligence that drew out and organized its consequences."[4]

In spite of his prudence and his rectifications (clearly signaled in his writing by expressions such as "in part," "doubtless," and "at least"), Mornet postulated a necessary connection between the Enlightenment and the Revolution. The reasons for the Revolution were, of course, not entirely contained in philosophy, but without transformations in "public thought" wrought by "the intelligence," that event could not have occurred when it did. This led Mornet to a working hypothesis that for the last fifty years has haunted both the intellectual history and the cultural sociology of the eighteenth century.

The Chimera of Origins

Doubts have arisen, however, that insinuate that the question may have been badly put. First of all, under what conditions is it legitimate to set up a collection of scattered and disparate facts or ideas as "causes" or "origins" of an event? The operation is not as self-evident as it may seem. On the one hand, it supposes a sorting-out process that retains, out of the innumerable realities that make up the history of an epoch, only the matrix of the future event. On the other hand, it demands a retrospective reconstruction that gives unity to thoughts and actions supposed to be "origins" but foreign to one another, heterogeneous by their nature and discontinuous in their realization.

Following Nietzsche, Michel Foucault has offered a devastating criticism of the notion of origin understood in this sense.[5] Assuming the absolute linearity of the course of history, justifying a never-ending search for beginnings and annulling the originality of the event as already present before it happens, recourse to this category obliterates both the radical discontinuity of abrupt historical changes and the irreducible discordance separating the various series of discourses and practices. When history succumbs to "the chimera of origins," it burdens itself, perhaps unconsciously, with several presuppositions: that every historical moment is a homogeneous totality endowed with an ideal and unique meaning present in each of the realities that make up and express that whole; that historical becoming is organized as an ineluctable continuity; that events are linked together, one engendering another in an uninterrupted flow of change that enables us to decide that one is the "cause," another the "effect." For Foucault, however, it was precisely these classical notions of totality, continuity, and causality that "genealogical" or "archaeological" analysis had to escape if it wanted to render an adequate account of rupture and divergence. Like the *wirkliche Historie* of Nietzsche, such an analysis "transposes the relationship ordinarily established between the eruption of an event and necessary continuity. An entire historical tradition (theological or rationalistic) aims at dissolving the singular event into an ideal continuity—as a teleological movement or a natural process. 'Effective' history, however, deals with events in terms of their most unique characteristics, their most acute manifestations."[6] If history is to replace a search for origins with "the systematic deployment of the notion of discontinuity,"[7] the very pertinence of the question with which we began is undermined.

This is all the more true since the notion of origin entails the further risk of proposing a teleological reading of the eighteenth century that seeks to understand it only in relation to the phenomenon deemed to be its necessary outcome—the French Revolution—and to focus only on the phenomenon seen to lead to this outcome—the Enlightenment. However, precisely what should be questioned is the retrospective illusion inherent in "the regressive movement that enables us to read premonitory signs when the event has arrived at completion and when we regard the past from a point of arrival that perhaps was not necessarily its future."[8] In affirming that it was the Enlightenment that produced the Revolution, the classical interpretation perhaps inverses logical order: should we not consider instead that it was the Revolution that invented the Enlightenment by attempting to root its legitimacy in a corpus of texts and founding authors reconciled and united, beyond their extreme differences, by their preparation of a rupture with the old world?[9] When they brought together (not without debate) a pantheon of ancestors including Voltaire, Rousseau, Mably, and Raynal, when they assigned a radically critical function to philosophy (if not to all the Philosophes), the revolutionaries constructed a continuity that was primarily a process of justification and a search for paternity. Finding the "origins" of the event in the ideas of the century—which was Mornet's program—would be a way of repeating, without knowing it, the actions of the persons involved in the event itself and of holding as established historically a filiation that was proclaimed ideologically.

Can the difficulty be circumvented by a reformulation that replaces the category of *intellectual* origins with that of *cultural* origins? Such a substitution would undoubtedly do much to increase the possibilities for comprehension. On the one hand, the notion of cultural origins assumes that cultural institutions are not simple receptacles for (or resistances to) ideas forged elsewhere. This permits us to restore a dynamic of their own to forms of sociability, means of communication, and educational processes that is denied them by an analysis like Mornet's that considers them only from the point of view of the ideology that they contain or transmit. On the other hand, an approach in terms of cultural sociology opens a large range of practices that must be taken into consideration: not only clear and well-elaborated thoughts but also unmediated and embodied representations; not only voluntary and reasoned engagements but also automatic and obligatory loyalties. This enables the revolutionary event to be placed within the long-term transformations of what Edgar Quinet designated "temperament" when he contrasted the inflexible nature of the religious reformers of the sixteenth century and the more malleable temper of the revolutionaries of the eighteenth century,[10] opening the way to an essential reflection on variations in the structure of personality, or, to use Norbert Elias's terminology, psychic economy.[11] But will this enlargement of perspective be enough to avoid the snares of teleological interpretation? "The postulate that 'what actually happened' did so of necessity is a classical retrospective illusion of historical consciousness, which sees the past as a field of possibilities within which 'what actually happened' appears *ex post facto* as the only future for that past," François Furet wrote,[12] putting us on guard against the a posteriori reconstructions that seem to be necessarily implied in any search for origins.

But is this danger avoidable? Must we, inspired by "counterfactual history," behave as if we were unaware of how the 1780s ended? Must we suspend judgment and suppose that the French Revolution never took place? It might be amusing, even profitable, to take up that challenge. But if we did, what question and what principle of intelligibility would we use to organize our interrogation of the many series of discourse and practice that intertwine to make up what is usually designated as the culture of eighteenth-century France? History stripped of all temptation to teleology would risk becoming an endless inventory of disconnected facts abandoned to their teeming incoherence for want of a hypothesis to propose a possible order among them. Whether we like it or not, then, we have to work within the terrain staked out by Mornet (and before him by the revolutionaries themselves) and consider that no approach to a historical problem is possible outside the historiographical discourse that constructed it. The question posed by *Les Origines intellectuelles de la Révolution française*—the question of the relationship of ideas formulated and propagated by the Enlightenment to the occurrence of the Revolution—will serve us as a set of problems that we both accept and place aside, that we receive as a legacy and continue to subject to doubt.

Taine: From Classical Reason to the
Revolutionary Spirit

Mornet's relationship with the historians who preceded him was of exactly the same order. There are two fundamental bibliographic references in his *Origines intellectuelles*: one that he reiterated, discussed, and refuted—Hippolyte Taine's *L'Ancien Régime* (1876)—the other discreet and mentioned almost in passing—*L'Ancien Régime et la Révolution*, by Alexis de Tocqueville (1856). Both works are central to revolutionary historiography. Mornet offered two criticisms of Taine. First, he reproached him for concluding too hastily that "the revolutionary spirit" was widespread early and for basing his judgment on texts that were too famous, too few, and, furthermore, misconstrued. For Mornet, reconstituting the progress of new ideas required a different approach: an attempt to measure the penetration of those ideas (or resistance to them) on the basis of a collection of evidence as vast as possible and taken not only from literature or philosophy but also from personal memoirs, printed periodicals, academic courses, debates in the academies and the Masonic lodges, and the *cahiers de doléances*. It is true that in this work Mornet's implementation of his call for rigor is often awkward and tentative, remains more enumerative than quantitative, and accepts the evidence of disparate and incomplete series. The concern Mornet expressed (which on the whole remains faithful to the program drawn up by Lanson in the 1900s)[13] has nonetheless provided a base for studies that have profoundly changed French cultural history in the last twenty or twenty-five years by leading it toward the massive documentary corpus, the treatment of data in time series, and the experience of ordinary people.

Mornet had a second reproach for Taine, however. When Taine stated that the "revolutionary spirit" already existed, completely formed, in Old Regime society, and was carried to its most extreme consequences by the Philosophes, he gave new life to the old plot theory and to the thesis of a planned revolution. Mornet found this idea unacceptable. "A Lenin, a Trotsky, wanted a particular revolution; first they prepared it, then they carried it out, then they directed it. Nothing like that occurred in France. The origins of the Revolution are one story, the history of the Revolution is another."[14] The remark is a valuable one. It opens the way to all the lines of thinking that distinguish the Revolution as it was inscribed within a long-term process as the necessary outcome of a constellation of causes that made it happen, on the one hand, and, on the other, the Revolution as an event instituting, by a dynamic of its own, a political and social configuration in no way reducible to the conditions that made it possible.[15] Even assuming that the Revolution had many origins (intellectual, cultural, or other), its own history still cannot be limited to them.

Mornet's double-pronged criticism doubtless missed the paradoxical originality of Taine's work—that is, the genealogy that traces the "revolutionary spirit" back to its matrix in French classicism. In a letter addressed to Boutmy in 1874, Taine described his projected work in the following terms:

[I want to] show that Boileau, Descartes, Lemaistre de Sacy, Corneille, Racine, Fléchier, etc. are the ancestors of Saint-Just and Robespierre. What held them back was that monarchical and religious dogma was intact; once that dogma was worn down by its excesses and overthrown by the scientific view of the world (Newton, via Voltaire), the classical spirit inevitably produced the theory of abstract, natural man and the social contract.[16]

Beyond the Enlightenment, the Revolution was rooted in the triumph of *la raison raisonnante* of classicism. By substituting an "abstract world" for "the plenitude and complexity of actualities," replacing the real individual as he actually exists in Nature and in history by "man in general," the classical spirit gave philosophical thought its framework at the same time that it undermined the customary and historical foundations of the monarchy.

The negation of reality that lies at the heart of classicism reached its completion in an acculturating eradication called for by the men of the Revolution:

> In the name of Reason, of which the State alone is the representative and interpreter, they undertake to unmake and make over, conformably to reason and to reason alone, all customs, festivals, ceremonies, and costumes, the era, the calendar, weights and measures, the names of the seasons, months, weeks and days, of places and monuments, family and baptismal names, complimentary titles, the tone of discourse, the mode of salutation, of greeting, of speaking and of writing, in such a fashion, that the Frenchman, as formerly with the Puritan or the Quaker, remodelled even in his inward substance, exposes, through the minutest details of his conduct and exterior, the dominance of the all-powerful principle which refashions his being and the inflexible logic which controls his thoughts. This constitutes the final result and complete triumph of the classic spirit. [17]

Must this be seen as the exuberance or inebriation of a counter-revolutionary philosophy rewriting national history in the light of its inevitable, destructive, and detestable outcome? Perhaps not, or not merely. By tracing the "revolutionary spirit" not directly to Enlightenment reforms but to tradition itself—to tradition in its forms most respectful of authority, royal and divine—Taine set aside the *topos* forged by the Revolution, which, in its search for founding heroes, picked only Descartes (proposed but not admitted to the revolutionary Pantheon) to stand beside the Philosophes. Filiations that failed to surface in the consciousness of history's protagonists and that wove unknown relationships underneath their proclaimed ideologies are more interesting than the ones they claimed and exalted. In this regard, Taine aided the conceptualization of the cultural process that included the Revolution, setting it in a longer time span than was taken into account either before him or after Mornet. Furthermore, when Taine characterized classicism in terms of its rejection of reality and its negation of the social world, he provided an outline for later analyses that defined this "dereification" as the distinctive trait of French literature in the seventeenth and eighteenth centuries. "The classic tragedy of the French represents the ultimate extreme in the separation of styles, in the severance of the tragic from the everyday and real, attained by European literature."[18] This pronouncement of Erich Auerbach's is like a reminiscence of Taine's statement. For Auerbach as well, the classical aesthetic (which also ruled the literature of the Enlightenment, and of which tragic drama was simply an exemplary expression) substituted a universal, absolute, and mythical humanity for concrete, daily experience, practical politics, and individual existences. Twenty years before Taine, and considering a shorter time span, Tocqueville conceived of the same opposition between the abstract world of reason and "the plenitude and complexity of actualities," using another pair of contrasted categories: "literary politics" and "experience of public affairs."

Tocqueville: Literary Politics and Experience of Public Affairs

For Tocqueville, it was essential to express that the Revolution was, paradoxically, the ineluctable outcome of both an extremely long evolution of the administrative centralization undertaken by the monarchy and a brutal, violent, and unexpected rupture:

> Chance played no part whatever in the outbreak of the Revolution; though it took the world by surprise, it was the inevitable outcome of a long period of gestation, the abrupt and violent conclusion of a process in which six generations had played an intermittent part. Even if it had not taken place, the old social structure would nonetheless have been shattered everywhere sooner or later. The only difference would have been that instead of collapsing with such brutal suddenness it would have crumbled bit by bit. At one fell swoop, without warning, without

transition, and without compunction, the Revolution effected what in any case was bound to happen, if by slow degrees. Such then was the achievement of the Revolution.[19]

Although its significance was entirely contained in the process that was its beginning and its cause, the Revolution was nonetheless a violent break whose moment and radicality cannot be deduced from that process. To account for this, Tocqueville advanced other reasons, which he sketched in book 3 of *L'Ancien Régime et la Révolution*, where he attempted to fit together the emergence of the event and the later developments—many centuries in the making—that conferred meaning and necessity to that event. In order to do so, he emphasized a short-term chronology (the thirty or forty years preceding the Revolution) and attempted to discern the cultural shifts that produced rapid transformations in ideas and feelings. The new role taken on by the intellectuals was not the least of those changes.

Tocqueville analyzed the intellectuals' role in book 3, chapter 1, "How towards the middle of the eighteenth century men of letters took the lead in politics and the consequences of this new development."[20] The chapter's point of departure is a fundamental opposition between the effective exercise of government by the agents of the monarchical administration (whom Tocqueville called, with some anachronism, *fonctionnaires*) and the "abstract, literary politics" developed by the men of letters who had become the arbiters of opinion. In France after 1750, authority had been cut off from power, politics had been separated from administration, and public discussion took place outside governmental institutions. In Tocqueville's view, such a situation dangerously juxtaposed politics without power and a power without authority. It had two results: on the one hand, it led to substituting "abstract theories and generalizations regarding the nature of government" for the lessons of "practice" and "experience," a respect for "the complex of traditional customs," and "experience of public affairs." Banished from the sphere of government, and hence lacking any hold on administrative decision making, political life could only be transposed or "canalized" into literature—*refoulée dans la littérature*, Tocqueville wrote, indicating both repression and transfer. On the other hand, the break between administrative power and "literary politics" invested "men of letters"—the "philosophers" and "our writers"—with a function and a responsibility that formerly (or elsewhere) devolved upon the normal "leaders of public opinion." Unlike England, where "writers on the theory of government and those who actually governed cooperated with each other" and where the "professional politicians" continued to direct public opinion, in France at the end of the Old Regime men of letters became a sort of substitute aristocracy that was both all-powerful and without real power.

The reason for this paradox lies in the process of centralization. When it destroyed the "free institutions" that Tocqueville qualified as "commonly described as feudal," and when it weakened "public life" by removing "the nobility and bourgeoisie" from the exercise of power, the monarchy itself created the conditions that authorized "philosophical" hegemony. On the one hand, the government, which had done away with the entire administration after emptying the Estates General, the provincial assemblies, and the municipal councils of their substance, found itself deprived of people experienced in the art of politics because there was now nowhere to acquire that experience. On the other hand, the power of the state was faced with a public opinion that had arisen out of the rubble of the old public liberty and was fascinated by "literary politics." The elites, stripped of all representative institutions and thrust out of public affairs, turned away from the society that had been theirs to move within the ideal world constructed by men of letters: "Thus alongside the traditional and confused, not to say chaotic, social system of the day there was gradually built up in men's minds an imaginary ideal society in which all was simple, uniform, coherent, equitable, and rational in the full sense of the term." When the social world was stripped of its reality (an idea from which Taine would profit) "these literary propensities were imported into the political arena"—that is, the dual movement of abstraction and generalization tended to reduce the "complex of traditional customs" to a few "simple, elementary rules deriving from the exercise of the human reason and natural law." The politicization of literature was thus at the same time a "literization" of politics transformed into an expectation of rupture and a dream of an "ideal world."

Literary politics and theoretical education, products of the process of centralization, became a common ideology among groups equally deprived of any participation in government. Hence they contributed noticeably to minimizing the differences between nobles and bourgeois, making the two groups comparable. Tocqueville thus set the new political thought and its diffusion of general and abstract theories into the perspective (fundamental in his eyes) of the narrowing of the gaps between provinces and classes:

> No doubt it was still possible at the close of the eighteenth century to detect shades of difference in the behavior of the aristocracy and that of the bourgeoisie; for nothing takes longer to acquire than the surface polish which is called good manners. But basically all who ranked above the common herd were of a muchness; they had the same ideas, the same habits, the same tastes, the same kinds of amusements; read the same books and spoke in the same way.

Tocqueville's judgment is clear, as seen in the title of book 2, chapter 8: "How France became the country in which men were most like each other."

We must heed the rest of Tocqueville's thought, however: ". . . they differed only in their rights."[21] Community of minds made the exhibition of privilege and prerogative both more necessary and more unbearable. Behind identical thoughts and social practices there still lay fiercely antagonistic interests and a determined ostentation of distance. With the reinforcement of "democratic despotism"—a paradoxical category that, as Tocqueville used the term, refers to the dual process of administrative centralization and the abolition of differences—the solidarities and interdependence necessarily produced by a society of hierarchical structure and liberty gave way to competing individual interests. Although a shared culture brought uniformity to preferences and behavior patterns, it did nothing to attenuate the distances separating the French, "in many respects so similar." On the contrary, the disappearance of political liberty so clearly signified the decomposition of the body social that a common culture exacerbated hostility and increased tension.

Why this protracted discussion of Tocqueville? There are at least three reasons. The first is preventive: Tocqueville denounced any temptation to envisage the philosophy of the Enlightenment as an ideology exclusive to a conquering bourgeoisie in confrontation with the aristocracy. He contrasted this reductive view, which was to have some success after him, with another that saw the new ideas as having a spirit shared by "all who ranked above the common herd." Rational and reforming thought, far from indicating difference and distance, was common to the upper classes, whose rivalry was all the stronger for their shared attachment to "literary politics."

Second, Tocqueville's book clearly designates something that Mornet was unable to see: the cultural effects of transformations in the forms of the exercise of power. When Tocqueville gave a central and determinant place to a changing political configuration (in the destruction by the despotic centralized administration of the liberty inherent in a government based on representative institutions), he suggested a subtle way of thinking about positions and tensions in the intellectual and cultural area. Viewing the construction of the absolutist state and the development of critical thought as two autonomous and parallel histories is too simple an opposition. It was precisely because it tended to monopolize all exercise of government that the royal power, become administrative and centralized, produced both intellectual politics and public opinion.

Third and last, Tocqueville helps us to formulate the articulation between the historical awareness of those who made history and the significance of their actions, of which they themselves were unaware. The illusion of rupture that is the foundation and explicit meaning of the revolutionary act has its roots in the imaginary and abstract politics constructed by the writers of the eighteenth century outside the institutions that commanded "real society." Understanding the cultural practices of the century is thus necessarily a matter of attempting to grasp how they managed to make possible the will for and the awareness of absolute innovation that characterized the Revolution: "No nation has ever before embarked on so resolute an attempt as that of the French in 1789 to break with the past, to make, as it were, a scission in their life line and to create an unbridgeable gulf between all they had hitherto been and all they now aspired to be."[22] Any reflection on the "cultural origins" of that event must thus also consider that eschatological impulse and that certitude of inauguration.

The Political Culture of the Old Regime

Any attempt to reformulate the question that Mornet posed fifty years ago inevitably leads to taking a fresh look at the categories that he took for granted and to constructing other categories that for him had little pertinence. The notion of "political culture" is one such category. Faithful to Lanson, the entire plan of *Les Origines intellec-tuelles de la Révolution française* was aimed at discerning the dynamics of a diffusion after 1750, and even more after 1770, that gradually introduced the new ideas into all cultural institutions and social milieux. Thus Mornet was interested in forms of intellectual so-ciability, in book readership and newspaper circulation, in what was taught in schools, and in the progress of Freemasonry. His book notes the introduction of these institutions, measures participation in them, and remarks on innovations, thus opening up a new field of research that the retrospective cultural sociology of the 1960s took up with greater rigor and urgency. In doing so, however, Mornet's *Origines* created a reductive dichotomy that set "principles and doc-trines" against "political realities," thus returning to a bland form of Tocqueville's distinction between general theories and practical expe-rience in public affairs. His scheme left no place for political culture, if that culture is understood as "constituted within a field of dis-course, and of political language as elaborated in the course of political action."[23]

To consider the politics of the Old Regime as a set of concurrent discourses within an area unified by identical references and by the constitution of goals accepted by all the protagonists opens two perspectives. On the one hand, it becomes possible to connect the two domains that Tocqueville so clearly—perhaps too clearly— separated: the "government" and "literary politics." To counteract the vision of an all-powerful, inexorable, and seamless administrative centralization, we should stress the importance of the political and "constitutional" conflicts that shook the foundations of the monarchy after 1750. Similarly, to counter the idea of an abstract, homoge-neous, unique public policy we need to note the vivacity of rival currents within philosophical discourse that presented contrasting representations of social and political order. It is certain, in any event, that contemporaries were quite aware of the radical transformation of discourse and political debate, starting with the Jansenist crisis and the withdrawal of the sacraments from the priests who had refused to subscribe to the papal bull *Unigenitus*, and with the strengthening of parlementary resistance. Not only did intellectual ferment expose the secret workings of the state, thus depriving it of powers of restraint over people's minds; more important, the discussion that had been launched focused on the very nature of the monarchy and its founding principles.[24]

Furthermore, setting up the politics of the Old Regime as a discrete field of discourse—not to be merged either with philosophical thought or with the exercise of state authority—allows us to reinvest the intellectual sociability of the century with a political content, even though the manifest practices of that sociability seem distant from conflicts over power. There are two ways to portray that politicization. The first identifies the various associations of the eighteenth century (clubs, literary societies, Masonic lodges) as places in which to experiment and elaborate a democratic sociability that found its most complete and explicit form in Jacobinism. The *sociétés de pensée* of the Enlightenment developed individualistic and egalitarian modes of operation that could not be reduced to the representations underlying the society of "orders" and "estates." Set up to produce a necessarily unanimous public opinion, and endowed with a function of representation totally independent of the traditional sources of authority such as the provincial Estates, the parlements, or the sovereign himself, which thought to seize that role, the *sociétés de pensée* have been seen as the matrix of a new political legitimacy incompatible with the hierarchical and corporative legitimacy that the monarchical system demanded. Thus, even while their discourses affirmed respect for authority and adherence to traditional values, in their practices the new forms of intellectual association prefigured revolutionary sociability in its most radical forms.[25]

This first model of politicization, which we might call the Cochin-Furet model, differs from another that could be designated the Kant-Habermas model. The latter sees intellectual sociability in the eighteenth century as founding a new public area in which the use of reason and judgment was exercised without putting limits to critical examination and without obligatory submission to the old authority. The various instances of literary and artistic criticism (in the salons, the cafés, the academies, and the newspapers and periodicals) formed a new, autonomous, free, and sovereign public. To understand the emergence of the new political culture is thus to remark the progressive politicization of the public literary sphere and the shift in criticism toward the domains traditionally prohibited to it—the mysteries of religion and of the state.[26] Those two perspectives, although not incompatible, nonetheless mark two different ways of understanding the place of political culture within the forms of intellectual culture: the first localizing it in the operations automatically implied by the very modalities of voluntary association; the second founding it on the demands and conquests of public use of critical functions.

What Is Enlightenment?

Rethinking Mornet also necessarily implies questioning the notion of the "philosophical spirit" equated with the forward progress of enlightenment. The term seems easy to define as long as it is held to be a corpus of doctrines formulated by the Philosophes, diffused through all classes of the population, and articulated around several fundamental principles such as criticism of religious fanaticism, the exaltation of tolerance, confidence in observation and experimentation, critical examination of all institutions and customs, the definition of a natural morality, and a reformulation of political and social ties on the basis of the idea of liberty. Still, faced with this classical picture, doubt arises. Is it certain that the Enlightenment must be characterized exclusively or principally as a corpus of self-contained, transparent ideas or as a set of clear and distinct propositions? Should not the century's novelty be read elsewhere—in the multiple practices guided by an interest in utility and service that aimed at the management of spaces and populations and whose mechanisms (intellectual or institutional) imposed a profound reorganization of the systems of perception and of the order of the social world?

That perspective authorizes a reevaluation of the relationship between the Enlightenment and the monarchical state, since the state—the prime target of philosophical discourse—was doubtless the most vigorous initiator of practical reforms, as Tocqueville noted in book 3, chapter 6 of *L'Ancien Régime et la Révolution*, which bears the title "How certain practices of the central power completed the revolutionary education of the masses." Moreover, to think of the Enlightenment as a web of practices without discourse (or at least without those varieties of discourse traditionally and spontaneously defined as "enlightened") is to give oneself a way to postulate distances and even contradictions between ideological declarations and the "formality of practices" (to make use of one of Michel de Certeau's categories).[27]

To move from the "intellectual" to the "cultural" is thus, to my mind, not only to enlarge an inquiry or change its object. Fundamentally, this movement implies casting doubt on two ideas: first, that practices can be deduced from the discourses that authorize or justify them; second, that it is possible to translate into the terms of an explicit ideology the latent meaning of social mechanisms. Mornet used the second of these two procedures when he attempted to restore the "subconscious of Masonry"; Cochin used it when he designated the implicit ideology of intellectual and social practices of the *sociétés de pensée* as Jacobin. The first procedure, which is typical of all the literature devoted to the Enlightenment, sees the diffusion of philosophical ideas as leading to acts of rupture directed at the established authorities, on the assumption that actions are engendered by thoughts. Against these two procedures (which operate both to reduce and translate) we might postulate a different articulation of the series of discourse and regimes of practice on the basis of which social and intellectual positions are organized in a given society. From the one to the other there is neither continuity nor necessity, as seen, for example, in the contradiction between the liberating ideology of the Enlightenment and the mechanisms that, while they claimed to be based in that ideology, set up multiple restraints and controls.[28] If the Revolution did indeed have cultural origins, they resided not in any harmony (either proclaimed or unacknowledged) that supposedly united annunciatory acts and the ideology governing them, but in the discordances that existed between the (moreover, competing) discourses that in representing the social world proposed its reorganization, and the (moreover, discontinuous) practices that, as they were put into effect, created new differentiations and new divisions.

As a study of the propagation of the "philosophical spirit," Mornet's book makes extensive use of the notion of opinion. The fluctuations and evolution of opinion were the measure of the penetration of the new ideas. When those new ideas became "general public opinion" or "public thought," the cause was won for the Enlightenment and the way was thrown open for "intelligence" to give form and expression to political contradictions. Thus Mornet granted to opinion traits that opposed it, term by term, to the production of ideas: opinion was impersonal and anonymous, whereas ideas could be assigned to an individual and advanced in his or her name; opinion was dependent and active, whereas ideas were original and innovative intellectual creations. In Mornet's view, it was inconceivable to think of opinion in other terms, and he handled the notion as if it were a historical invariant, present in all societies, that offers history the sole task of taking note of its diverse and changing contents.

This postulate is no longer satisfactory. First of all, the diffusion of ideas cannot be held to be a simple imposition. Reception always involves appropriation, which transforms, reformulates, and exceeds what it receives. Opinion is in no way a receptacle, nor is it soft wax to be written upon. The circulation of thoughts or cultural models is always a dynamic and creative process. Texts, to invert the question, do not bear within them a stable and univocal meaning, and their migrations within a given society produce interpretations that are mobile, plural, and even contradictory. There is no possible distinction (Mornet to the contrary) between diffusion, grasped as a progressive enlargement of the milieux won over by the new ideas, and the body of doctrines and principles that were the object of that diffusion and that could be identified outside of any appropriation. Moreover, "general public opinion" is not a transhistorical category that only requires particularization. As an idea and as a configuration, it was constructed in a specific historical situation on the basis of discourses and practices that assigned particular characteristics to it. The problem is thus no longer whether opinion was receptive to the philosophical spirit or resistant to it, but to comprehend the conditions that, at any given moment in the eighteenth century, led to the emergence of a new conceptual and social reality: public opinion.

2

THE PUBLIC SPHERE AND PUBLIC OPINION

A READING (WHICH NECESSARILY WILL BE AN INTER-pretation) of Jürgen Habermas's classic work *Strukturwandel der Öffentlichkeit* (in English translation, *The Structural Transformation of the Public Sphere*) offers a first guide to how the notion of public opinion was constructed in the eighteenth century. [1] Habermas stated his thesis clearly: at the heart of the century (in some places sooner, in others later) there appeared a "political public sphere," which he also called "a public sphere in the political realm" or a "bourgeois public sphere." Politically this sphere defined a space for discussion and exchange removed from the sway of the state (that is, from the "sphere of 'public authority'" or "public power") and critical of the acts or the foundation of state power. Sociologically it was distinct from the court, which belonged within the domain of public power, and from the people, who had no access to critical debate. This is why this sphere could be qualified as "bourgeois."

The Political Public Sphere

Several organizing principles governed the political public sphere, which issued directly from the public literary sphere and was based in the salons and cafés and in periodical literature. Its first definition was as a space in which private persons made public use of their reason: "The bourgeois public sphere may be conceived above all as the sphere of private persons come together as a public." [2] A fundamental link thus existed between the emergence of a new form of "publicness"—which was no longer simply that of the exhibition or celebration of state authority—and the constitution of a domain of the private that included the intimacy of domestic life, the civil society founded upon exchange of merchandise and labor, and the sphere given over to the critical exercise of "public reason."

The process of privatization typical of Western societies between the end of the Middle Ages and the eighteenth century is thus not to be considered merely as a retreat of the individual into the various convivialities (conjugal, domestic, or sociable) that removed him from the demands and surveillance of the state and its administration. Doubtless there was a basic distinction between the private and the public in that the private person did not participate in the exercise of power and took his place in spheres not governed by the monarch's domination. But it was precisely that newly conquered autonomy that made it possible and conceivable to constitute a new "public" founded on the communication established between "private" persons freed of their duties to the ruler.

Such a communication postulates that the various participants are by nature equal. The political public sphere thus ignored distinctions of "orders" and "estates" that imposed hierarchy on society. In the exchange of judgments, in the exercise of critical functions, and in the clash of differing opinions an a priori equality was established between individuals that differentiated between them only for the self-evidence and coherence of the arguments they advanced. To the fragmentation of an order organized on the basis of a multiplicity of bodies, the new public sphere opposed homogeneity and uniformity; in place of a distribution of authority strictly modeled on an inherited social scale, it offered a society that accepted only its own principles of differentiation.

The exercise of public reason by private individuals was to be subjected to no limit, and no domain was to be forbidden. The critical exercise of reason was no longer reined in by the respect due to religious or political authority, as the exercise of methodical doubt had been. The new political public sphere brought on the disappearance of the division instituted by Descartes between obligatory credences and obediences, on the one hand, and, on the other, opinions that could legitimately be subjected to doubt. The first of the "maxims" in the "provisional code of morality" with which

Descartes armed himself was to "obey the laws and the customs of my country, retaining the religion which I judged best, and in which, by God's grace, I have been brought up since childhood."[3] This led Descartes to a fundamental distinction: "After thus assuring myself of these maxims, and having put them aside with the truths of faith, which have always been most certain to me, I judged that I could proceed freely to reject all my other beliefs."[4] In the public sphere constructed a century later this reservation disappeared, since no domain of thought or action was to be "put aside" and removed from critical judgment.

Such judgment was exercised by the institutions that made the public into a tribunal of aesthetic criticism—the salons, the cafés, the clubs, and the periodicals. The publicity these groups provided, wresting from the traditional authorities in such matters (the court, the official academies, a small circle of connoisseurs) their monopoly on the evaluation of artistic production, involved both an enlargement and an exclusion: an enlargement because the large number of outlets for publicity (periodicals in particular) created a critical community that included "all private people, persons who—insofar as they were readers, listeners, and spectators [supposing they had wealth and culture], could avail themselves via the market of the objects that were subject to discussion";[5] an exclusion because "wealth and culture" were not everyone's lot, and the majority of people were kept out of the political debate that derived from literary criticism because they lacked the special competence that made possible "the public of private persons making use of reason."[6]

It was the process of exclusion that gave full importance to the debates centering on the concept of representation during the eighteenth century. Eliminated from the political public sphere by their "literary" inadequacy, the people needed to make their presence felt in some manner, "represented" by those whose vocation it was to be their mentors or their spokesmen and who expressed thoughts the people were incapable of formulating. This was all the more true since all the various lines of political discourse that founded the sphere of public power developed, each in its own way, a theory of representation. Following Keith Baker, we can distinguish three such theories: the absolutist theory, which made the person of the king the only possible representative of a kingdom divided into orders, estates, and bodies; the judiciary theory, which instituted the parlements as interpreters of the consent or the remonstrances of the nation; and the administrative, or "social," theory, which attributed the rational representation of social interests to municipal or provincial assemblies founded not on privilege but on property.[7] In light of these contrasting and competing definitions (all of which, however, focus on the effective or desired exercise of governmental and state authority), the new public sphere defined an alternative mode of representation that removed the concept from any institutional setting—monarchical, parlementary, or administrative—and that postulated the self-evidence of a unanimity designated by the category "public opinion" and faithfully represented by enlightened men who could give it voice.

The Public Use of Reason

Reading Habermas opens an entire field of reflection that leads, first, to questioning the articulation between the concepts of public and private, and, from there, to pausing to consider the text that served Habermas as the matrix for his demonstration: Kant's response to the question "What is Enlightenment?" which appeared as an article in the *Berlinische Monatsschrift* in 1784.[8] Kant discussed the conditions necessary to the progress of Enlightenment, which he defined as humanity's emergence from its nonage. His answer rested on two observations. First, an emancipation of this kind supposes that individuals will take control of the use of their own understanding and will be capable of freeing themselves from "statutes and formulas, those mechanical tools of the rational employment or rather misemployment of . . . natural gifts" that hinder the exercise of the mind. Enlightenment thus requires a rupture with obligatory thought patterns inherited from the past and the duty of all to think for themselves.

But—and this is Kant's second observation—for the majority of men this is not an easy conquest, thanks to the force of ingrained habit, "which has become almost [their] nature," and to the weight of the accepted authority of mentors to whom humanity has entrusted responsibility for doing its thinking: "Therefore, there are few who have succeeded by their own exercise of mind both in freeing themselves from incompetence and in achieving a steady pace." The progress of enlightenment could not result from a reform of understanding embarked on by separate, isolated individuals left to their own devices. "But that the public should enlighten itself is more possible; indeed, if only freedom is granted, enlightenment is almost sure to follow." Thus the progress of enlightenment required the constitution of a community to back up each individual's advances and in which the daring moves of the most forward-looking could be shared.

At this point in his argument Kant proposed a distinction between the "public use" and "private use" of reason that, as he formulated it, entails an apparent paradox. Private use of reason is "that which one may make of it in a particular civil post or office which is entrusted to him." Private use of reason is thus associated with the exercise of a charge or an office (Kant offered the examples of the army officer under orders and the pastor teaching his congregation) or with the citizen's duty toward the state (for example, as a taxpayer). The exercise of understanding in such circumstances could legitimately be restrained in the name of "public ends" that guarantee the very existence of the community to which the officer, the pastor, or the taxpayer belong, in what Kant called "the interest of the community." This obligatory obedience, which leaves no room for criticism or personal reasoning, is not prejudicial to enlightenment, because it facilitates avoidance of the disruption of the social body that would necessarily be engendered were discipline refused.

Why, though, should this use of reason, which seems the most "public" sort of reason in terms of the old definitions that identified "public" as partaking in state or religious authority, be designated by Kant as "private," thus inverting the accepted meanings of these terms? Using the example of the churchman teaching the faithful, Kant sketched his reasons for this paradoxical definition: "The use . . . which an appointed teacher makes of his reason before his congregation is merely private, because this congregation is only a domestic one (even if it be a large gathering)." The category "private" thus refers to the nature of the community in which use is made of understanding. An assembly of the faithful, a particular church, an army, even a state, all constitute single, circumscribed, and localized entities. In that they differ radically from the "society of world citizens," which occupies no determined territory and the composition of which is unlimited. Social "families," whatever their size and their nature, are thus so many segments fragmenting the universal community; they must therefore be considered as belonging to the order of the "private," in contrast to a "public" defined not by participation, as agent and subject, in the exercise of any particular authority but by identification with humanity as a whole.

Placed on a universal scale in this manner, the public use of understanding contrasts term for term with the "private" use exerted within a relation of specific and limited domination. "By the public use of one's reason I understand the use which a person makes of it as a scholar before the reading public"; "as a scholar"—that is, as a member of a society without distinctions of rank or social condition; "before the reading public"—that is, addressing oneself to a community not defined by being part of an institution. The "public" necessary for the advent of enlightenment and whose liberty cannot be limited is thus constituted of individuals who have the same rights, who think for themselves and speak in their own names, and who communicate in writing with their peers. No domain should be out of reach of their critical activity—not the arts and sciences nor "religious matters" nor "lawgiving." The enlightened prince (read Frederick II) is enlightened precisely because he allows this public use of reason to develop without constraint or restriction, thus permitting men to reach full maturity. A tolerance of this sort in no way endangers "civil order," which is guaranteed by the limits imposed on the use made of reason in the duties required by social status or profession. Furthermore, tolerance has the merit of providing a striking example: "This spirit of freedom spreads beyond this land, even to those in which it must struggle with external obstacles erected by a government which misunderstands its own interest" (as was the case in the kingdom of France, which Kant perhaps had in mind without saying so).

Kant broke with two traditions in this text. First, he proposed a new articulation of the relation of the public to the private, not only by equating the public exercise of reason with judgments produced and communicated by private individuals acting as scholars or "in their quality as learned men" (as Habermas held), but also by defining the public as the sphere of the universal and the private as the domain of particular and "domestic" interests (which may even be those of a church or a state). Second, Kant shifted the way in which the legitimate limits put on critical activities should be conceived. Such limits, then, no longer lay in the objects of thought themselves, as in Cartesian reasoning, which starts from the postulate that there are domains forbidden to methodical doubt; they lay in the position of the thinking subject legitimately constrained when he was executing the duties of his charge or of his status, necessarily free when he acted as a member of "a society of world citizens."

That society was unified by the circulation of written works that authorized the communication and discussion of thoughts. Kant insisted on this point, systematically associating the "public use of one's reason" with the production or reading of written matter. As an educated person, every citizen must be allowed to "make his comments freely and publicly, i.e., *through writing*, on the erroneous aspects of the present institution" (emphasis added). Here the "public" was not construed on the basis of new forms of intellectual sociability such as clubs, cafés, societies, or lodges, because those groups doubtless retained something of the "domestic congregation" by gathering together a specific, discrete community. Nor was the "public" constituted in reference to the ideal of the city in classical antiquity, which presupposed being able to listen to the spoken word and deliberate in common, and which involved the physical proximity of all members of the body politic. For Kant, only written communication, which permitted exchange in the absence of the author and created an autonomous area for debating ideas, was admissible as a figure for the universal.

Kant's conception of the domain specific to the public use of reason was drawn from the notion and the functions of the *Respublica litteratorum*, a concept that united the lettered and the learned, through correspondence and through print, even before the Enlightenment.[9] Founded on the free engagement of the will, on equality among its interlocutors, and on the absolutely disinterested exercise of the intellect, the Republic of Letters (invented not by the Philosophes but by men of learning in the preceding century) provided a model and a support for free public examination of questions regarding religion or legislation. At the same time, reference to the notion of freely engaged will marks the distance separating the theoretical universality of the concept of public and the actual composition of that body. In Kant's time, the "reading public" was not the whole of society by any means, and the public capable of written production was even smaller. Kant explained the distance that he implicitly recognized between the public and the people as a whole by saying that "as things now stand, much is lacking which prevents men from being, or easily becoming, capable of correctly using their own reason in religious matters with assurance and free from outside direction" (or, we might add, in matters pertaining to the arts, the sciences, or legislation as well). "The whole community" only potentially constituted "a society of world citizens." When those two entities coincided, one could augur the advent of "an enlightened age."

The Public or the People

Kant held the distinction between the public and the popular to be temporary, transitory, and characteristic of a century that was "an age of enlightenment" but not yet "an enlightened age." For other thinkers of the eighteenth century, however, the two constituted an irreconcilable dichotomy. "The public was not a people," Mona Ozouf stated as she showed how, during the last decades of the Old Regime, public opinion was defined in precise contrast to the opinion of the greater number. Lexical contrasts show this particularly forcefully: Condorcet contrasted "opinion" with "populace"; Marmontel opposed "the opinion of men of letters" and "the opinion of the multitude"; d'Alembert spoke of "the truly enlightened public" and "the blind and noisy multitude"; Condorcet, again, set "the opinion of enlightened people which precedes public opinion and ends up by dictating to it" against "the popular opinion."[10] Public opinion, set up as a sovereign authority and a final arbiter, was necessarily stable, unified, and founded on reason. The universality of its judgments and the constraining self-evidence of its decrees derived from that unvarying, dispassionate constancy. It was the reverse of popular opinion, which was multiple, versatile, and inhabited by prejudice and passion.

These writers reveal a strong persistence of older representations of "the people"; a negative image of the public to which all opinions

must submit. The definition of *peuple*, which varies little in dictionaries of the French language from Richelet to Furetière and from the
Dictionnaire de l'Académie to the *Dictionnaire de Trévoux*, emphasizes
the fundamental instability attributed to popular opinion throughout the eighteenth century.[11] For example, the 1727 edition of
Furetière's *Dictionnaire Universel* gives: "The people is people everywhere; that is, foolish, restless, fond of novelties." Two examples
follow: "The people has the habit of hating in others the same
qualities that it admires in them (Voiture)," and "There is no happy
medium in the humor of the people. If it does not fear it is to
be feared, but when it trembles it can be scorned with impunity
(d'Ablancourt)." Subject to extremes, inconstant, contradictory,
blind, the *people* in eighteenth-century dictionaries remained true to
its portrayal in classical tragedy: always quick to change course, from
one minute to the next docile or furious, but always manipulable.
Thus in the last act of Corneille's *Nicomède*, first performed in the
winter of 1650 and published in 1651, popular revolt was simply a
weapon disputed by the mighty. Revolt is first fomented by Laodice:

> Par le droit de la guerre, il fut toujours permis
> D'allumer la révolte entre ses ennemis.
>
> 'Tis by the laws of war permitted always
> To kindle revolt among one's foes.

Next, it is perhaps to be defused by Prusias, if he listens to Arsinoé's
advice:

> Montrez-vous à ce peuple, et flattant son courroux,
> Amusez-le du moins à débattre avec vous.
>
> Show thyself unto the people
> And, bowing to their wrath, at least beguile them
> By arguing with them.

Finally it is snuffed out by a gesture from Nicomède:

> Tout est calme, Seigneur: un moment de ma vue
> A soudain apaisé la populace.
>
> All is calm, sire. The people instantly
> Have been appeased by the mere sight of me.[12]

Burdened with these deep-rooted representations, the people could not easily be seen as a political agent, even when discourse was not deliberately disparaging. The article "Peuple," compiled by Jaucourt for the *Encyclopédie*, stands as proof of this.[13] The article proposes a strictly sociological definition: the people are exclusively "the workers and the plowmen," excluding men of law and men of letters, businessmen, financiers, and even that "species of artisans, or rather, mannered artists who work on luxury items." Considered as forming "always the most numerous and the most necessary part of the nation," this worker and peasant people, pitied and respected, was considered in no way capable of participating in government by counsel and representation but rather as linked with the sovereign in a relationship of fidelity offered in exchange for safeguard, of attachment in return for the assurance of a "better subsistence." The article continues: "Kings have no more faithful subjects and, dare I say, better friends. There is more public love in that order perhaps than in all the others; not because it is poor but because it knows very well, in spite of its ignorance, that the authority and protection of the prince are the only gage of its security and its well-being."

The *Encyclopédie* does not acknowledge the notion of "public opinion." The term *opinion* can be found in it as a logical category ("a judgment of the dubious and uncertain mind," opposed to the self-evidence of science) or, in the plural, as a technical term in the language of justice.[14] The term *public* is used only as a qualifier, as in "the public good" or "the public interest," the safeguarding of which is entrusted "to the sovereign and to the officials who, under his orders, are charged with this responsibility."[15] We need not force the analysis to the extent of contrasting the *Encyclopédie*'s definition of "the people" with a notion of "the public" that did not yet exist in this philosophic *summa* of the eighteenth century (proof, incidentally, of the late affirmation of the newer notion). Nonetheless, when it reiterates the traditional images of the people as either loving or rebelling, the *Encyclopédie* manifests the continuing validity of a representation that considered the harsh demands of the popular condition incompatible with participation in the reasoned conduct of government.

When the power of public opinion did emerge—defined as the superior authority to which all particular opinions must bow, even those of the king and his administration—the distinction between public opinion and popular opinion became essential. As Keith Baker has indicated, the concept of public opinion arose in discussions that took place around 1750, first in the controversy over the refusal of the sacraments to the Jansenists, then over the liberalization of the grain trade, and finally over the financial administration of the kingdom.[16] Powerless to forbid public debate, the monarchy itself was forced to enter into it to explain, persuade, and seek to win approval and support.

A new political culture thus took shape, recognized as a novelty by contemporaries in that it transferred the seat of authority from the will of the king alone, who decided without appeal and in secret, to the judgment of an entity embodied in no institution, which debated publicly and was more sovereign than the sovereign. This increased the acuity and the urgency of new questions: How could one distinguish this authority that had devolved on the public from the violent differences between rival factions so detestably illustrated in England? Who were the true spokesmen for the opinion that had become public in this manner: the men of letters who fashioned it, the magistrates of the Parlement who formulated it, or the enlightened administrators who carried it out? Finally, how was one to evaluate the self-evidence of its decrees that was the guarantee of consensus? Although everyone recognized the existence of public opinion and postulated its unity, there was no unanimous answer to these questions because public opinion was both a voice that demanded to be heard and a tribunal that had to be persuaded.

The Tribunal of Opinion

In 1775, in his maiden speech before the Académie française, Chrétien-Guillaume Malesherbes forcefully expressed the idea—by then commonly accepted—that public opinion was to be considered a court of justice more imperious than any other:

> A tribunal has arisen independent of all powers and that all powers respect, that appreciates all talents, that pronounces on all people of merit. And in an enlightened century, in a century in which each citizen can speak to the entire nation by way of

print, those who have a talent for instructing men and a gift for
moving them—in a word, men of letters—are, amid the public
dispersed, what the orators of Rome and Athens were in the
middle of the public assembled.[17]

There are several arguments contained in this comparison. First, it
invested the new judges—"in a word, men of letters"—with an
authority that ordinary judges did not have. Their competence knew
no bounds and their jurisdiction no limits; their freedom of judgment was guaranteed because they were in no way dependent upon
the power of the ruler; their decrees had the force of self-evident
propositions. Setting up men of letters as the magistrates of an ideal
and supreme tribunal in this manner was to invest them with the
fundamentally judiciary legitimacy of all the traditional powers,
beginning with those of the king and the Parlement. Thus the power
of "men of letters" was no longer exclusively founded—as in the
Système figuré des connaissances humaines of the *Encyclopédie*—on the
submission of the "science of God, or natural Theology, which it has
pleased God to correct and to sanctify by Revelation" to a "science of
being in general," the first branch of the "philosophy or the science
(for these words are synonyms)" that was "the portion of human
knowledge which should be related to reason." This subjection permitted the role of guide for humanity to be transferred from the
scholastics to the philosophers.[18] With the invention of public opinion, "the enlightened nation of men of letters and the free and
disinterested nation of the philosophers" found itself entrusted with a
veritable public office.[19]

Reference to the judiciary had another function, however. It aimed
at establishing a connection between the universality of judgments
and the dispersal of persons, and at constructing a uniform opinion
that, unlike that of the ancients, had no physical location in which it
could express or experience its unity. As for Kant later, it was the
circulation of printed matter that made it possible for Malesherbes,
in the remonstrances that he presented in May 1775 in the name of
the Cour des Aides, to envisage the constitution of a unified public in
a nation in which people were necessarily separated from each other
and formed their ideas individually: "Knowledge is being extended
by Printing, the written Laws are today known by everyone, every-

one can comprehend his own affairs. The Jurists have lost the empire that other men's ignorance gave to them. The Judges can themselves be judged by an instructed Public, and that censure is much more severe and more equitable when it can be exercised in a cool, reflective reading than when suffrages are constrained in a tumultuous assembly."[20] By associating the public nature of the written word— vastly increased by the presses (an indispensable resource in combating the "clandestinity" of the administration)—with the supreme authority of the judgments pronounced by opinion binding even on the judges, Malesherbes converted the congeries of particular opinions that emerge from solitary reading into a collective and anonymous conceptual entity that is both abstract and homogeneous.

Condorcet developed the same idea in the opening pages of the eighth "epoch" of his *Esquisse d'un tableau historique des progrès de l'esprit humain*, written in 1793. He launched his argument by contrasting the spoken word, which touches only nearby listeners and excites their emotions, with the printed word, the circulation of which creates the conditions for unlimited and dispassionate communication:

> Men found themselves possessed of the means of communicating with people all over the world. A new sort of tribunal had come into existence in which less lively but deeper impressions were communicated; which no longer allowed the same tyrannical empire to be exercised over men's passions but ensured a more certain and more durable power over their minds; a situation in which the advantages are all on the side of truth, since what the art of communication loses in the power to seduce, it gains in the power to enlighten.

Printing thus made possible the constitution of a public realm that was unreliant on proximity—a community with no visible presence: "The public opinion that was formed in this way was powerful by virtue of its size, and effective because the forces that created it operated with equal strength on all men at the same time, no matter what distances separated them. In a word, we now have a tribunal, independent of all human coercion, which favours reason and justice, a tribunal whose scrutiny it is difficult to elude, and whose verdict it is impossible to evade."[21] That tribunal, in which readers were the judges and authors the interested parties, was a manifestation of the universal because "all men who speak the same language can become alive to any questions discussed anywhere."[22] Even though Condorcet gave the most "democratic" definition of it, public opinion, ideally universal, had to come to terms with obvious cultural rifts, and it was not an easy matter to make the absolute concept coincide with the realities of the social world: "And so, though there remained a great number of people condemned to ignorance either voluntary or enforced, the boundary between the cultivated and the uncultivated had been almost entirely effaced, leaving an insensible gradation between the two extremes of genius and stupidity."[23] The very terms Condorcet used ("though"; "almost entirely") clearly indicate the persistence of a distance that was, however, considered to have been abolished.

Thus from the seventeenth century to the eighteenth century there had been a radical shift in the manner of conceiving the public. In the age of "baroque" politics the traits that defined the public were the same as those that typified the theater public: heterogeneous, hierarchized, and formed into a public only by the spectacle that they were given to see and to believe. This type of public was potentially composed of men and women from all social levels; it brought together all whose adherence and support were sought—the mighty and the common people, shrewd politicians and the ignorant plebs. It was also a public to be "led by the nose"; to be "seduced and deceived by appearances," according to Naudé, the self-appointed theoretician of a politics in which the most spectacular effects always masked the maneuvers that produced them and the goals they sought.[24] Ensnared, held captive, and manipulated in this manner, the spectators of the *theatrum mundi* in no way constituted a "public opinion" (even if the expression can be found before 1750, for example, in Saint-Simon).

When the concept of "public opinion" did emerge, it effected a dual rupture. It countered the art of pretense, dissimulation, and secrecy by appealing to a transparency that was to ensure the visibility of intentions. Before the tribunal of opinion all causes were to be argued without duplicity: causes that evidently had justice and reason on their side would necessarily triumph. But all citizens were not (or not yet) adept at exercising their judgment in this fashion or at joining together to form enlightened opinion. Thus a second rupture rejected the public that mingled in the theaters, where the inexpensive places in the pit ajoined the boxes and where everyone had his own interpretation—subtle or rough-hewn—of a spectacle destined for all, in favor of the more homogeneous public that served as the tribunal to judge literary or poetic merits and talents. When opinion was thought of as actor rather than as acted upon, it became public and lost its universality, and by that token it excluded many people who lacked the competence to establish the decrees that it proclaimed.

The Constitution of the Public

Constituting the public as an entity whose decrees had more force than those of the established authorities supposed several operations. Two examples should suffice to illustrate them. The first operation, which concerns the memoirs published in great numbers by both lawyers and litigants from 1770 onward, was to take the judicial comparison literally. Malesherbes justified this operation in his remonstrances of 1775, in which he spoke against the criticism of judges who thought that "the public should not be constituted as the judge in the courts": "Basically, the common order of justice in France is that it be rendered publicly. It is to a public hearing that all cases should normally be brought; and when one takes the Public as a witness by means of printed Memoirs, all that does is to augment the public character of the hearing."[25] In all cases, an affair being examined by a normal tribunal should be exposed before opinion. To take a specific case that set private persons against one another and was subjected to the secret procedures of justice and transform it into a public debate charged with letting the truth shine through and, in effect, with shifting the context in which judgment took place necessitated the adoption of several strategies.

The most fundamental strategy consisted in endowing the cause one was defending with general and exemplary value. Lacretelle, a lawyer, said as much: "Any particular affair that leads to general considerations and that is apt to become a major focus of public attention must be considered as a major event in which experience testifies with full authority and public opinion rises up with all its influence." An admiring witness tells us that this was also Lacretelle's practice: "Instead of shutting himself within the narrow circle of an ordinary subject, he soars above the constitutive laws of the various governments; he sees only major outcomes; each particular case becomes in his hands the program of a question of state." The debt that a court noble refused to pay to his commoner creditors thus became an ideal occasion for denouncing unjust privilege, just as the arbitrary imprisonment of a Breton gentleman was an opportunity to denounce the *lettres de cachet*.[26]

Two other things had to be accomplished before specific cases could be endowed with universal significance. First, the secrecy of judicial procedure had to be broken by mobilizing the potential of the circulation of printed texts on the largest possible scale. This accounted for both the large press runs of judicial memoirs (three thousand copies at the least, often six thousand, and occasionally ten thousand or more) and their low price (when they were not distributed free). Second, a different writing style had to replace the customary legal prose, a style that took its models and references from successful genres and gave narration a dramatic form, or else a style based in first-person narrative that lent veracity to the defendant through an exhibition of the "I," as in the literature of the times. Universalizing the particular, making public what had been secret, and "fictionalizing" discourse were the techniques that lawyers used to appeal to opinion and, in doing so, to proclaim themselves the authorized interpreters of that opinion.

The traditional direct, discreet, and exclusive relationship that bound individuals to the king—the guarantor and guardian of domestic secrets—gave way to a totally different mechanism in the public exposition of private differences.[27] From that point of view, judicial memoirs are the exact inverse of the *lettres de cachet* accorded by the sovereign in response to requests from families interested in stifling "disorders" that sullied their honor. The memoirs displayed what the *lettres* concealed; they expected from the judgment of opinion what the *lettres* hoped to gain from the omnipotence of the monarch; they converted into a civil suit the scandals that the *lettres* were charged with burying. The "politicization" of the private sector thus seems to have arisen out of a development that based the very existence of a new public sphere on a process of "privatization" in which individuals gradually conquered autonomy and freedom from state authority.

The second operation, the emergence of the public as a higher court of judgment, is clear in the evolution of artistic criticism. After 1737, when the Salon became a regular and well-frequented institution, its very existence transferred legitimacy in aesthetic appreciation away from the narrow milieux that up to that point had claimed monopoly (the Académie royale de Peinture et Sculpture, aristocratic and ecclesiastical clients, collectors, and the merchants who sold to them) toward the mixed and numerous public who passed judgment on the paintings hung on the walls of the Salon carré of the Louvre. Setting up that throng of visitors as a tribunal of taste was not without its problems. As Thomas Crow wrote, one question was central in the minds of all those who backed the expectations and the tastes of the new spectators against the old authorities:

> What transforms [an] audience into a public, that is, a commonality with a legitimate role to play in justifying artistic practice and setting value on the products of that practice? The audience is the concrete manifestation of the public but never identical with it. . . . A public appears, with a shape and a will, via the various claims made to represent it; and when sufficient numbers of an audience come to believe in one or another of these representations, the public can become an important art-historical actor.[28]

Transforming spectators into a "public" encountered strong resistance from the Académie, the connoisseurs, and even the artists themselves. The move was nonetheless achieved, more or less successfully, by independent critics (often anonymous, on occasion clandestine) whose numbers increased after the 1770s and whose writings circulated discernibly more widely than the comments Denis Diderot reserved for the subscribers to Melchior Grimm's *Correspondance littéraire*. Just like the public that was both invoked and represented by the lawyers who wrote judicial memoirs, the public that was thought to regulate taste in the fine arts found its earliest interpreters in the critics who set it up as the aesthetic lawgiver.

Even if, or because, it was defined as a conceptual entity, and not in sociological terms, the notion of public opinion that invaded the discourse of all segments of society—political, administrative, and judicial—in the two or three final decades of the Old Regime operated as a powerful instrument both for division and for social legitimization. In reality, public opinion founded the authority of all who, by affirming that they recognized its decrees alone, set themselves up as mandated to pronounce its judgments. It was in constructing opinion into a unified, enlightened, and sovereign public that men of letters, as Tocqueville wrote, "took the lead in politics." Universal in its essence, the public capable of making critical use of reason was far from universal in its actual composition. The public sphere, emancipated from the domain in which the ruler held sway, thus had nothing in common with the shifting opinions and blind emotions of the multitude. Between the people and the public there was a clear break. From Malesherbes to Kant, the line of demarcation ran between those who could read and produce written matter and those who could not.

3

THE WAY OF PRINT

WO NEARLY CONTEMPORARY TEXTS PERMIT US A FIRST examination of the relationship between the emergence of the public sphere and the circulation of the printed word. The first is Malesherbes's *Mémoires sur la librairie*, written in 1758 and 1759, after Malesherbes had been appointed director of the book trade in 1750.[1] The second is the memoir on freedom of the press written by Diderot toward the end of 1763 at the request of the Paris booksellers' professional association, the Communauté des Libraires parisiens, and in particular at the request of the *syndic* of that organization, the bookseller Le Breton, one of the publishers of the *Encyclopédie*. This second memoir became known after the nineteenth century by the title *Lettre sur le commerce de la librairie*, the title of the autograph manuscript.[2] The two texts were addressed to similar figures as well as having nearly contemporary dates of publication. Malesherbes wrote his *Mémoires* for a powerful person, probably his own father, Guillaume de Lamoignon, who had been chancellor since 1750 and by that token was responsible for supervision of the book trade. De Lamoignon then transmitted the *Mémoires* to the dauphin. Diderot's memoir was to be sent in the name of the Communauté des Libraires to Antoine de Sartine, who had replaced Malesherbes as director of the book trade in 1763 when, after his father's fall from grace, he had resigned the position in order to give all his time to his responsibilities as first president of the Cour des Aides. In both cases, then, the texts were written for high levels of the royal administration for the purpose of submitting grievances or proposals for reform but with no intention that they would be published (in fact, Malesherbes's *Mémoires* were not published until 1809, and Diderot's *Lettre* only in 1861).

Diderot, however, had thought in 1769 of publishing his memoir in a collection of assorted pieces. In a letter addressed to Madame de Meaux he described it in these terms: "I might add to that [collection] a piece that I wrote on the freedom of the press, in which I expose the history of the regulations governing the book trade, the circumstances that produced them, what should be kept, and what ought to be eliminated."[3] By "freedom of the press" Diderot meant the liberty to publish printed matter of any sort—books, lampoons, or periodicals. The expression was also used by Malesherbes, who criticized excessive censorship: "People are afraid of offending the ministers, as if they were not amply compensated by the eminence of their positions for the small discomforts to which freedom of the press might expose them" (*M*, p. 121). For Malesherbes as for Diderot, then, the central question was freedom to print, since both authors held free publication necessary for the advent of the truth: "Books do harm; but the human spirit is making progress that tends toward the general good. There are detours, but in the long run the truth prevails" (*M*, p. 110); "I will not dispute whether those dangerous books [prohibited books] are as dangerous as people say; whether lies and sophistry are not sooner or later recognized and treated with contempt; whether the truth, which can never be stifled, spreading gradually, winning by nearly insensible degrees over the prejudice that it finds in place, and becoming general only after a surprising lapse of time, can ever have any real danger" (*L*, p. 87).

The Crises of the 1750s

A close reading of these lines reveals traces of the three crises that shook the entire system of censorship and the policing of books toward the end of the 1750s and, beyond these, the royal power itself. The first crisis was strictly political, and its roots lay in the refusal of the sacraments to the Jansenists. On one side, the archbishop of Paris ordered his clergy in 1751 to administer extreme unction only to priests who could present a *billet de confession* signed by a priest who adhered to the papal bull *Unigenitus* condemning Jansenism; on the other side, the Parlement of Paris protected the priests who were being harassed. Since the king annulled several of the decisions of the Parlement (in particular, the decrees providing for the arrest of priests who refused to administer the sacraments), the authority of that body became the major issue in the controversy. The quarrel became particularly bitter in December 1756, when Louis XV promulgated several declarations and edicts at his *lit de justice* that struck squarely at the claims of the Paris magistrates. Events were precipitated by Damiens's attempted regicide on 5 January 1757, by the arrest on 11 January of two officials of the Parlement of Brittany who held out stubbornly against the fiscal declaration of July 1756, and by the exile on 27 January of sixteen members of the Parlement of Paris who had been relieved of their functions at the king's *lit de justice* in December. The crisis lasted through the summer of 1757 and ended only with the rehabilitation of the Parlement in September.[4] It provides the background that gives deeper significance to two other affairs that both Malesherbes and Diderot had in mind as they wrote their memoranda on the book trade.

On several occasions Malesherbes alluded in his memoir to a conflict that arose between the Parlement and the king regarding Helvétius's *De l'Esprit*. Approved (pending a few cuts) by the two censors to whom it had been submitted, the work had received a *privilège* in May 1758 and had come off the presses two months later. It was then that the scandal broke concerning the "irreligion" of the work, which treated morality as an experimental science governed by the varying requirements of the public good rather than according to the universal commandments of the church. A decree of the king's council dated 10 August 1758 revoked the work's *privilège*, and both Helvétius and First Censor Tercier, who had seen nothing condemnable in the manuscript, were obliged to make a public retraction. Despite the council's decree, the Parlement decided on 23 January 1759 to judge the work, along with several others also held to be suspect. On 6 February Helvétius's work was sentenced to be burned; the sentence was carried out four days later.[5] The affair had a great impact, both because it laid bare the incoherence of the operation of royal censorship and because it revealed the pretensions of the Parlement, which arrogated the right to judge and condemn a book even after its *privilège* had been revoked by the king.

A similar conflict was brewing concerning the *Encyclopédie*. Although it was protected by the three *privilèges* obtained by its publishers in April 1745, January 1746, and April 1748, it appeared, with *De l'Esprit*, among the works that the Parlement undertook to judge. In February 1759 their decision—less severe than in the case of Helvétius's work—submitted the seven volumes that had already appeared to the examination of censors designated by the Parlement. The king, however, revoked the *privilège* by a decree of the council on 8 March (written by Malesherbes). The council intended not only to defeat the censure of the sovereign court by removing its reason for being but also to protect the enterprise of the *Encyclopédie* by tolerating the clandestine printing and distribution of the volumes and, in September of that year, by according a *privilège* for the volume of plates.

Malesherbes recounted the affair in his *Mémoire sur la liberté de la presse*, written at the end of 1788:

> They [the censors named by the Parlement] had nothing to censure. The booksellers took a decision that they might have taken earlier. They had [the work] printed without censors' review, in a foreign land, or secretly within the kingdom (I have never sought to penetrate this mystery), and they had the entire work printed at once in order not to have to endure suits over each volume. When the work appeared in this fashion, there was no one to whom one could complain, so zeal cooled, and no one opposed its entry or its distribution, and every copy arrived at its destination to the subscriber. (*M*, p. 269)

"I have never sought to penetrate this mystery" is a phrase with an interesting corollary: obviously, nothing could be more false than to hold that the Philosophes and the monarchical administration were irrevocably opposed forces engaged in all-out combat.

Malesherbes had already come to the rescue of the *Encyclopédie* once before, in 1752. At that time, ecclesiastical and parliamentary wrath had struck a young priest from Montauban, the abbé de Prades, whose thesis for a theology degree at the Sorbonne was originally approved but later was censured and condemned to be burned for containing ten heretical propositions. As it happened, the abbé de Prades, who had been stripped of his titles and threatened with bodily seizure, was the author of the article "Certitude" in volume 2 of the *Encyclopédie,* which was about to come off the presses. Transferring the young cleric's condemnation to the collective enterprise (whose first volume had met with harsh criticism from the church, the Jesuits in particular), the council decreed on 7 February that distribution of the first two volumes was forbidden since they contained several maxims "tending to destroy the royal authority, to establish the spirit of independence and revolt, and, in obscure and equivocal terms, to praise the foundations of error [and] the corruption of mores, religion, and unbelief."[6] In its apparent severity, the decree inspired by Malesherbes preserved what mattered most, since the *privilège* granted to the work was not revoked. Even better, it led to storing the manuscripts of the succeeding volumes in Malesherbes's own house when they were threatened with seizure. The scene was described by Madame de Vandeul, Diderot's daughter:

> M. de Malesherbes advised my father that the next day he would give orders to remove his papers and his files. "Your announcement upsets me terribly; never will I have the time to move out all my manuscripts, and besides, it is not easy to find people, within twenty-four hours, who will agree to take charge of them and with whom they will be safe." "Send them all to me," answered M. de Malesherbes. "No one will come looking for them there!" In fact, my father sent half of his office to the man who was ordering the inspection.[7]

In like fashion, seven years later it was the highest authorities of the state who protected the cause of the *Encyclopédie.* The director of the book trade accorded, as Diderot put it, "a tacit tolerance, inspired by the national interest" for the publication of the work without *privilège,* and the lieutenant general of the police (Sartine at the time) closed his eyes to its sale.[8]

Administration and Justice; Police and Commerce

Two opposed pairs of beliefs governed Malesherbes's reasoning in the *Mémoires sur la librairie.* The first set justice against administration;

the second opposed police (that is, surveillance and regulation) and commerce. He considered it essential to "provide regulations for the book trade that determine to what point the administration must go but that also leave the course of justice free" (*M*, p. 85). There should be a clear and uncontested separation between the "administration" of the chancellor and the council, which alone had authority over the granting of *permissions* and *privilèges* (and therefore over the censors), and the rights of the Parlement, which applied "regulated justice" to decide the cases submitted to it by the *ministère public* (the public prosecutor's office) or by individuals. Where the affairs of the book trade were concerned, then, the point of contention was the division of powers within the monarchic state; and the major fear was that the Parlement might encroach upon the legitimate prerogatives of the administration.

On several occasions Malesherbes declared his anxiety concerning the sovereign court's possible use of the control over publishing that it arrogated to itself. First, he feared that the Parlement might reach a point of "so limiting the authority of the chancellor in this matter that it is really on the Parlement that the people's ability to speak by way of print depends—an ability that it would be very dangerous to leave in the hands of a body that already has altogether too much power over people's minds" (*M*, p. 85). Elsewhere he stated: "If the claims of that body are contrary in some ways to the royal authority, if it is not believed totally impartial on important questions, and if print is believed to be an appropriate means of moving minds, it is very dangerous to put in its [the Parlement's] hands weapons that could not easily be taken away from it when desired" (*M*, p. 91).

Even though Malesherbes did not yet use the expression "public opinion" in this text, using instead such terms as *l'esprit général de la nation*, *les esprits*, or, separately, *l'opinion* and *le public*, he showed a clear awareness of the transformations that had occurred in the political sphere in the mid-eighteenth century. The mysteries of the state, formerly protected by the king's secret, were henceforth made public by the various parties that attempted to capture the support of opinion. For Malesherbes, as for Jacob-Nicolas Moreau in the same period,[9] the monarchy itself had an obligation to enter into the fray and mobilize the resources of printing to reconquer an opinion that had been seduced by the Parlement. This was why freedom to publish works concerning administrative questions was absolutely necessary: "It seems to me that the cries of a submissive public are to be feared only by underlings whose faults want clarification, and are never [feared] by the absolute master who heeds them only as much as he wishes. I also think that those cries are raised to an equal degree when the public is left in ignorance, with the difference that the best operations cannot be justified" (*M*, p. 122). Malesherbes said elsewhere:

> Other persons say that there are some financial operations against which it is dangerous to let [people] write, for fear of [their] decrying them; but the minister of finance will never lack writings in his favor that will easily refute the sophisms that might be written against him. And I am wont to think that the operations that a pamphlet might harm, without another pamphlet destroying its effect, are flawed operations. (*M*, p. 126)

"The age of print," as Malesherbes wrote in his 1775 *Remontrances*, had irremediably modified the conditions of the exercise of power. It had given the nation "the taste for and the habit of self-instruction through reading,"[10] hence it had endowed the French with the faculty of reasoning and judging. By that token it had made discussion and criticism public. This seemed obvious to Malesherbes, and toward the end of the 1750s, as a faithful servant of the king, he invited his sovereign to draw the appropriate conclusions from this revolutionary change: the king would do well to strengthen his authority by mobilizing the resources of the printing industry to his own advantage and by winning over popular approval. Fifteen years later, the same revolutionary change underlay the demands of the legal profession speaking for the sovereign courts in denouncing secrecy in the procedures of the royal administration.

The second tension that structured Malesherbes's reflections resulted from the contrasting demands of surveillance and commerce. He gave explicit expression to this tension when he discussed regulations to limit the number of printshops. "Thus," he stated, "what would be most advantageous for the printing trade, looking to *commerce*, would be to leave it free. Looking to *police*, one finds that it would be better to have fewer printers" (*M*, p. 147; emphasis added).

The contradiction was by no means exclusive to the book trade; all thinking concerning provisioning, for example, was shot through with it. Ensuring regular provisionment and avoiding speculation in foodstuffs required an increasing number of regulations and prohibitions, which limited the freedom of the grain merchants and the millers who furnished flour. Policing the grain trade in this manner, however, carried the risk of discouraging commercial initiative and turning business away from the city markets. What was needed was confidence in the free play of competition and in the principle of an abstract market, defined only by the law of supply and demand rather than by the constraints and controls put on transactions made in officially designated hiring squares and market halls. If that happened, though, commerce, freed of all hindrance, might seek excessive profits by raising prices unreasonably, and hence anger the people—the consumers. The monarchy, torn between these two perils, never could decide one way or the other, and it alternated between attempts at liberalizing the grain trade (for example, in the 1760s or under Turgot in 1774) and returning to stricter regulation.[11]

The comparison between the grain trade and the printing trade—between bread and the book—is valid in two senses. First, neither merchandise was an ordinary commodity. Ferdinando Galiani asserted that bread "belongs to police and not to commerce,"[12] and Joseph d'Hémery, the inspector of the book trade, echoed his sentiments, declaring, "Nothing [is] more contrary to the interests of the government than regarding the book trade as an object of commerce."[13] Second, even though one group had a professional corporate organization and the other did not, grain merchants and printer-booksellers shared the same economic logic: they desired both liberty and protection, both unhindered enterprise and the security brought by the patronage of the authorities who conceded authorizations and privileges and preserved competitive appetites. The regime of privileges and permissions, the system of preliminary censorship, and the regulatory framework of the book trade go far to explain the strong and lasting bond between the book trade and the monarchical administration. That bond doubtless relied on an even deeper reality, however, in an economic mind-set typical of the Old Regime that saw enterprise as always taking place at the expense of others, that saw no contradiction in a demand for free commerce and a search for privilege, and that associated the most audacious speculation with willingly accepted dependency.

Between severe surveillance and the granting of freedom, Malesherbes unhesitatingly preferred the second policy: "It is not in rigor that a remedy should be sought; it is in tolerance. The book business is today too extensive and the public is too avid for books to be able to restrain commerce to a certain point, over a taste that has become dominant" (M, p. 104). Tolerance was necessary for three reasons. First, it was a precondition for the respect of prohibitions: "I know of only one means of enforcing prohibitions: it is to make very few of them" (M, p. 104); or, "My entire administrative system is founded on the toleration of many small abuses in order to prevent great ones" (M, p. 110). Second, tolerance alone could eliminate the fraud that enriched foreign booksellers and printers who, with the aid of accomplices equally interested in profits, imported books that could not be printed within the kingdom. Finally, the progress of knowledge, manners, and the human mind depended upon generous freedom to publish. Censorship should thus be restricted to a narrow range of categories: texts questioning the king's authority, obscene books (carefully distinguished from works that were at the most "free" or "licentious," which it was better to tolerate tacitly), and "works that strike at the foundations of religion."

Malesherbes thus observed the Cartesian preference for excluding the verities of the faith and the principles of the state from the exercise of methodical doubt when he traced the boundaries of the domain of legitimate censorship. His line of demarcation is not without a certain irony that reveals his true thoughts:

> Moreover, [theology] is not a science susceptible to progress. Unity, simplicity, and constancy are its principal attributes. All new opinion is at least dangerous and always useless. Let one not fear, then, that the rigors of the censors will prevent the theologians from perfecting their studies. The science of religion acquired full perfection the moment it was given to us, and the taste for discoveries has never been anything but harmful to it. (M, pp. 129–30)

In all other domains tolerance must be entire, implying in return the ability to bring authors before "regulated justice." That liberty was required by the very functioning of the "Republic of Letters" (the expression appears in Malesherbes's text), and it could be measured by "what can be observed in judicial order": "Every philosopher, every author of a dissertation, every man of letters must be considered as the advocate one must always heed, even when he advances principles that one believes false. Cases are at times argued for centuries: the public alone can judge, and in the long run it will always judge well when it has been sufficiently instructed" (*M*, p. 118). In this manner the public was equated with a tribunal even before the 1770s, when (as we saw in chapter 2) the comparison, become a commonplace, was shifted slightly to give men of letters judges' robes rather than the garb of the lawyer who must submit to the judge's verdicts.

Regulating the Book Trade

When he passed from the administration of censorship to measures for policing printing and book selling, Malesherbes proposed the revision of three regulatory texts: the *Réglement du Conseil pour la librairie et imprimerie de Paris* of February 1723, known as the *Code de la librairie*; the *Déclaration concernant les imprimeurs* of May 1728; and, recently promulgated on the initiative of the loyalist members of Parlement who had remained in that court after the resignation or exile of their fellows, the *Déclaration* of April 1757, which established in its first article that "all those who are proved to have composed, caused to be composed, or printed pieces tending to attack religion, to disturb minds, to attack our authority, and to trouble the order and tranquillity of our States will be punished with death." Such extreme severity, inspired by the immediate interest of judges who were "continually torn to shreds in pamphlets written in favor of those who had resigned or been exiled," could not possibly be enforced. The text made no distinction between degrees of guilt; it confused clandestine printers and authorized printers, master printers and journeymen, printers and booksellers, all of whom were unequally open to sanction. It also stipulated a death penalty out of all proportion with the crime: "The death penalty for a misdemeanor expressed in such vague terms as those of having composed works tending to disturb minds [*émouvoir les esprits*] displeased everyone and intimidated no one because it was felt that a law that harsh would never be enforced" (*M*, p. 137).

Malesherbes's proposals for palliating both this unenforceable law and the shortcomings of previous regulations (which were limited to the capital alone) were organized around three basic ideas that provide a good introduction to the operation of the book business in the eighteenth century. Traditionally, a limited number of print shops were authorized to operate in each city, but printing establishments were permitted in a large number of cities (142, according to the inquiry ordered by Sartine in 1764). Malesherbes suggested the opposite practice: drastically restrict the number of cities with printing establishments and increase the number of print shops in the larger cities. His reasoning was that "surveillance can only be carried out diligently in cities where there are intendants." In several "considerable" cities that were not seats of an intendance, regulation of the book trade would have to be entrusted to an inspector of the book trade, who might be a judge, though in this case the responsibility was attached to his person, and not to his office, so that the fundamental distinction between administrative and judicial functions was preserved. Malesherbes's advice was not followed. The number of cities that had at least one printing establishment remained the same during the last decades of the Old Regime (149 are cited in the *Etat général des imprimeurs du royaume* of 1777, drawn up at the request of Le Camus de Néville, the newly appointed director of the book trade),[14] thus leaving a broad scattering of presses available for clandestine printing.[15]

Malesherbes also worked to base the control of the book trade on full, rigorous, and systematically kept administrative records. Printers were to keep a register accurately recording business dealings that would be forwarded on a yearly basis to the intendant. The registers were required to list the number of their presses, the names of the workers they employed, and the jobs they had worked on each day. In the larger cities, where employment was extremely irregular and depended largely on innumerable print jobs for the city (notices, posters, announcements, and the like), a composite list of print workers (foremen, correctors, compositors, and pressmen) could be drawn up by the *chambre syndicale* of the print trade or by the police and substituted for the registers kept by master printers. Such composite lists were to provide names and basic information for the *garçons* employed by the printers and were to note the renewal of annual contracts for journeymen retained from the previous year. Each journeyman was to receive from the *syndic* of the printers' association (the *communauté*) a *permission* on a *papier tout imprimé* stating his name, his vital statistics, and his number in the record books. This paper was to be presented on demand to officials of the *chambre syndicale* or the police. The keeping of an accurate list of workers employed by master printers was designed to make it more difficult for the clandestine presses to find the manpower they required. All sellers of books who were not authorized—hence known—booksellers were to be registered as well: Parisian street vendors and haberdashers, peddlers and dry-goods sellers, who came under the regulations of the Code de la librairie, but also "book merchants who [had] access to houses" and the peddlers who plied the fairs in the provinces, who had formerly been tolerated and subjected to no real control.

The carefully elaborated bureaucratic dispositions suggested by Malesherbes aimed at establishing a control not adequately ensured by the severance papers (*billets de congé*) stipulated in the Code de la librairie of 1723, which prevented journeymen from freely leaving their masters, or by the very severe decrees of 1724 and 1732 obliging masters to keep weekly lists of their workers. Malesherbes's project, which, despite the reappearance of its dispositions in the 1774 law, remained largely unapplied, shows a clear intent to shore up a new conception of book trade regulation by an administrative rationale that relied on files, uniform registration procedures, and the comparison of written reports. The effort was not very different from the almost contemporary attempt of Joseph d'Hémery, the inspector of the book trade, when he undertook to create a file of all the Paris authors of his day. The 501 reports that d'Hémery wrote between 1748 and 1753, transcribed on identical printed forms (with six headings: name, age, birthplace, description, address, "history") and filed in alphabetical order, were for him a precious tool in his hunt for "bad subjects"—active and unrepentant pamphleteers. [16]

Between Law and Necessity: Tacit Permissions

Malesherbes also suggested the retention of tacit permissions, but he stated that they needed reform, saying that "in the last thirty years . . . [they] have become almost as common as the use of public permissions" (*M*, p. 159). The practice of tacit permission arose from a contradiction between the law, which prohibited the publication of any work without the inclusion of a printed notice of the permission and approval that authorized publication of the work, and necessity. "There are circumstances in which one did not dare authorize a book publicly, and in which one nevertheless felt that it would not be possible to prohibit it" (*M*, p. 209). This meant that the administration granted permissions that were not stipulated by the regulations, at first purely verbally, with no written records, and later registered under the camouflage of "the list of works printed in foreign lands whose distribution is permitted in France." The subterfuge did not satisfy Malesherbes, because a bookseller-printer was given no title to prove that he had indeed received permission. This led to problems, both because some printers were prosecuted when they had full rights to publish and because others fallaciously claimed they had verbal permission when none had been given. To reconcile the need to give some guarantee to the printer and the impossibility of establishing tacit permissions by a written declaration, which would implicate the authority of the chancellor and the king, the director of the book trade proposed "an oblique route": "works tacitly permitted" could be considered "as works for which a permission, signed and sealed, was to be given but has not yet been sent"—a permission, of course, that never would be sent (*M*, p. 212). The printer-bookseller would not be obligated to print a notice in each work of a permission that he had not yet received, but he could nevertheless produce a paper attesting that the text he had printed had been examined by the censors (whose names were not to be given) and tacitly authorized by the administration.

The proposal was never adopted, but recourse to tacit permissions increased as time went on: the annual average of those permissions granted, which was only 6 between 1719 and 1729, rose to 17 between 1730 and 1746, to 79 between 1751 and 1763, and then to 178 between 1764 and 1786. For the two latter periods, the total number of authorizations granted represents 59 percent and 56 percent, respectively, of all requests received, barely less than the proportion of accepted requests for official *privilèges* and *permissions*.[17] There were two reasons for such a policy. The first was economic, as Malesherbes noted in his *Mémoire sur la liberté de la presse* of 1788: "The interests of commerce did not permit allowing foreign book-sellers to grow wealthier every day by the distribution of these books, to the detriment of French booksellers" (*M*, p. 247). The second reason was intellectual, since "a man who had never read any books other than those that had originally appeared with the express attach-ment of the government [that is, covered by a properly sealed and registered permission], as the law prescribes, would be nearly a century behind his contemporaries" (*M*, p. 241). Malesherbes then cited his predecessors, d'Argenson and Chauvelin. "The enlightened magistrates who were responsible for the book trade" had notably increased not only tacit permissions but also simple tolerance:

> Often one felt it necessary to tolerate a book, yet did not want to admit that it was tolerated; thus express permission was with-held. . . . In this case, the decision was made to tell the bookseller that he could publish the work, but secretly; that the police would pretend to be unaware of it, and would not have it seized. And as it was impossible to foretell how irritated the clergy and the courts might be, he was advised to remain always ready to make his publication disappear the moment he was warned to do so, and he was promised that he would be given advance notice before his premises were searched. I am at a loss to know what name to give this sort of permission, the use of which has become common. Strictly speaking, these are only assurances of impunity. (*M*, p. 249)

It was with an "assurance" of this sort, for example, that Malesherbes pro-tected the publication and sale of *Emile* in 1762 before the book was con-demned by the Parlement and a decree to arrest its author was issued.[18]

Administration of the book trade under the Old Regime thus rested on a dangerous paradox: it was too lax in its censorship, yet its laxity was too repressive. In his 1788 *Mémoire* Malesherbes gave a lucid analysis of the corrosive effects of such a system. On the one hand, it had led the state to undermine its own authority, since with the tacit permissions it was "the government itself that taught the booksellers and the printers that they could disobey a specific law" (the obligation to give printed notice of the permission authorizing publication in the work itself). In the case of simple toleration, it was the lieutenant general of the police who "encouraged them to take measures to escape the clutches of the law" (*M*, pp. 248, 250). On the other hand, Malesherbes showed that the strict measures that were maintained were even more intolerable because they operated at a moment in which everything—or nearly everything—could be printed freely and sold publicly. "Patiently endured so long as it seemed beyond redress, a grievance comes to appear intolerable once the possibility of removing it crosses men's minds. For the mere fact that certain abuses have been remedied draws attention to the others and they now appear more galling; people may suffer less, but their sensibility is exacerbated."[19] Here Tocqueville gives a perfect description of the expectations and frustrations engendered by a publishing regimen that set tolerance against the law.

The practice of the administrators responsible for the book trade thus nearly satisfied the desire that Diderot expressed at the end of his memoir on freedom of the press: "Thus I think that it is useful for letters and commerce to increase tacit permissions indefinitely, subjecting the publication and the distribution of a book only to a sort of propriety in order to satisfy small minds" (*L*, p. 88). Diderot's arguments were identical to Malesherbes's (though written with more verve). Prohibitions were inefficacious and ruinous—inefficacious because they turned against themselves:

> I see that the stricter the proscription is, the more it raises the price of the book and the more it excites curiosity to read it; the more the book is bought, the more it is read. How many books are there whose condemnation made them known, though their mediocrity had condemned them to oblivion. How many times would the bookseller or the author of a book that bore a privilege have said to the highest police magistrates, if they had dared, "Sirs, be merciful, just a little decree that condemns me to be torn up and burned at the foot of your staircase." When the condemnation of a work is announced, the press workers exclaim, "Good! One more edition! (*L*, p. 87)

Prohibition was ruinous because it brought the greatest profits to the foreign booksellers who took over prohibited titles and, surveillance or not, imported them into France: "Dear Sir [Sartine, Malesherbes's successor as director of the book trade], line all your frontiers with soldiers; arm them with bayonets to repel all the dangerous books that present themselves, and those books—you will forgive my expression—will slip between their legs or jump over their heads to reach us" (*L*, p. 81). Thus Diderot recommended that censors be chosen among men of letters recognized by their peers and that tacit permissions be granted with great liberality and considered as true *privilèges*.

Publishing Privileges and Literary Proprietary Rights

Diderot's *Lettre sur la liberté de la presse* was written at the request of the Parisian printer-booksellers, who wanted to present their grievances to the director of the book trade and to defend the rights they had acquired. They were not overly enchanted with the work Diderot had done, and they rewrote the text, cutting it severely, before they presented it to Sartine under the title *Représentations et Observations en forme de Mémoire sur l'Etat ancien et actuel de la Librairie et particulièrement sur la propriété des privilèges* (Representations and observations in the form of a memoir on the former and current state of the book trade, in particular, on the ownership of privileges), which clearly shows the difference between Diderot's intention to plead for "freedom of the press" and the Parisian bookseller-printers' first concern to defend interests that they felt would be threatened if the renewal of *privilèges* was discontinued. The publishing community in Paris had been apprehensive in 1761 when, by decree of the council, the *privilège* for La Fontaine's *Fables* was transferred away from the bookseller who had purchased it to two female descendants of La Fontaine. After that, the trade took care to assert the legitimacy of the *privilège*, which gave the bookseller who had obtained it exclusive and perpetual publishing rights for any given title.

This explains the tensions present throughout Diderot's memoir, in which he championed the book trade's *privilèges*, even though the *Encyclopédie* was generally hostile toward commercial and manufacturing monopolies, which it considered obstacles to the free play of economic laws. Diderot himself pointed out this embarrassing contradiction: "It would be a strange paradox indeed, in a time in which experience and good sense concur to prove that all hindrance is harmful to commerce, to suggest that *privilèges* alone can lend support to the book trade. Nothing, however, is more certain; but we will not be intimidated by words" (*L*, p. 39). He also asserted the need for strict control of the book trade, proposing to reduce the number of authorized booksellers, even though he was known to favor the abolition of trade associations. Finally—and this is not the least of the paradoxes—he came forward as a zealous spokesman for the demands of the Parisian booksellers, even though his relations with them had never been comfortable. Each time an agreement or contract was drawn up with the printers who published the *Encyclopédie* (Le Breton, David, and Briasson, in 1747, 1754, 1759, and 1762), he had a difficult time extracting better terms from these men who paid him wages and whom he called *mes corsaires*.[20] Relations came to a crisis in 1764, when Diderot realized that Le Breton had made cuts in certain articles without telling him and after the proofs had been corrected.

   The simple fact that Diderot worked for wages is not sufficient to account for the contradictions in his treatise. Even while he was putting his talents at the service of the Parisian printer-booksellers, Diderot was, in effect, attempting to establish authors' rights on a firmer footing and to protect their interests. In order to do so he needed first to establish the *privilège* as property rather than a favor accorded by the royal power. Eliminating the advantages that had traditionally been attached to it—in particular, the monopoly over publication of the title for which it was granted—would be "to treat the publisher's *privilège* like a grace freely accorded or refused, and to forget that it is merely the guarantee of a true ownership, which could be violated only with injustice" (*L*, p. 58). Reiterating the arguments of earlier works written in support of the printers' claims, Diderot put literary property on a contractual basis. Since it was freely acquired or sold, it was completely comparable to landed property or real estate: "I ask you, Sir, if the person who has bought a house does not have exclusive ownership and enjoyment of it" (*L*, p. 40). Such property was thus inalienable since it could neither be transferred nor shared against the will of the owner. This proprietary right was nonetheless different from other exclusive rights, since it did not reserve to one printer the right to print books in general, or even books on one particular subject, but concerned only specific titles: "It involves one manuscript, one asset legitimately ceded, legitimately acquired, of a work bearing a *privilège* which belongs to one buyer alone, which cannot be transferred either in whole or in part to another without violation [of his right], and ownership of which does not prevent [others] from writing and publishing ad infinitum on the same topic" (*L*, p. 44).

Restricted in this manner, the *privilège* should be the usual procedure in the book trade. To prove this point, Diderot enumerated the negative effects of "publishing by competition," in which permissions, by themselves, involved no exclusive right of publication. The printers would risk ruin because their profits would shrink when sales were divided among the various editions competing for the market. The art of the book would be downgraded because of "economic emulation" engendered by the desire to publish at the lowest possible cost: "Books would become very common, but before ten years [passed] you would have them all as miserable in their typefaces, paper, and correction as the *Bibliothèque bleue*—an excellent way to ruin in a brief span of time three or four important industries" (*L*, pp. 48–49). Furthermore, following good mercantilist logic, it was the state itself that would be the long-term victim of an evolution that would leave foreigners with the monopoly over better-quality editions and discourage French printers from any risky enterprise: "One moment of persecution and confusion, and every bookseller will take care of his needs far away, according to the size of his business. No longer exposing himself to losing his investment in his product, what could he do that would be more prudent? The State will be impoverished, however, by the loss of the workers and by a decline in production on your soil, and you will send out of your lands the gold and silver that your soil no longer produced" (*L*, p. 75).

In declaring the need for an exclusive and inalienable *privilège* for the printer-booksellers, Diderot was attempting to argue for recognition of each author's full ownership of his work. Since the author ordinarily could not print his own works ("to keep account books of receipts and expenditures, answer, exchange, receive, send—what occupations for a disciple of Homer or Plato!," [*L*, p. 45]), he had to use the services of the booksellers; but the contractual relationship between them was, precisely, proof of the writer's rights to his own work ("the most precious portion of himself, the one that would never perish," *L*, p. 41). "I repeat: the author is master of his work, or no one in society is master of his wealth. The bookseller possesses it as it was possessed by the author" (*L*, p. 42). Thus it was the author's ownership that founded the legitimacy of the *privilège*, and, inversely, it was the indefeasibility of that *privilège* that, indirectly, proved the author's rights.

The Autonomy of the Literary Field

In its manner, Diderot's strategy illustrates the transformation of the authors' predicament during the last three or four decades of the Old Regime. The older model offered two possibilities: either the writer enjoyed an economic independence ensured him by his social position or his fortune, or he was the protégé of a patron who ensured him an occupation and a living in return for his fidelity. In neither case did the man of letters live directly from his pen. The overwhelming majority of the 333 writers kept under surveillance by d'Hémery (and whose source of income can be identified) were divided between these two situations. More than half (55 percent) had revenues that had nothing to do with their literary activities: 12 percent were clerics, 17 percent were nobles, 18 percent were men of the law, of the administration, or attorneys, 3 percent were professors, 2 percent were physicians, and 3 percent had independent incomes. One-third held a position (tutor, journalist, secretary, librarian, and so forth) that they owed to the good graces of a protector. The rest—12 percent—were a mixed group of artisans, domestic servants, and employees in subalternate positions. Nine writers—3 percent of the total—were women.[21]

To judge by the survey of *gens de lettres* (that is, authors of at least one published title) published in *La France littéraire* in 1784, the two largest groups in d'Hémery's files still led the list among the 1,393 authors whose socioprofessional position was mentioned. Clerics accounted for 20 percent of all writers in the *France littéraire* survey, nobles for 14 percent, lawyers and administrators for 15 percent, physicians and apothecaries for 17 percent, engineers and architects for 2 percent, professors for 11 percent. Those whose occupation depended directly upon royal or aristocratic protection were a minority of 10 percent—less than in d'Hémery's files. This figure shows either a decline in patronage or, more probably, a difference in the definition of *author*, which was more strictly literary and philosophical in the Parisian inspector's view, and more inclined to include provincial notables in *La France littéraire*.[22]

Still, Diderot's treatise registers the appearance of another type of literary figure—the author who hoped to make his living from the "commercial value" of his productions; that is, by means of the agreements he signed with the booksellers who published his works and the remuneration he received for them. "One could not get rich, but one could acquire ease if these sums were not spread over a great number of years, did not vanish as soon as they were paid, and were not all gone when years have passed, needs increased, eyes dimmed, and [one's] wits worn thin. Still, it is an encouragement! And what sovereign is wealthy enough to replace them with his liberalities?" (*L*, p. 64). Thus, even if the tradition that portrayed the munificent ruler as the protector of letters continued to be considered normal, new requirements that posited the author's rights to a just recompense for his writing labors were becoming established.

In order for that right to be recognized, the writer's ownership of his manuscript had to be clearly established. This explains Diderot's tactic in founding the legitimacy of that ownership on the legitimacy of its cession. It also explains the connection, which Diderot saw as obligatory, between the author's ability to command a just recompense and the existence of laws "that assure the businessman the undisputed and permanent possession of the works that he acquires" (*L*, p. 64). Both his somewhat paradoxical defense of printers' *privilèges* and his reasons for agreeing to lend his talents to the service of the Parisian booksellers (from whom he received small thanks) become clearer as well. In the book trade under the Old Regime, the writer's economic independence could only result from safeguarding the monopolies conceded to the booksellers who published his works:

> Abolish those laws. Render the proprietary rights of the acquirer uncertain, and that misdirected policy will strike the author. What will I get from my work, especially if my reputation is not what I suppose it to be, when the bookseller fears

that some competitor, without running the risk of trying out my talent, without venturing the funds for a first edition, without granting me the least honorarium, can take over immediate enjoyment of it after six years [the average length of a *privilège* with no renewal] and sooner if he dares? (*L*, p. 64)

There are two external signs of the authors' emergent "professionalism" analyzed by Diderot. First, as the eighteenth century progressed, the sources list an increasing number of authors with no indication of social position or employment. This is true of 101 of the 434 writers (23 percent) sketched by d'Hémery between 1748 and 1753, but it is true of 1,426 (or 50 percent) of the 2,819 authors listed in *La France littéraire* in 1784. There is a good likelihood that many of the authors listed with no profession or sinecure were attempting to live, as best they could, by their pens. It was from their ranks that the collaborators required by the great bookmaking enterprises after the 1750s were recruited—the encyclopedias, dictionaries, *bibliothèques*, *cabinets*, extracts, and translations—as well as the pamphleteers who fed the foreign presses with incendiary pieces against the government, the mighty, the court, the royal family, or the sovereign himself.

Voltaire would later take on the role of merciless scourge of the "unhappy class who write in order to live."[23] Without social status or honor, the *canaille de la littérature* was defenseless before the demands of the booksellers: "A hundred authors compile to get their bread, and twenty fools extract, criticize, apologize, and satirize these compilations to get bread also, because they have no profession." To live by writing—or to attempt to do so—was not for any author worthy of the name, as it showed obscure birth, a base soul, and little talent:

> These poor people are divided into two or three bands, and go begging like mendicant friars; but not having taken vows, their society lasts only for a few days, for they betray one another like priests who run after the same benefice, though they have no benefice to hope for. But they still call themselves authors! The misfortune of these men is that their fathers did not make them learn a trade, which is a great defect in modern policy. Every man of the people who can bring up his son in a useful art, and does not, merits punishment. The son of a mason becomes a

Jesuit at seventeen; he is chased from society at four and twenty, because the levity of his manners is too glaring. Behold him without bread! He turns journalist, he cultivates the lowest kind of literature, and becomes the contempt and horror of even the mob. And such as these, again, call themselves authors!

After 1760 the terms used in publishing contracts changed—a second sign of literary "professionalization." Clauses remunerating the author by granting him a certain number of copies of his work to offer current or prospective patrons disappeared in favor of monetary compensation when the printer-bookseller acquired the manuscript. The sums paid varied enormously according to the genre of the work and the reputation of the author, but they rose after 1750, sometimes reaching five or six thousand livres. The best-paid authors were the dramatists, who were paid not only a fixed sum for the manuscript but also had a right to a percentage of the take from performances (established at one-ninth—after 1780, one-seventh—of the gross for a five-act play).[24] Within a system founded on literary activities that were either dependent upon revenues connected with a social status unrelated to literature or else subject to the vagaries of patronage, a literary market began to take shape that set up its own hierarchy of values and created conditions that made possible the independence of men of letters.[25]

It was doubtless changes in the authors' status that signaled the real existence of a relatively autonomous literary field free from social pressures and organized according to its own principles, hierarchies, and rewards. Admittedly, in the seventeenth century, between 1635 and 1685, there had been instances (even competing instances) of the consecration of an author that amounted to a first institutionalization of literary merit. There were the salons and the academies, which broke with the encyclopedic model of humanism and drew a distinction between the *littérateur* and the scholar; there was the patronage system, which substituted the recognition of talent for the obligations of the patron-client relationship; there was the emergence of a larger public that permitted notable successes without the support of the learned community or the court, and which, at least for some sorts of works, promised handsome royalties to authors.[26]

Was this network of institutions enough to give the literary field any real autonomy? Probably not, and for two reasons. First, the various forms of literary consecration were gradually taken over and controlled by the monarchy. Thus academic legitimacy was taken over by the Académie française, and patronage was dominated by royal largesse. Second, the aristocratic model of the writer who was provided for through his social status and the logic of the patronage system was strong enough to prevent the formation of a literary market capable of ensuring economic independence to authors. The literary life of the classical age was thus directly subject to external political and social powers.

Literature as a way of life won a certain autonomy only in the latter half of the eighteenth century, when fierce editorial competition, encouraged by demand from a nation hungry for reading matter, combined with the new ambitions of authors attempting to live by their pens to create a market that obeyed its own rules and compensated writing directly rather than indirectly through pensions and sinecures. One of the six decrees of the king's council on 30 August 1777 that instituted basic reforms in the administration of the book trade recognized this new situation, though in its own manner. The decree, "providing regulation of the length of publishing privileges," differed from the demands of the Parisian booksellers formulated by Diderot in that it defined the *privilège* as a "grace founded in justice" or "an enjoyment accorded," not "a rightful proprietorship," and, far from authorizing indefinite extensions of publishing privileges, it forbade them except in the case of editions republished with at least one-fourth of their bulk devoted to additional materials.

The decree was innovative, first, in distinguishing between the period of validity for *privilèges* granted at the request of the author and in his or her own name—"he will enjoy his privilege, for himself and his heirs, in perpetuity"—and those granted to printers, in which case the *privilège* "could not be for a shorter period than ten years," but would be valid only "during the life of the authors, in the event that they survive the expiration of the privileges." Even if not all authors could publish and sell their own works (Diderot remarked, "I have written and on several occasions printed on my own account. And I can assure you, by the way, that nothing is less harmonious than the active life of the merchant and the sedentary life of the man of letters [*L*, p. 45]), the decree of 1777, by asserting the perpetual and transmissible right of the author to his work (if he did not sell it to a printer-bookseller) marked a step forward in the recognition of literary ownership as the fruit of one's labors (*travail* is the word used in the decree) and a source of revenue.

This was all the more true when, the following year, a new decree of the council, promulgated at the request of the Académie française, eliminated the restrictions placed on the publishing activities of writers. It declared:

> Any author who has obtained the *privilège* for his work in his own name will not only have the right to sell it himself [the only possibility envisaged in the 1777 decree] but may also, and as often as he wishes, have his work printed by any printer and also have it sold for him by any bookseller he chooses, without any agreement or contract he may make for the printing or distribution of an edition of his work being considered a transfer of his *privilège*.[27]

This decree recognized a practice that some authors had sought to impose, even at the cost of a lawsuit brought by the Communauté des Imprimeurs et Libraires, which claimed total monopoly on the sale of printed works.[28]

Moreover, the decree of 1777 set up a public domain—still extremely limited, of course, but new. It stipulated that "all booksellers and printers may obtain, after the expiration of the *privilège* for a work and the death of its author, a permission to print an edition, without the granting of this same permission to one or to several [persons] preventing anyone else from obtaining a similar permission"— which was a way of instituting free competition among booksellers for all titles not covered by an exclusive *privilège*. The measure was intended to favor provincial booksellers, who had been reduced "to abuses and counterfeits" by the publishing monopolies generously accorded to their powerful Parisian competitors since the reign of Louis XIV. It fell short of its aims because the publishing trade outside the capital had deteriorated so much, but it introduced one of the preconditions necessary to the development of an open and competitive literary market.

Printing: Enslaved and Emancipatory

By the end of the century the obstacles set up by the administrators of the book trade in an attempt to hinder the full development of this market had become intolerable. Figaro's famous monologue in the last act of Beaumarchais's *Le Mariage de Figaro* stands as proof of this. [29] The publishing business figures prominently in the previous career that Beaumarchais invented for the man who had become the *valet de chambre* of Count Almaviva and the *concierge* of the castle of Aguas-Frescas. Under the veil of a fictional Spain, Figaro attacks the entire monarchical system of censorship and control of the printing trade. Of the five careers that he had taken up after a childhood spent among the Gypsies who had kidnapped him (a detail that prepares the recognition scene in 3:16, where Marceline turns out to be his mother and Bartholo his father), three have had to do with writing. Figaro had first been a surgeon with no hope of establishing a practice except as a veterinarian. Disillusioned with the patronage system, which had betrayed his hopes ("I learn chemistry, pharmacy, surgery, yet the whole influence of a great lord hardly succeeds in securing me the practice of a veterinary"), he decides to write for the theater. But "to please the Mohammedan princes," the censors prohibit his play, a comedy "satirizing life in the harem." "There goes my play up the spout," he cries, and his exclamation echoes the fate of the *Mariage de Figaro* itself, which was written in 1775 and submitted to the judgment of six successive censors. Performance at court was prohibited, but it was finally performed in September 1783 at a private party given by the comte d'Artois, and in Paris in April 1784 it was performed by the Comédiens français ordinaires du Roi, who had accepted it four years earlier.

"A public debate starts up about the nature of wealth, and since one needn't own something in order to argue about it, being in fact penniless, I write on the value of money and interest." His ironic reference to the fashion for political economy fed by controversies between mercantilists, physiocrats, and liberals makes Figaro one of the throng of pamphleteers who churned out occasional pieces. Not only the censors threatened the writer, however: "Immediately, I find myself inside a coach looking at the drawbridge of a prison and leaving hope and freedom behind." The text plays here with an image that was strongly implanted in the collective consciousness of readers of the end of the eighteenth century: the Bastille, the symbol of a despised despotism. Books denouncing the horrors of the royal prison were among the best-sellers of the times.

Between 1782 and 1784, just when Beaumarchais's play was being performed, a seller of prohibited books named Bruzard de Mauvelain sold thirty copies in Troyes alone of Linguet's *Mémoires sur la Bastille* (1783), twenty-one copies of Mirabeau's *Des lettres de cachet et des prisons d'Etat* (1778), eighteen copies of the *Remarques historiques et anecdotes sur le château de la Bastille* by Brossays du Perray (1774), and another eighteen copies of a *Mémoire sur les maisons de force*.[30] These pamphlets and others like them propagated hatred of the arbitrary power with which the "potentates who last four days in office," as Figaro put it, placing the blame on the ministers, frustrated the legitimate rights of individuals and a necessary freedom of opinion. Such works forged a powerful set of images that made the royal prison a detested lair of cruelly arbitrary power, barbarous oppression, and atrocious torture.[31]

The literary motif was not without a basis in fact, since it was between 1750 and 1779 that imprisonment in the Bastille "for publishing offenses" (*pour affaires de librairie*) reached its height. In those thirty years alone, 383 of the 941 booksellers, printers, journeymen, peddlers, and authors locked up for such infractions of justice during the entire period 1659–1789 (40 percent of the total number, and more than 100 prisoners per decade) were held in the state prison. Authors (pamphleteers, fiction writers, gazetteers) made up more than one-third of this total (141 persons out of 383) during those three decades. The prisoners' stay in the state prison was usually brief, though it was longer for writers (more than six months on the average after 1750) than it was for men and women of the book trade (less than a hundred days on the average). The total number of persons imprisoned for having written, printed, or sold prohibited texts still made up 40 percent of the boarders in the Parisian fortress during the latter half of the century, with the exception of the 1780s, when both the number of prisoners in the Bastille and the proportion of people imprisoned for matters relating to the book trade declined. The figures show that the tolerance displayed by the administrators of the book trade did not in any way exclude repressive rigor. It was, in fact, when Malesherbes was director of the book trade, and, as we have seen, a director extremely sympathetic to the Philosophes, that the number of people incarcerated for publishing offenses began to grow.[32]

When Figaro emerges from prison, he attempts for the third time to live by his writing talents: "I sharpen my quill once more, and ask people what is in the news." He opts for journalism and announces a periodical, for "at public expense, free trade and a free press have been established in Madrid, so that, provided I do not write about the government, or about religion, or politics, or morals, or those in power, or public bodies, or the Opera, or the other state theatres, or about anybody who is active in anything, I can print whatever I want with perfect freedom under the supervision of two or three censors." His *Journal inutile* is stillborn, for it violates privileges already accorded: "I see a thousand poor devils of subsidized hacks in arms against me. I am put down and once again unemployed."

Discouraged in his literary career and betrayed once more by patronage ("Despair nearly had me by the throat when someone thought of me for a vacant place. Unfortunately I was qualified for it. They needed an accountant and put in a dancer"), Figaro abandons the disappointments of honest ambitions for the somewhat less honest profits of gambling: "The only way out was to turn thief. I set up as croupier of a gambling den. Ah, then, my dears, I was in the swim! I dine out and people known as respectable courteously open their houses to me, keeping for themselves only three quarters of the take." We are now back to the opening theme of the monologue, in which Figaro compares himself with the count and denounces not inequality of rank and "estate," which he recognizes as necessary to keep the monarchy from degenerating into despotism, but behavior that laughs at the ethical responsibilities that that privilege imparts. Abandoning his trade once more, after an attempted suicide, Figaro returns to his first trade ("I take up my razors and lancet"). We all know what happens next from *The Barber of Seville* and *The Marriage of Figaro*.

The principal target of Figaro's criticism in his monologue is thus the regulation of the printing trade, with its preliminary censorship in the hands of the central authority, its *privilèges* and monopolies that shriveled new initiatives, and its severe regulation. As to freedom of the press: "How I should like to hold in the hollow of my hand one of these potentates who last four days in office and are ready to ordain punishments! When a healthy fall from grace had sobered his pride, I'd let him know that printed nonsense is dangerous only in countries where its free circulation is hampered; that without the right to criticize, praise and approval are worthless, and that only petty men fear petty writings." Calling for a free press meant urging the demolition of a system that hindered freedom to speak and that, far from expressing the government's strength, betrayed its vulnerability. However, to demand the disappearance of the institutions sustaining the administration of the book trade was also to plead for the independence of literary activity and writers. Beaumarchais, who founded the Bureau de législation dramatique, which aimed at protecting the interests of dramatic authors against the claims of the actors of the Comédie française, and was an ardent defender of writers' rights, thus used Figaro to speak out for the legitimacy of the literary career and the freedom of the press that was the precondition of that legitimacy.

The printing trade was thus in irons and had to be liberated from the shackles that restrained it and the control that subjugated it. If such a liberation was thinkable, it was because the progress of enlightenment depended upon an art that dissipated all errors and overturned all oppression. At the height of the Revolution, Condorcet, following the lead of others (I am thinking of the *Histoire de l'origine et des premiers progrès de l'imprimerie,* published by Prosper Marchand, The Hague, 1740),[33] celebrated the indomitable force of printing:

Has not printing freed the education of the people from all political and religious shackles? It would be vain for any despotism to invade all the schools; vain for it to issue cruel edicts prescribing and dictating the errors with which men's minds were to be infected, and the truths from which they were to be safeguarded; vain for the chairs dedicated to the moral enlightenment of the vulgar or the instruction of the young in philosophy and the sciences to be obliged under duress to put forward nothing but opinions favourable to the maintenance of this double tyranny: printing would still be able to diffuse a clear and independent light. The instruction that every man is free to receive from books in silence and solitude can never be completely corrupted. It is enough for there to exist one corner of free earth from which the press can scatter its leaves.[34]

Was it that "corner of free soil" that nurtured the texts that caused the collapse of the ancient edifice? Do books really make revolutions?

4

DO BOOKS MAKE REVOLUTIONS?

T HE THREE AUTHORS WHO ACTED AS OUR GUIDES IN
chapter 1 had a ready answer to this question. They can speak
for themselves.

Alexis de Tocqueville:

Never before had the entire political education of a great nation
been the work of its men of letters, and it was this peculiarity
that perhaps did most to give the French Revolution its excep-
tional character and the régime that followed it the form we are
familiar with. Our men of letters did not merely impart their
revolutionary ideas to the French nation; they also shaped the
national temperament and outlook on life. In the long process
of molding men's minds to their ideal pattern their task was all
the easier since the French had no training in the field of
politics, and they thus had a clear field. The result was that our
writers ended up by giving the Frenchman the instincts, the
turn of mind, the tastes, and even the eccentricities of the
literary man. And when the time came for action, these literary
propensities were imported into the political arena. [1]

Hippolyte Taine:

Philosophy winds through and overflows all channels public
and private, by manuals of impiety, like the "Théologies porta-
tives," and in the lascivious novels circulated secretly, through

epigrams and songs, through daily novelties, through the amusements of fairs and the harangues of the Academy, through tragedy and the opera, from the beginning to the end of the century, from the "Oedipe" of Voltaire to the "Tarare" of Beaumarchais. It seems as if there was nothing else in the world. At least it is found everywhere and it floods all literary efforts; nobody cares whether it deforms them, content in making them serve as a conduit.[2]

Daniel Mornet:

Philosophy made it possible for those who chose to take up politics to discourse about it. Political pamphlets doubtless circulated at all times during the Old Regime, even when censorship was most severe and most effective, but they were fairly rare and they circulated with some difficulty. After 1770, however, and particularly after 1780, the freedom to write that the Philosophes had demanded was nearly total in fact. . . . That is why the hundreds of libels published with not the least philosophical intent and utterly anodyne treatises were among the causes that had the strongest effect upon opinion: they displayed political problems before it and gave it a taste for reflection on [political matters].[3]

A common idea underlies these three statements: reading is endowed with such power that it is capable of totally transforming readers and making them into what the texts envisage. Thus these three authors, each in his own way, understood the shaping of opinion in prerevolutionary France as a process of internalization, on the part of more and more readers as the century progressed, of ways of thinking proposed by the philosophical texts. Borne by the printed word, the new ideas conquered people's minds, molded their ways of being, and elicited questions. If the French of the late eighteenth century fashioned the Revolution, it is because they had in turn been fashioned by books. Furthermore, those books provided an abstract discourse remote from the practice of daily affairs and a criticism of tradition destructive to authority. This is my working hypothesis, although I reserve the right to express a few doubts along the way.

Increased Readership

Figures show—to begin with the most massive set of data—that booksellers offered a more numerous and increasingly avid reading public a profoundly transformed product. As far as the readers are concerned, the most important point here is perhaps not so much the overall rise in literacy (the rate rose from 29 percent to 47 percent for men and from 14 percent to 27 percent for women between 1686–90 and 1786–90) as it is the increasing evidence of printed matter in social milieux in which people had formerly owned few books. During the course of the century, in fact, there was an increase in both the proportion of the population that owned books (particularly among craftsmen and shopkeepers) and the size of their libraries. In Paris, books, which at the beginning of the century appeared in only 30 percent of inventories after death for domestic servants and 13 percent for journeymen workers, figured in 40 percent and 35 percent, respectively, of such inventories in 1780. In the towns and cities of western France, the proportion of inventories after death that mention printed works rose, between the end of the seventeenth century and the middle of the eighteenth century, from 10 percent to 25 percent in estates evaluated at less than 500 livres; from less than 30 percent to more than 40 percent in estates worth between 500 and 1,000 livres; from 30 percent to 55 percent in those between 1,500 and 2,000 livres; and from 50 percent to 75 percent in those evaluated at more than 2,000 livres. The size of the collections grew as well: between the end of the seventeenth century and the 1780s, the mode in libraries belonging to the *bourgeoisie à talents* shifted from a bracket of 1–20 volumes to one of 20–100 volumes; among the clergy the modal number of books owned increased from 20–50 volumes to 100–300 volumes; in the libraries of nobles and men in the legal professions the mode increased from between 20 and 50 volumes to more than 300 volumes. Although not all those who had achieved literacy could be counted as potential purchasers of books (especially in rural areas, where printed works were still only rarely found in peddlers' stocks), in the towns, at least, the market for books had grown and a larger number of readers demanded a larger number of texts.[4]

New commercial formulas arose to satisfy the demands of these readers (which often exceeded their means), such as the *cabinets de lecture* opened by booksellers after 1760 and book lenders' shops and stalls that enabled people to read without buying. Subscribers to the *cabinets de lecture* paid an annual fee of from ten to twenty livres in exchange for the right to read or borrow works that they might not be able to acquire themselves: gazettes and newspapers (which had a high subscription price), larger reference works such as dictionaries, encyclopedias, and almanacs, and the latest literary and philosophical works. The *cabinets de lecture* enabled subscribers to read extensively while spending little and made prohibited titles discreetly available. They were successful both in Paris and in the provinces and attracted a large clientele from among members of the liberal professions, the merchant classes, students, and professors, and even among the better-off craftsmen.[5] The book lenders, for their part, made books available to Parisians by the day or even by the hour. As Louis-Sébastien Mercier wrote in his *Tableau de Paris* (a work that will often serve as our guide in this chapter), "There are works that excite such a ferment that the bookseller is obliged to cut the volume in three parts in order to be able to satisfy the pressing demands of many readers; in this case you pay not by the day but by the hour."[6] Installed in small shops or working from stalls in the open, these *bouquinistes* probably reached the readers who were lowest on the social scale and who devoured novelties and political pamphlets in the public areas of France's major city. Thus, even though the private libraries revealed in the notaries' inventories increased in both number and size during the last decades of the Old Regime, they are insufficient to measure the hunger for reading matter that tormented even the humblest city dwellers.

A Transformed Product

The eighteenth-century book industry offered this proliferation of readers a totally transformed product. The most spectacular change in the book trade, as reflected in the requests for *permissions publiques* (both *privilèges* and simple permissions to publish), was the decline—first slight, then precipitous—of religious books. Religious titles, all categories included, accounted for one-half of the production of Paris printers at the end of the seventeenth century and still made up one-third of their output in the 1720s, but they accounted for only one-fourth of book production early in the 1750s and only one-tenth in the 1780s. Since the other general bibliographical categories (law, history, belles-lettres) remained fairly stable throughout the century, it was the arts and sciences, whose proportional share doubled between 1720 and 1780, that benefited the most from the decline in books of liturgy and piety. This shift is even more pronounced where tacit permissions were concerned and where works in the arts and sciences claimed the largest share. Although such works accounted for only a quarter of the requests for tacit permissions in the 1750s, following belles-lettres, toward the beginning of the 1780s they headed the list, with more than 40 percent of requests. With the sciences leading the field as far as official permissions—*permissions du sceau*—were concerned, and with political works heading the list in requests for tacit permissions, the arts and sciences advanced irresistibly, offering readers the opportunity to inventory and enlarge their knowledge, but proffering works of criticism and reform as well.[7]

Works published with a permission—"public" or tacit—nevertheless constituted only a part of what was available to the French reading public of the eighteenth century. A large number of books that the book trade designated "philosophical" were also in circulation. Printed by typographical societies situated beyond the confines of the kingdom (in Switzerland or in the German principalities), imported clandestinely, sold "under the cloak," and prohibited and actively pursued by the royal authorities, the works characterized in commercial correspondence and secret catalogues as "philosophical" were a mixed bag. First, there were philosophical texts in the general sense of the term: works that held up morality and politics, beliefs and authority, to critical examination. Second, there was a pornographic literature that relied upon the classics of the genre but also included new titles. Third, there was an entire assortment of satires, libels (*libelles*), and scandalmongering narratives (*chroniques scandaleuses*)—sensational texts often spiced with salacious passages that denounced the highhandedness and corruption of the powerful. "Philosophical" books, known to the police as "bad books," were a dangerous commodity. Those who transported, stocked, or distributed them ran heavy risks: confiscation, the Bastille, the galleys. And even though printing houses outside the kingdom were beyond the reach of the officers of the king of France, they could on occasion arouse the fury of the Protestant powers who governed them. This meant that discretion was needed to circumvent surveillance (or to corrupt the authorities); it also meant that "philosophical" books usually commanded a price twice that of other books.[8]

The magnitude of the output of prohibited works has long been underestimated in studies that attempt a quantitative analysis of book circulation on the basis of administrative archives (in this case, the registers listing permissions to print) or notarial inventories of libraries drawn up for estate appraisals. Permission registers lack the many titles for which the bookseller-printers would never have dreamed of requesting a permission (even a tacit permission), so sure were they that the authorities would turn them down. Estate inventories generally fail to mention the titles that zealous heirs spirited away, before the inventory was drawn up, in the interest of protecting the memory of the dear departed. Mercier corroborated this practice when he described the *huissiers-priseurs*, court functionaries who seized and appraised confiscated goods and presided over public auctions: "The licentious books and the obscene prints are put aside by the *huissier-priseur* and are not sold publicly, but the heirs divide them up and have no scruples about selling their father's bed, his shirts, and his suits of clothing."[9]

Thus the titles listed in the public permissions registers indicate only a part of what Old Regime readers might have read. Taking the year 1764 as an example, we can see that the proportion of total book production that failed to figure in the official registers is considerable. Out of the 1,548 titles that were published in French that year and that exist today, only 40 percent figure among the requests for permissions addressed to the director of the book trade. Close to two-thirds of the books printed were thus produced either with a secret and purely verbal authorization, with no authorization at all, or in violation of a prohibition.[10] The bookseller-printers based outside the kingdom captured the better part of the market for books that lacked public permissions. Mercier noted as much in his virulent criticism of the royal censors:

> These are the men most useful to the foreign presses. They enrich Holland, Switzerland, the Low Countries, etc. They are

so hesitant, so pusillanimous, and so punctilious that they dare give their approval only for *insignificant* works. And who could blame them for it, since they are personally responsible for what they have approved? It would mean running a danger without glory to act otherwise. Since they add weight, in spite of themselves, to a yoke that is already incommodious, the manuscript flies off to seek a country of reason and wise liberty.[11]

Mercier's remark is not just an often-repeated commonplace; it states an essential truth about publishing. As Robert Darnton wrote, "it is possible that the majority of French books produced during the second half of the century came from presses situated outside France."[12]

Pirated and Prohibited Books

We must distinguish clearly between the two groups of books—prohibited books and pirated books—that made up this illicit commerce. When the two sorts of works were seized on entering the capital, they received very different treatment, both from the corporate authorities of the book trade and from the police. Prohibited books were confiscated and marked for destruction. Pirated titles (that is, as the *Encyclopédie* defines them, works "printed by someone who does not hold the right to do so, to the prejudice of the person who holds [that right] through the ownership the author has ceded to him; [an] ownership rendered public and authentic by the King's Privilege or by other equivalent letters of the [king's] Seal") were either returned to the sender or turned over to the bookseller who held the *privilège* for the title, who could then sell the copies and pocket the proceeds. Everyone involved in the book trade was acutely aware of the difference. Foreign publishers prepared two catalogues of their offerings: a public one for pirated editions and a secret one for "philosophical" books, and clandestine book smugglers were quite aware that the risks they ran were not the same for the two sorts of merchandise.

Pirated books were a fundamental part of the book trade, and they fueled the activities of both the provincial presses (notably in Lyons and Rouen) and foreign presses (in Avignon, Switzerland, and Holland). They formed the basis of the publishing strategies of foreign typographical societies, which were always on the lookout—through their literary agents, traveling salesmen, and corresponding book-sellers—for titles in high demand that would make good reprints. They accounted for a large part of the booksellers' business, as attested by the large number of pirated books that emerged from the stockrooms when, in application of a decree in August 1777 concerning the book trade, there was a two-month grace period during which such works could be authorized by the application of an official stamp.[13] Records of the stamping process are extant for eight of the twenty *chambres syndicales* of the book trade, and these indicate that 387,209 copies were legally put back onto the market in this manner. The decree stipulated rigorous penalties for editions pirated after the grace period—"a fine of six thousand livres for the first infraction, an equal fine and abrogation of license (*déchéance d'état*) in case of a repeated offense," to which might be added damages and interest that the owner of the infringed *privilège* could obtain through the courts from the publisher of the pirated edition.

The king's "act of indulgence" (as the preamble to the edict termed it), which accorded the two-month grace period for the legalization of pirated books in circulation, reflects two things. First, it recognized the broad scope of a commerce that concerned not only provincial booksellers but their colleagues in the capital. Panckoucke, for example, ordered foreign pirated editions of his own publications and of titles that he sold for the royal presses (the Imprimerie royale), preferring their low cost to the expense of financing a new edition himself. Second, it is clear from the king's clemency that although pirating books was a commercial offense and a violation of the *privilège*, it was not a threat to political or religious authority because, by definition, the pirated titles had all been granted a public permission. Thus the act, through illicit commerce, increased the circulation of legally authorized works—which perhaps explains why some bookseller-printers' names and addresses appear in the works they pirated.[14]

The same was not true of the *libelles contre la morale* so vigorously attacked by Mercier (whose own *L'An Deux Mille Quatre Cent Quarante* and *Tableau de Paris*, ironically, figured among the "best-sellers" of the clandestine book trade):

[As for] the books that have that odious nature, it is better to put them to the pulper—that is, to mash them in a machine made for that purpose, which transforms these scandalous pages into useful cardboard boxes. They make up the tobacco boxes that everyone carries in his pocket. The impious and obscene work, pulped and varnished, is in the hands of the prelate: he plays and fiddles with the object of his former anathemas; he takes snuff from what formerly composed *Le Portier des Chartreux*.[15]

The Circulation of "Philosophical" Books

But was the corpus of prohibited books that flooded the kingdom principally made up of such *libelles contre la morale*, now totally forgotten, or of the texts that tradition considers the very expression of the philosophy of the Enlightenment? This question can be answered only partially and provisionally until such time as Robert Darnton publishes his promised study of the 720 titles most frequently mentioned in police archives and in the records of the typographical societies. In the meantime, three lists of prohibited books, taken as examples rather than as necessarily representative, can shed some light on the matter. The first is a listing of the works seized from a Parisian bookseller, Roch Moureau, on 31 July 1777. On the order of Lieutenant General Lenoir of the Paris police, sixteen titles (there were fifty-nine copies in all) were sent to the Bastille for storage before they could be pulped. What sorts of works were they? Five titles were pornographic works: some were classics of the genre (the *Académie des dames ou les entretiens galans d'Aloysia* of Nicolas Chorier, the Latin original of which dates from 1678); others were more recent titles (*La Fille de joye*, translated from the English in 1751, and *L'Arétin* of Du Laurens [1763]). Equal in number to the erotic repertory were political libels and scandalmongering narratives, among them two texts by Pidansat de Mairobert (the *Anecdotes sur la comtesse Du Barri* [1775] and the *Correspondance secrète et familière de M. de Maupeou* [1772]) and *L'Espion chinois,* by Ange Goudar (1764). Finally, there were the Philosophes: Voltaire (with three titles: *La Pucelle d'Orléans*, *La Bible enfin expliquée*, and the *Histoire du Parlement de Paris*), d'Holbach (*La Morale universelle, ou les devoirs de l'homme fondés sur la nature*), and Mercier (well represented with eleven copies of his *L'An Deux Mille Quatre Cent Quarante*).[16]

The order that the *marchand forain* Noël Gille, based in Montargis, sent to the Société typographique de Neuchâtel on 30 July 1777 covers the same repertory, though it is weighted differently. Although pornography is still much in evidence (with *L'Histoire de dom B*****, *portier des Chartreux*, *Margot la ravaudeuse*, and *Thérèse philosophe*, attributed to the marquis d'Argens, joining the *Académie des dames* and *La Fille de joye*), the Philosophes account for most of the 23 titles. Gille the book peddler ordered 6 titles by d'Holbach, 5 works by Voltaire (aside from *La Bible enfin expliquée*, the *Lettres philosophiques*, the *Evangile de la raison*, *Dieu et les hommes; oeuvre théologique mais raisonnable*, and the *Questions sur l'Encyclopédie*), the complete works of Helvétius, and various works of Jean-Jacques Rousseau. Only one libel is included in his order, but it is an extremely violent one: *Le Gazetier cuirassé, ou Anecdotes scandaleuses de la cour de France,* by Théveneau de Morande. It was published in London in 1771 but declared itself "printed a hundred leagues from the Bastille, at the sign of Liberty." Noël Gille used the societé's secret catalogue to write out his order (which, incidentally, was not filled by the Société typographique de Neuchâtel, which was not eager to do business with those whom it suspected—with reason—of being bad business risks). It seems clear that he had access to their catalogue, since the better part of the titles he requested (15 of 23) figure on a handwritten list of 110 titles headed *Livres philosophiques*, made up in 1775, that Robert Darnton found among the archives of the Société typographique. Using idiosyncratic spelling, phonetic except for the word *philosophique*, which was rewritten correctly, as if it were copied, the peddler requested that similar lists be sent to him regularly in the future:

> Sit vous voulet trete avec moi vous pouve manvoier votre cathalo sur tout les livres [filo] philosophique duquelle je poures vous faires eun debis au condisions que vous merranderrer les marchandise fran de porre jusqualion. [If you would like to do business with me you can send me your catalogue of all the philosophical books, from which I can give you an order, on

the condition that you send me the merchandise prepaid to Lyons.}[17]

In Troyes, the titles ordered and received between 1781 and 1784 by Bruzard de Mauvelain, a bookseller who dealt in works that circulated "under the cloak," show yet another picture. Out of a total of 120 works that he requested, 48 were ordered at least three times (996 book copies out of a total of 1,528 copies ordered). Three genres dominate in this corpus of prohibited books: libels and political pamphlets (314 copies), pornographic works (206 copies), and scandalmongering narratives (178 copies). There are fewer philosophical treatises (only 107 copies), and the category includes neither Voltaire nor Rousseau, inclining instead toward the materialists (La Mettrie, Helvétius, d'Holbach) and the popularizers of the Enlightenment (Mercier, with his two titles, and Raynal, with *L'Histoire philosophique et politique des établissemens et du commerce des Européens dans les deux Indes* [1770]).

Reorders show which sorts of clandestine literature were most avidly consumed. Heading the list, ordered eleven times for a total of eighty-four copies, was a libel attacking the depravity of the late king, *Les Fastes de Louis XV*, published in 1782. Next came a pornographic work, *Les Muses du foyer de l'Opéra* (five orders, forty-six copies), a chronicle describing the shocking mores of the great; *La Chronique scandaleuse, ou Mémoires pour servir à l'histoire des moeurs de la génération présente* written by Guillaume Imbert de Boudeaux and printed in 1783 "in Paris, in a corner from where one sees everything" (five orders, forty-five copies); and a licentious anticlerical poem of Charles Bordes published in 1777, *La Papesse Jeanne* (six orders, forty-four copies). Furthermore, as we saw in chapter 3, pamphlets denouncing the despotism of the monarchy (*lettres de cachet* and the state prison in particular) were sure sellers. The *Mémoires sur la Bastille* of Linguet, *Des lettres de cachet et des prisons d'Etat* of Mirabeau, the *Remarques historiques et anecdotes sur le château de la Bastille* of Brossays du Perray, and the *Mémoire sur les maisons de force* accounted for eighty-seven copies. Mauvelain's orders, unlike those of Noël Gille, eschewed the canonical texts of the Enlightenment in favor of a denunciatory literature aimed at the aristocracy, the court, and, ultimately, the king. [18]

Philosophy and "Low Literature"

Does this change in reading material show the effect of a radicalization of people's minds during the 1780s? Or does it show only that Mauvelain's specialized commerce in Troyes left the classics of the Enlightenment to other book dealers? It is difficult to know for sure. It is certain, in any event, that until the end of the Old Regime philosophical treatises and politico-pornographic *libelles* were linked in both the practical dealings of the book trade and the mechanisms of repression. The catalogue titled *Livres philosophiques* distributed by the Société typographique de Neuchâtel in 1775 stands as proof of this.[19] The 110 titles it contains quite naturally include a good number of works of the genre that Mauvelain's clients found most to their liking: licentious works and political pamphlets and chronicles. Fifteen pornographic titles are offered, including all the classics of the genre, ancient and modern, from *La Putain errante*, a translation of Aretino, to *Thérèse philosophe*, from the *Vénus dans le cloître, ou la religieuse en chemise* to the *Histoire de dom B****, portier des Chartreux* and its companion volume, the *Histoire de la tourière des carmélites*. In the category of political denunciation, libels like the *Mémoires authentiques de Mme la comtesse Du Barry* (London, 1772) accompany multivolume series such as *L'Espion chinois* (six volumes) and the *Journal historique de la révolution opérée dans la constitution de la monarchie française par M. de Maupeou* of Pidansat de Mairobert and Mouffle d'Angerville (seven volumes in all, three of which had appeared when the catalogue was drawn up).

What is most striking in the secret catalogue of the Société typographique de Neuchâtel, however, is the massive presence of the Philosophes. The foundations of the new thought are represented by Fontenelle (if indeed the work given as *La République des incrédules* is his posthumous *La République des philosophes*), Boulainvilliers, Hobbes (d'Holbach's translation of *Human Nature*), and Bayle (through an *Analyse raisonnée* of his works in eight volumes by François-Marie de Marsy and Jean-Baptiste-René Robinet). Also represented are Diderot (with the *Lettre sur les aveugles*, the *Lettre sur les sourds et muets*, and the *Bijoux indiscrets*), Rousseau (*Le Contrat social* and the *Oeuvres diverses*), the popularizers of the Enlightenment (Raynal, Du Laurens, Mercier, Bordes), and the materialist current (four titles of Helvétius,

De l'Esprit among them, the *Oeuvres philosophiques* of La Mettrie, and, above all, fourteen works written or translated by d'Holbach). But the author who dominates the catalogue is Voltaire, with thirty-one titles that range from the *Lettres philosophiques* of 1734 to the *Romans et contes philosophiques* and the *Questions sur l'Encyclopédie*, published in the early 1770s.

Voltaire is also the author best represented in the second document I cite here: a catalogue drawn up between June and September 1790 by the Parisian bookseller Poinçot, who had been given the responsibility of inventorying the confiscated books stored in the Bastille in 1785 in the last campaign for the destruction of dangerous books of the Old Regime.[20] Poinçot had received this commission after he had volunteered that it "was possible to make use, to the profit of the City, of the great mass of printed matter heaped up pell-mell and without order, which would be lost in the humidity and the dust if haste were not made to rescue it."[21] The list, which covers books confiscated during the five years preceding the Revolution, is divided into four inventories and includes 564 items, which correspond to 393 different titles. It mentions a certain number of new titles along with the works already cited. In the pornographic repertory, for example, we find *La Foutromanie, poème lubrique,* by Sénac de Meilhan (A Sardanapolis, 1775), the *Errotika Biblion* of Mirabeau (A Rome de l'Imprimerie du Vatican, 1783), and *Le Rideau levé, ou l'éducation de Laure* (A Cythère, 1786). The pamphlets include libels directed at the queen (*Les Amours de Charlot et de Toinette* [1779] and the *Essais historiques sur la vie de Marie-Antoinette d'Autriche, reine de France* [1781]).

In the storerooms of the Bastille, as in the warehouses of the Société typographique de Neuchâtel, the works of the Philosophes shared the fate of the *chroniques scandaleuses*. The two listings even show similar results: Voltaire heads the list of books in the Bastille in 1790 with eighteen works. Next comes d'Holbach (eight titles), then Rousseau (four titles, including *Du Contrat social*, the *Discours sur l'origine et les fondements de l'inégalité parmi les hommes,* and *Emile*), and, with one or two titles each, Helvétius, Diderot, Condorcet, Raynal, and Mercier. Although only seven prisoners were inmates in the state prison on 14 July 1789, all the classics of the Enlightenment were there, victims of censorship and the king's police along with the pamphlets that Mercier so scorned:

A totally flat, totally atrocious, totally calumnious libel appears under the cloak; it is immediately bid up. People pay a crazy price for it; the peddler, who does not know how to read and is only trying to earn bread for his poor family, is arrested. He is thrown into the Bicêtre [prison], where his fate is predictable. The more the pamphlet is prohibited, the more avid people are for it. When you read it and you see that nothing compensates for its base temerity, you are covered with shame for having run after it. You hardly dare say, "I have read it." It is the scum of the basest literature, and what thing has not its scum?[22]

Thus the fundamental dichotomy dividing the literary field—we need only recall Voltaire's diatribes—into authors worthy of the name and *folliculaires* belonging to the "unhappy class who write in order to live" established no radical break between what the two groups wrote. Admittedly, the distinction justified strategies that made scorn for *la basse littérature* the essential sign of quality in a writer. As Mercier's *Tableau de Paris* tells us: "Among the ancients public consideration was alive; our glory is dim in comparison with the honors paid for services rendered to humankind. To slough off the burden of gratitude among us, people cry at every hand, 'The number of authors is immense!' Yes—of those who usurp that name or who have produced one lone tract in their lives. But in fact there are in France no more than thirty writers constantly pursuing their art." Mercier went on in a note to draw a distinction between writers "worthy of the name" who deserved to share "public consideration" (and its retributions) and "compilers, journalists, translators at so much the page" who failed to merit that honor.[23] It is not difficult to guess in which category the author of the text implicitly placed himself. When the writers excluded from the Republic of Letters internalized the distinction themselves, the opposition between the "High Enlightenment" and the "Low-Life of Literature" (the terms are Robert Darnton's), between the established Philosophes and the "gutter Rousseaus" (*les Rousseau des ruisseaux*), lent structure to literary rivalries, pitting the frustrated ambitions of the "low-lifers" against the well-endowed positions monopolized by the "High Enlightenment" writers.

Still, in both the commercialization and the repression of "philosophical" books, both sorts of writers knew a common fate, in fortune and misfortune alike. Defined as one specific corpus within all book production, such works may perhaps have shared a horizon of reading that responded to expectations arising from the attraction of prohibition and the seductions of irreverence or transgression. The coherence of this set of extremely heterogeneous works was not a matter exclusively of how they were viewed by the bookseller, the police, or the reader; it was rooted in the authors' writing practices as well. For one thing, even the best-known authors did not hesitate to use the forms most common to low literature. Thus Voltaire was a past master in both the use and the subversion of the defamatory *libelle*, the antireligious satire, and the political pamphlet, all the while juggling pseudonyms, false attributions, and parodic signatures. Second, genres were by no means clearly separated. Not only did philosophic discourse often invade pornographic texts (at times even infiltrating titles, as with *Thérèse philosophe, ou Mémoires pour servir à l'histoire du P. Dirrag et de Mlle Eradice*); the Philosophes themselves indulged in the licentious genre (as in Voltaire's *La Pucelle d'Orléans* or Diderot's *Bijoux indiscrets*, published in "Monomotapa" in 1748). This free circulation of forms and motifs doubtless reinforced the perception of "philosophical" books as a unified set of texts. Does this mean that they should be taken as the torches that set the Revolution ablaze?

From Reading to Belief

Most assuredly yes, according to Robert Darnton, who has little doubt that the large-scale diffusion of this critical and denunciatory literature, which increased in both its flow and its virulence during the two final decades of the Old Regime, profoundly transformed the representation of the monarchy by undermining its founding myths, by ridiculing the rituals through which it was expressed, and by accustoming the French to think of themselves as the victims of an arbitrary and decadent state. Thus "philosophical" books, whatever their intent, produced a veritable "ideological erosion" that may have made the revolutionary rupture inevitable. According to Darnton,

> The political tracts worked a dozen variations on a single theme: the monarchy had degenerated into despotism. They did not

call for a revolution or foresee 1789 or even provide much discussion of the deeper social and political issues that were to make the destruction of the monarchy possible. Inadvertently, however, they prepared for that event by desanctifying the symbols and deflating the myths that had made the monarchy appear legitimate in the eyes of its subjects.[24]

Thus there was a close connection between the deep penetration of corrosive and profanatory prohibited works and the exhaustion of systems of belief that guaranteed the king the respect and love of his people.

But does this view perhaps invest reading with a force and an efficacy that it may not have had? Let us return to Mercier for a moment. In his eyes, several things seriously diminished the force of persuasion of denunciatory works. First, the social sphere in which they circulated was much more restricted than for licentious works:

> Much criticism has been leveled at philosophical books, read by a small number of men, and which the multitude is totally unable to understand. The indecent engraving triumphs publicly. Every eye is struck by it; [the eye] of innocence is troubled, and modesty blushes. It is time for severe relegation to within the merchant's folders of what they have the impudence to display even outside their shops. Think of it: maidens and honest women also pass by in the streets!"[25]

Next, Mercier argued, interest in denunciatory literature was ephemeral: "Where is the libel that, after fifteen days, has not been flayed by public opinion and abandoned to its own infamy?"[26] Finally, he argued the public's incredulity: "Formerly it was fairly common to find a number of critical posters on the affairs of the day. . . . Caricatures of this sort are no longer affixed to walls; they have passed into pamphlets distributed on the sly. . . . Satirical thrusts are now found only in pamphlets [and] the fashionable world finds them amusing without giving them too much credit."[27] Louis-Sébastien Mercier was far from postulating that the readers of "philosophical" works gave full credence to the representations that the texts attempted to impose. His description of the way they were read recalls the characterization of popular reading by the English sociologist Richard Hoggart, who spoke of "an oblique way" of receiving a text that involves "skepticism," "unbelief," and "silent resistance."[28] The images in the libels and the topical pamphlets were not graven into the soft wax of their readers' minds, and reading did not necessarily lead to belief. If a connection existed between the massive distribution of an aggressively disrespectful pamphlet literature and the destruction of the image of the monarchy, it was doubtless neither direct nor ineluctable.

Shared Books and Contradictory Choices

Another proof of the need for caution in linking philosophical books and revolutionary thought is the presence of the same philosophical reading matter (in all senses of the term) among readers who made highly contradictory choices in the face of the revolutionary event. This happened in the case of Rousseau's work, which was known and loved among the common people. In his *Journal of My Life* the journeyman glazier Jacques-Louis Ménétra mentioned only six works, and three of them were by Rousseau (the *Contrat Social*, *Emile*, and *La Nouvelle Héloïse*). He claimed to have been on familiar terms with the author when Rousseau was in Paris for the last time, between 1770 and 1778: "We went into the café de la Régence He asked for a pitcher of beer He asked me if I knew how to play chess I said no He asked me if I knew how to play checkers I said a little He joked He said that was right for my age We played I lost I listened and I heard people all around who kept saying But that is Rousseau that's surely his brother."[29] The ardent Rousseau-ism of Parisian *sans culottes*, fueled by Jacobin discourse, the radical newspapers, and Rousseau's promotion to the Pantheon, was rooted in the reading preferences of the most "popular" readers of the Old Regime.

At the other end of the social scale, aristocratic readers were also devotees of Rousseau. One indication of this is the number of nobles (court nobles, provincial nobility, men ennobled through service to the crown) among Rousseau's correspondents; at 36 percent of all correspondents, they are as numerous as members of the Third Estate.[30] Another sign is the cult of Rousseau's memory in the gardens of Ermenonville, where, at the invitation of the marquis de

Girardin, the great names of the aristocracy came on pilgrimage. Yet another indication is the longstanding attachment, the Revolution notwithstanding, of counterrevolutionary émigrés to both the man and his work (*Social Contract* excepted).[31]

Rousseau not only provided reading matter for both plebeians and aristocrats; he was also the favorite author of some members of the commercial middle class, who took him for their *maître à penser*. This is evident in the letters that Jean Ranson, a La Rochelle merchant, addressed to Ostervald, one of the directors of the Société typographique de Neuchâtel. For Ranson, Rousseau was a veritable mentor: "Everything that *l'Ami* Jean-Jacques has written about the duties of husbands and wives, of mothers and fathers, has had a profound effect on me, and I confess to you that it will serve me as a rule in any of those estates that I should occupy." Rousseau's death deeply affected him: "So, Monsieur, we lost the sublime Jean-Jacques. How it pains me never to have seen or heard him. I acquired the most extraordinary admiration for him by reading his books. If some day I should travel near Ermenonville, I shall not fail to visit his grave and perhaps to shed some tears on it."[32] One point of reference—the work and, even more, the person of Rousseau, the guarantor of the truth of his statements—thus inspired different and even contradictory interpretations, just as it prompted contradictory allegiances.

The same is true concerning the *Encyclopédie*. Where its subscribers can be identified (as in Besançon and in Franche-Comté for the quarto edition of Neuchâtel), there are two lessons to be drawn. First, it is clear that because of its high price (even when the cost was lowered by a smaller format), the *Encyclopédie* could be purchased only by notables. Even more than the great merchants (a minority among subscribers), it was the society of the traditional elites (clergy, military nobles, members of the Parlement, men of the law and of the liberal professions) who made up the work's true public. Second, although some of those who acquired the *Encyclopédie* were dedicated to the revolutionary cause, the majority was doubtless indifferent or hostile to it.[33] Subscribing to the work emblematic of the Enlightenment thus implied no commonality of choice or of action among its readers, any more than its massive presence in the milieux most closely tied to the Old Regime state signified a radical rupture with traditional ways of conceiving of society.

Finally, the books owned by émigrés and condemned persons that were confiscated by the revolutionary authorities after 1792 attest to the strong and durable attachment to the philosophical corpus on the part of victims or enemies of the Revolution. What they read was not fundamentally different from the reading matter of the most deeply committed revolutionaries. Thus Buffon and the *Encyclopédie* accompanied Maréchal de Broglie to prison, and in the Temple Louis XVI read Montesquieu and Voltaire along with Corneille and La Fontaine.[34] These facts, which confirm Tocqueville's intuition ("basically, all who ranked above the common herd were of a muchness; they had the same ideas, the same habits, the same tastes, the same kinds of amusements; *read the same books* and spoke in the same way"),[35] make it impossible to attribute too direct a role to books. The new representations that they proposed did not become imprinted on the readers' minds, and in all cases they were open to varied use and multiple interpretations. It is thus perhaps risky to credit the incontestable success of philosophical works with the increase in distance between French society and the monarchy.

That distance was not necessarily the result of an intellectual operation, but it may easily have been set up in the immediacy of ordinary practices, actions taken without deliberation, and words that had become commonplaces. Mercier astutely pinpointed such spontaneous downshifts, which were all the more profound for being unconscious. They were discernible in ready-made formulas downgrading royalty by use of the expression *à la royale*: "A vulgar expression and frequently employed. Beef *à la royale*, cakes *à la royale*, boot scrapers *à la royale*; the cooked meats man puts the word in golden letters over his shop door; the pork products vendor sells hams and sausages *à la royale*; one sees nothing but *fleurs de lys* crowning stewing hens, gloves, boots, and ladies' shoes, and the teas vendor cries, A la royale!" No hostility toward the monarchy was implied in all this. To the contrary, as Mercier noted, "*à la royale* means, in the figurative sense, *good, excellent, most excellent,* because the common people do not suppose that the mediocre, in any form, could have the temerity to draw near to the court."[36] Still, common usage desacralized the attributes and symbols of royalty, depriving it of all transcendent significance. Elsewhere, Mercier noted:

Among the iron-mongers of the quai de la Mégisserie there are storehouses of *old shop signs* appropriate for decorating the entrance of all the taverns and smokers' dens of the faubourgs and the suburbs of Paris. There all the kings of the earth sleep together: Louis XVI and George III exchange fraternal embraces; the king of Prussia lies with the empress of Russia; the emperor is level with his electors; there, finally, the [papal] tiara and the turban mingle. A tavern owner arrives, pokes all these crowned heads with his foot, examines them, and picks at random the likeness of the king of Poland; he bears it away, hangs it up, and writes underneath, *au Grand Vainqueur.*[37]

The scene—and it matters little whether it was actual or imaginary—indicates that the image of royal majesty demanded no particular reverence and evoked no fear. This suggests another relationship between the shifts in sensibility and the large-scale circulation of texts undermining royal authority. Why could not the infatuation with philosophical books have been made possible only because a previous symbolic and affective disinvestment had worked to make them acceptable, comprehensible, and a matter of course? In this case philosophical books, far from producing a rupture, would result *from* a rupture.

There is in this notion a first reason to question the efficacy so often supposed for the philosophical text. There is a second reason also, however. Although the texts, and most particularly the political libels, were indeed mechanisms intended to produce desired effects, the techniques they used were always deciphered through expectations, interpretive tools, and levels of comprehension that varied from one reader to another or that could lead any one reader to lend a different and even contradictory status to a given work at a later point in time. Reading the philosophical literature backward, starting from the revolutionary event, runs the risk of attributing to it a univocal denunciatory and persuasive meaning. Eighteenth-century readers did not necessarily believe in the truth of what they were given to read (for example, on the arbitrary acts of a monarchy become despotic or on the depravity of the sovereign and his court), but their incredulity in no way diminished their avid appetite for forbidden books.

The pornographic *libelles* that focused on the great, the royal favorites, the queen, and the king serve to illustrate this point. Such texts operated on several levels and lent themselves to a plural reading. First, they followed the traditional conventions of the erotic genre: they used a codified vocabulary to express sexual pleasure; they played with the literary forms of the age and invested them with an unexpected content; they usually contained one character whose gaze stood in for the reader's. With the political libel, however, although these mechanisms are still recognizable as such, they are put to the service of an overriding purpose. Still, their message is not immediately perceptible. This is clear in the earliest pamphlets attacking Marie-Antoinette (the *Amours de Charlot et de Toinette* or the *Essais historiques sur la vie de Marie-Antoinette d'Autriche, reine de France*). Like the *mazarinades* more than a century earlier,[38] these texts did not necessarily aim at making people believe that the queen truly was as she was pictured; rather, they attempted to justify her adversaries in the court by disqualifying her. Readers aware of the struggles among the various courtly coteries understood that the meaning of such texts was not literal but lay in the effects they had on court politics. Other, more easily manipulated, readers might believe the accusations leveled against a queen described as governed by her senses and unfaithful to her duty. Thus a set of themes was put into place (amplified after 1789 by the revolutionary pamphleteers) that unflaggingly associated the image of a ravenous, bloodthirsty queen with the image of a lascivious and dissolute woman.[39] These varying horizons of reading, which accorded a variety of statuses to any one text, were to some extent determined by the way in which the "philosophical" books themselves were organized, with overlapping genres, crisscrossing motifs, and the blending of levels of discourse such as political denunciation, pornographic description, and philosophical reflection. This very plurality, inscribed in the texts themselves, makes it impossible to conclude that they were read in an identical manner by all their readers or that their interpretation could be reduced to any one simple ideological statement.

Did the Revolution Construct the Enlightenment?

Should not the terms of our initial question perhaps be reversed to sustain the idea that it was the Revolution that made the books and philosophy—that is, that it was on the basis of the revolutionary event that a corpus of works was constituted and authors selected who were held to have prepared and announced it? The ways and means of this retrospective construction of the Enlightenment by the Revolution are many. Election to the Pantheon was the most spectacular of these but also the most selective, since only two writers from past centuries—Voltaire and Rousseau—were glorified as *grands hommes*, all others proposed (Descartes, Fénelon, Buffon, Mably) having been rejected by the revolutionary assemblies.[40] Thus those two authors were recognized as true precursors of the Revolution. This is implicit in the inscriptions engraved on the sarcophagus containing Voltaire's mortal remains when they were transferred to the Pantheon on 11 July 1791, in a moment of unanimous national sentiment and alliance between the Revolution and the constitutional church. On one side the inscription reads:

> He combatted atheists and fanatics
> He demanded the rights of man against the
> servitude of feudalism;

The other side reads:

> Poet Historian Philosopher
> He enlarged the human spirit and taught it
> that it must be free.[41]

This is similar to what Robespierre said of Rousseau in his discourse "Sur les rapports des idées religieuses et morales" of 7 May 1794 (which, incidentally, lashed out at the materialist "sect" of the encyclopedists):

> Among those who, in the times I speak of, stood out in the career of letters and philosophy, one man [Rousseau], by the elevation of his soul and by the grandeur of his character, showed himself worthy of the ministry as preceptor of humankind. . . . Ah! if he had been witness to this revolution whose precursor he was and that bore him to the Pantheon [on 12 October 1793], who can doubt that his generous soul would have embraced with transport the cause of justice and equality![42]

The canon for precursors was not limited to the two authors elected to the Pantheon. It also included a variety of genres, such as the anthologies, or *florilèges*, published in the almanacs and the literary journals,[43] and works of extracts that offered selections from one author or a group of authors.[44] Véron's political catechism, *Au peuple. Des vérités terribles, mais indispensables, tirées de J.-J. Rousseau, Mably, Raynal, etc. et de tous les philosophes amis des principes de l'égalité*, belongs to the second genre, while the poem "Les philosophes," which appeared in *L'Almanach des Muses* for 1794 and celebrated Fontenelle, Voltaire, Diderot, Franklin, and Rousseau, belongs to the first. In political celebrations in the year II, busts of the Philosophes and the martyrs for liberty also figured in this retrospective quest for legitimacy. Thus in Roye, Picardy, ceremonial honors were paid to Voltaire, Rousseau, Buffon, Benjamin Franklin, Marat, and Lepeletier de Saint-Fargeau, and their praises were sung in "civic couplets."[45] The same was true of a number of widely circulated printed objects such as decks of cards (in the year II, the printer Gayant replaced the kings with "philosophers"—Voltaire and Rousseau, but also Molière and La Fontaine), revolutionary almanacs, ABCs, and catechisms. The *Alphabet des sans culottes, ou premiers éléments d'éducation républicaine*, also of the year II, offered the following exchange:

Q: Who are the men who by their writings prepared the revolution?
A: Helvétius, Mably, J. J. Rousseau, Voltaire, and Franklin.
Q: What do you call these great men?
A: Philosophers.
Q: What does that word mean?
A: Sage, friend of humanity.[46]

In one sense, then, it was the Revolution that "made" the books, and not the other way around, since it was the Revolution that gave a premonitory and programatic meaning to certain works, constituted, after the fact, as its origin.

From the Book to Reading: Desacralized Reading

That fact, however, does not invalidate our first question, which we can now reformulate thus: What place should one accord to the circulation of printed matter in the intellectual and affective transformations that rendered the sudden and radical break with absolute monarchy and a corporatively organized society thinkable, admissible, and decipherable? Even more than the critical and denunciatory representations massively proposed by the "philosophical" books, in all their diversity, should we not emphasize the transformations that profoundly modified the ways people read? The hypothesis of a *Leserevolution* has been advanced for Germany of the latter half of the eighteenth century.[47] According to this hypothesis, the new style of reading showed several characteristics that distinguished it from traditional practices: the reader's increased mobility before more numerous and less durable texts; the individualization of reading when, in essence, it became a silent and individual act taking place in privacy; the religious disinvestment of reading, which lost its charge of sacrality. A communitarian and respectful relation to the book, made up of reverence and obedience, gave way to a freer, more casual, and more critical way of reading.

Debatable and much debated, this hypothesis nonetheless accounts adequately for the transformation of reading practices in eighteenth-century France. With the tripling or quadrupling of book production between the beginning of the century and the 1780s, the multiplication of institutions that enabled clients to read without having to buy, and the increasing flood of ephemeral print pieces (the periodical, the libel, the topical pamphlet), a new way of reading, which no longer took the book as authoritative, became widespread. The motif, so often chosen by late-eighteenth-century writers and painters, of patriarchal, biblical reading at the *veillée*, when the head of the peasant household read out loud to the assembled family, was one way of expressing regret for a lost manner of reading. In the representation of an idealized peasant world dear to the lettered elite, communitarian reading signified a world in which the book was revered and authority was respected. Use of this mythic figure is an obvious criticism of the way city people read—typically insatiably, negligently, and skeptically.[48]

One last time Louis-Sébastien Mercier comes to our aid to define a cultural change—or, what is just as important, belief in such a change. His judgment appears contradictory. On the one hand, he deplored the loss of a diligent, attentive, and patient manner of reading: "In Paris hardly anyone reads any work that has more than two volumes. . . . Our worthy forebears read novels in sixteen volumes, and still they were not too long for their evenings. They followed with transport the manners, the virtues, [and] the combats of ancient chivalry. As for us, soon we will be reading only from [decorated fire-] screens."[49] On the other hand, Mercier noted that reading had invaded all social practices and that since it had become the commonest of habits it had obliged the book to change form:

> The mania for *small formats* has replaced the one for the immense margins that were all the rage fifteen years ago. Then one had to turn the page at every instant; all you bought was white paper, but it pleased [book] lovers. . . . Fashion has changed: no one looks for anything but *small formats*; in this way, all our pretty poets have been reprinted. These little books have the advantage of being able to be pocketed to furnish relaxation during a walk, or to ward off the boredom of travel, but at the same time, one must carry a magnifying glass, for the print is so fine that it requires good eyes.[50]

In the long run, Mercier's seemingly contradictory remarks converge in a common notion: when reading penetrated the most ordinary circumstances of daily life and avidly consumed texts that were soon abandoned, it lost the religious reference that had long inhabited it. In this way, a new relationship between reader and text was forged; it was disrespectful of authorities, in turn seduced and disillusioned by novelty, and, above all, little inclined to belief and adherence. The new manner of reading was accompanied by the exercise—both on a large scale and in the immediacy of practice—of Kant's "public use of one's reason" on the part of "private persons."[51] Thus the crux of the matter is not the content of "philosophical" books, which quite possibly did not have the persuasive impact generously attributed to them, but rather a new mode of reading that, even when the texts it took on were in total conformity with religious and political order, developed a critical attitude freed from the ties of dependence and obedience that underlay earlier representations. In that sense, transformations in reading practices were part of a larger-scale change in which historians have been wont to discern a process of dechristianization. It is to that larger movement that we now turn.

5

DECHRISTIANIZATION AND SECULARIZATION

WHEN HE REFLECTED ON HOW THE REVOLUTION and religion were connected, Tocqueville advanced two apparently contradictory ideas: antireligious sentiment had become "vehement and widespread"—*une passion générale et dominante*—among the French of the eighteenth century; nevertheless, the Revolution "followed the lines of a religious revolution" to define "a species of religion" fueled by a new belief in man's "innate virtue." On the one hand, when it had spread to all classes in the nation, "the total rejection of any religious belief" typical of the French had undermined the power of Christianity, thereby preparing that sudden break with tradition, authority, and the old hierarchies that characterized the Revolution in its founding radicality. On the other hand, however, disengagement from the old faith in no way signified a total loss of religious reference. To the contrary, it was the transposition of the "habitual nature of religions," Christianity in particular, to new values (faith in virtue, confidence in the perfectibility of humankind) and new expectations (the regeneration of the human species, the transformation of society) that made the French Revolution unique, formed as it was of ardent proselytism and a vocation for universals.[1] As Tocqueville put it: "When religion was expelled from their souls, the effect was not to create a vacuum or a state of apathy; it was promptly, if momentarily, replaced by a host of new loyalties and secular ideals that not only filled the void but (to begin with) fired the popular imagination."[2]

Tocqueville's analysis poses two questions that this chapter will attempt to answer. First, must we fully subscribe to the idea that the disengagement from Catholicism dates from the eighteenth century, with the corollary that prerevolutionary France was already profoundly indifferent to religion, and even aggressively irreligious? Second, when representations and practices formed outside the teachings of the church or even in opposition to church dictums were invested with a high religious charge, must we consider this transfer of sacrality an absolutely new phenomenon created by the revolutionary event?

Another question requires clarification before these two can be answered, since they presuppose that Christian beliefs, before falling into universal discredit, as Tocqueville said, truly and profoundly inhabited the souls of the French. The hypothesis of dechristianization assumes that France had previously been christianized; but, as Jean Delumeau has remarked, "Have we not for too long called 'Christianity' what was in fact a mixture of practices and doctrines with frequently but little connexion with the gospel message? If this is so, can we still properly talk of 'dechristianization'?"[3] Behind the appearance of respectful conformity, was the France of the Old Regime truly a Christian land?

A Religion of Stability

The terms *christianization* and *dechristianization* are used in the present text not to refer to what Christianity might be in its essential definition (a definition that is not the historian's task to determine), but to designate changes in deeds and behavior that occurred within a particular historically and culturally determined way of teaching, interpreting, and experiencing the religion of the Gospels, the most outstanding characteristic of which was doubtless its near unanimity in practice. In fact, with certain differences from one diocese to another, the clergy of the Catholic Reformation managed to impose two things on the faithful: regular and disciplined attendance at Mass and scrupulous performance of their Easter duties.

These two practices changed greatly from the end of the Middle Ages to the eighteenth century (as seen in the case of Flanders, which is quite probably generally applicable).[4] During the Middle Ages, Sunday Mass never gathered all the members of the parish, and everyone failed to attend at one time or another. Moreover, attendance varied enormously from one season to another, at its highest during Lent and dropping to its lowest during the summer. Finally, the obligation of annual confession and Holy Communion at Easter, instituted by the Lateran Council of 1215, was only poorly respected. In the cities and towns perhaps as much as half the population failed to fulfill the Easter duties, if we accept the estimates of Jacques Toussaert, who calculated that 10 percent of Christians abstained totally, 40 percent communicated only irregularly at Easter, 40 percent regularly received Holy Communion at Easter, and 10 percent went beyond the prescribed minimum. In rural areas, observance of the council's decree seems to have been higher, but it was also irregular, varying from nearly unanimous observance one year to observance by only a small minority the following year.

The Catholic Reformation's most obvious result was to impose regularity and universality on acts that, two or three hundred years earlier, were only irregularly performed. As pastoral visits during the seventeenth and eighteenth centuries attest, those who failed to perform their Easter duties had become very few, usually making up less than 1 percent of their communities. The negligent belonged to the highest and lowest levels of society, since we find among them gentlemen and officeholders who were refused the sacraments for reasons of notorious ill conduct (in particular, living openly with a concubine) and some whose itinerant occupations made belonging to a parish difficult, such as sailors, woodcutters, agricultural day workers, and shepherds. Attendance at Sunday Mass was high as well, favored by the enforcement of laws that closed taverns during Mass and prohibited work on the obligatory day of rest.[5]

Regular instruction from the parish clergy, backed up by the dramatic preaching of the missions, used the threats of excommunication or refusal of Christian burial to bring about this major change in collective behavior. Questionnaires drawn up for episcopal visits allow us to date this drive for christianization and even to note when it succeeded. It is possible, for example, to analyze how often questions were asked concerning frequency of attendance at the sacraments, especially Easter Communion.[6] Between 1550 and 1620 the question was asked in only 29 percent of the dioceses visited. Later, preoccupation with the matter increased and the question was asked in 58 percent of parishes between 1610 and 1670, and in 78 percent between 1670 and 1730. After this period of the strict imposition of new behavior patterns, following church dictates, the frequency of the question declined (asked in only 57 percent of parishes between 1730 and 1790), as though the religious authorities in a number of regions considered the battle won. Except for certain dioceses in the north and northeast of France slower to be conquered by Tridentine influence than those of the Midi, the church seems not to have doubted that henceforth all Catholics in the kingdom would conform to the model of the "good Christian" who attends Mass scrupulously and habitually performs his or her Easter duties. These widespread practices, elementary though they were, doubtless shaped a basic identity among the faithful, in which the repetition of the same gestures implanted in everyone a direct awareness of belonging and furnished a vital reference point that lent meaning to the world and to existence. As Alphonse Dupront wrote: "First there was the religion of daily life, that of ordinary days, set to a fixed rhythm, that of the Lord's day, and structured liturgically, in a correspondence between the drama of the redemption story and the yearly astral cycle so nearly perfect that it had become almost unconscious."[7] This "religion of stability" was specific to a cultural situation different both from that of earlier times, which had not yet reached that stage, and from a later situation of religious conformity in which Christianity was reduced to the great rites of passage of baptism, marriage, and burial.

But does this necessarily indicate universal religious fervor? In reality, behind the unanimous acts, documentable everywhere (here, from the mid-seventeenth century, there, after about 1730), lay profound differences in the relationship between the faithful and the institution of the church—the primary, if not the exclusive, mediator where relation with the sacred was concerned. There were differences between dioceses, and even within a given diocese, not in the practice of Easter Communion, which was nearly universal, but in the presence or absence of freer and more voluntary participation in religious life. This was true of priestly vocations as well, and, for example, of the founding of lay confraternities. The diocese of La Rochelle, the classic example, shows a sharp distinction in both categories between the more heavily wooded northern half of the diocese, where vocations were numerous and sodalities of the Rosary prospered, and the south, a region of plains and marshes where priests were in short supply and there was only a scattering of confraternities.[8] Thus it is clear that if the Catholic Reformation christianized the basic framework of both personal and collective experience, there were strong geographical variations in Christian zeal.

Changes in Sensibility: Death and Life

Although deviance from this model during the eighteenth century can be understood in terms of dechristianization, unanimous respect for Sunday and Paschal obligations did not disappear. Under cover of this respect, however, fundamental changes were transforming thinking about essential matters. The first decisive upset affected attitudes toward death. In Catholic lands, wills provide us with a massive, homogeneous, and socially representative documentary source reflecting those attitudes. Indeed, time-series studies of testamentary clauses show that between 1730 and 1780, both in Paris and in Provence, all the gestures that the clergy of the Catholic Reformation had inculcated in the faithful during the seventeenth century gradually fell into disuse.[9] First, the sums that testators left to fund masses for the repose of their souls decreased; next, there was widespread indifference toward the place of burial that received the mortal remains; finally, even requests for masses for the reduction or mitigation of the trials of purgatory ceased. In Provence, bequests for such masses, which had figured in 80 percent of wills between the late seventeenth century and the mid-eighteenth century, appeared in only 50 percent in the 1780s. Moreover, in the wills that did provide for such masses, the number of masses requested fell from four hundred to one hundred. Thus disintegration struck a set of practices based on two fundamental acts—the stipulation of the consecrated ground of a church or a monastery as the place of burial and the allocation of a notable portion of the estate (perhaps 4 percent in Paris between 1670 and 1720) to fund masses and charitable bequests.

Attitudes did not change at the same rate everywhere, of course. Such shifts occurred earlier in the capital than in the provinces, and more rapidly in cities than in rural areas. They were more noticeable among male testators than among females, and more marked among craftsmen and seafaring men or tillers of the soil—even among the more prosperous merchants—than among the traditional elites. Still, the change is a good indication that at least a large part, if not all, of the population diverged from a fundamental belief imposed by the Catholic Reformation—fear of the terrible sufferings of purgatory, leading to a demand for intercession in order to abbreviate them. When the acts commanded by these beliefs were abandoned, the structure of Christian discourse in testamentary preambles and invocations lost its coherence, since wills often omitted the formula "by the merits of the death and the passion of Christ" that had rooted the recommendation of the soul to God in a strongly christocentric piety, founded in the mystery of the Incarnation. Was this divergence from earlier practice unique to France? Continued fidelity to the older model among testators in the Countship of Nice, which lay close to secularized Provence but was among the states of the House of Savoy, indicates that it was. At the end of the eighteenth century, as at its start, nine out of every ten wills in the Countship of Nice contained a request for masses for the repose of the soul of the departed, and although the number of masses provided for shows some variation during the century, it shows no clear decline.[10] The same was true in Savoy itself, where testaments deposed with the senate in Chambéry show only a very slight decline in the proportion of wills with bequests for masses, shifting from 91 percent between 1723 and 1767 to 88 percent between 1768 and 1777, then to 86 percent between 1778 and 1786.[11] Habits thus seem to have been quite different on different sides of the frontier, even in nearby regions, which suggests the singularity of dechristianization in France.

Recourse to contraceptive practices brought a second series of ruptures with past customs that involved behavior patterns at their most intimate and demonstrated a declining observance of religious morality and weakened clerical control. Highly dependable demographic data attest to a reduced birthrate in a number of places after 1760. When women's average age at their last pregnancy is clearly lower than their average age at the termination of fertility, we can be fairly sure that voluntary birth control is being practiced. This was true in Rouen, where the proportion of "contraceptive" couples (thus defined) shifted from a range of 5 to 10 percent at the end of the seventeenth century to a range of 20 to 30 percent in the first third of the eighteenth century, to over 50 percent on the eve of the Revolution. It was true in the villages of French Vexin and in rural areas near Paris and in upper Normandy. Finally, it was also true in modest-sized towns such as Meulan or Vic-sur-Seille in Lorraine. Thus it is clear that even before the Revolution, during the three final decades of the Old Regime, contraception that was intended to put an end to childbearing (as distinguished from prolonging the interval between births) had become established, at least in northern France.[12] This new demographic pattern, which seems to have affected towns and cities before rural areas, and notables before merchants and crafts-men, was obviously an important break with a Christian sexual ethic that connected sexual relations with the intention to beget children.

Paradoxically, however, the teaching of the church may be seen, from two quite different perspectives, as the basis for this deviation from previous norms. First, by emphasizing the basic impurity of sexual relations, putting a high value on celibacy and continence, and closely associating the flesh and sin, the Counter-Reformation church developed an "asceticism of repression" (in the psychological sense) that, although it may have made delayed marriage and conjugal abstinence possible, also favored the practice of failing to complete intercourse. A circuitous casuistry held this practice, which necessitated strict control of the body, to be less sinful, or, in any event, to be a way to conceal weakness of the flesh. Hence the hypothesis that there was a strong correlation between the rise in contraceptive practices and the spread of rigoristic Jansenist preach-ing emphasizing guilt. As Pierre Chaunu put it: "Place on the map the zones of widespread Jansenism, of early and persistent dechris-tianization, and of rapid, continuous, and steep declines in fertility, and you will see that they superimpose perfectly."[13]

From the second perspective, the new family morality proposed by the church insisted on the need to protect women from too-frequent pregnancies, which endangered their lives, and on parents' obliga-tions to their children. Parents were enjoined to care for their infants and ensure them a decent upbringing and a proper start in life. This may well have led to a change in people's priorities, working to restrict family size, and hence to recourse to the cumbersome expedient of coitus interruptus as a means to that goal. In this view, a system of values less hedonistic and individualistic than has been thought was thus put into effect, turning the new teachings of the church favoring protection of women and children against the church's own sexual morality. Accordingly, when the eighteenth-century clergy taught the faithful new responsibilities, they brought about the ruin of the traditional Christian commandments, now ignored by couples who had become freer and more independent (perhaps even more so in areas where Jansenism was strong).[14] Although the two interpretations differ in their analyses, they nonetheless share the notion that the faithful appropriated the rhetoric of the church and turned it against the church's purposes.

Two other facts confirm the weakening of the norms of Catholic morality. First, even if the rate of prenuptial conceptions was high in the seventeenth century (or, in any event, higher than it was long thought to be), the rate rose after 1760 or 1770, reaching 10, 15, or even 20 percent of first births, with particularly high prenuptial birthrates in communities with a large worker population. Second, illegitimate births increased after the 1750s, not only in cities and towns but in the villages as well. Illegitimacy rates ran from 6 to 12 percent of all births in the larger cities (a figure that would doubtless be a good deal higher if births out of wedlock were restricted to first births, nearly always the case in illegitimate births). The figures for rural areas are lower (from 1.5 percent to 4 percent of births), but this is partly because country girls preferred the anonymity of the city for bringing their illegitimate children into the world. The long-term curve for illegitimate births clearly attests to a strong decline between the mid-sixteenth century and the period from 1650 to 1730 (when the rates were lowest), which undeniably reflects the success of the church's offensive against infractions of Christian conjugal morality. However, the same figures show a universal rise in illegitimate births—thus of sexual relations outside marriage—beginning in the 1750s and 1760s.[15]

Was this freer conduct unique to France, or could it be found in other Christian lands? In England, although voluntary limitation of births was not clearly in evidence before the nineteenth century, the rates for illegitimate births in rural areas, always higher than in France, doubled between the 1730s and the 1790s. The transformations that the first industrial revolution brought to people's lives and matrimonial customs particular to Britain (such as the continued practice of authorizing sexual relations before marriage between engaged couples) in part explain this rise, but it may also reflect a weaker social control on the part of the church—in this case, the Church of England. [16] If we add that contraceptive practices are well documented at the end of the eighteenth century in both French Switzerland and in the Rhine Valley, we can state that throughout northwestern Europe, where literacy was long established and widespread, people freed themselves sooner from Christian moral theology, both Catholic and Reformed. France may well have been both the pioneer and the epicenter of this disengagement, since it separated sexual behavior from church morality earlier and more systematically than elsewhere.

The Crisis in Christian Vocations

If France underwent a unique process of secularization between 1750 and 1775, it was doubtless because both sensibility and sociability had changed. Secularized Christians not only turned away from the teachings and ethics of the Catholic church, they neglected church institutions as well. A crisis in religious vocations was a first sign of this. Ordinations declined after the mid-eighteenth century in nearly all dioceses, reaching their lowest point in the 1770s. In spite of a timid rise during the following years, the French church on the eve of the Revolution faced a veritable dearth of priests, in striking contrast to the expanding recruitment at the height of the Catholic Reformation, which continued well into the eighteenth century. A number of religious orders underwent a similar decline in professions during the same decades.

The decline in the number of priests was accompanied by a change in the social categories from which the clergy was recruited. By the end of the century a growing proportion of priests were the sons of country people and peasants. Sons of officeholders, members of the liberal professions, and *bourgeois,* who had accounted for a large proportion of parish priests in the seventeenth century, rejected the ecclesiastical career when it was embraced by "merchants" (many of them rural) and peasants. [17] Thus a large segment of the population of France changed its attitude toward the priestly state during the forty years preceding the Revolution. Economic considerations—devaluation, for example, due to the combined effects of rising prices and fixed revenues from benefices—may have turned some sons of *officiers* and urban merchants away from a career in the church. The fundamental reason doubtless lies elsewhere, however—in a secularization of people's mind-sets that made them abandon the more spectacular religious engagements.

The changing composition of penitential confraternities, abandoned by the notables after 1770, is another illustration of this secularization. In Provence the officeholders, merchants, and burghers who traditionally served as rectors and vice rectors of the confraternities deserted religious organizations en masse in favor of Masonic lodges. Even though this shift was facilitated by similarities in the practices (secrecy, conviviality, independence) and functions (mutual aid, charity, discussion) of these two forms of sociability, this collective transfer of membership is nonetheless a sure sign of movement away from a type of association that had flourished under the Counter-Reformation and had constituted a major technique for the social organization of the faithful. [18]

The decline in new membership in the Marian congregations that the Jesuits had established in their colleges to effect a radical reform of piety, not only among their students but even more among the men and youths of the towns where they were established, was a further sign of crisis in lay devotional associations. [19] Even before the expulsion of the Society of Jesus, recruitment had fallen off in the congregations of Paris, Rouen, Dijon, Reims, and Rennes, which were neglected by their old members as well. It is true that the congregants' zeal remained high in Alsace and in Lorraine, where the Marian associations expanded briskly until the suppression of the Jesuits by the papal brief of 1773. At that point new confraternal organizations on the same model (those of the Agony of Christ, for example) took over, setting themselves the task of implanting in rural parishes an ideal of the Christian life hitherto directed, for the most part, at city dwellers.

Thus it is undeniable that in certain areas at the eastern borders of the kingdom an attachment to institutions that inculcated Tridentine precepts in the faithful remained strong throughout the Old Regime—a fact that should warn against overly abrupt pronouncements concerning the universality of dechristianization on French soil. Everywhere else in France, however, defections and conflicts, which led not only to the rejection of Jesuit tutelage but to the abandonment of the congregations, provided clear signs that lay confraternal organizations had run their course.

Shifts in sociability were accompanied by a profound transformation in the production of printed matter, hence in the reading matter offered to the growing numbers of the newly literate. The production of titles published with an official *privilège* or public permission attests to the dramatic change discussed in chapter 4—the decline, then the collapse, of religious books' share of the book trade and, as a corollary, the triumph of works in the various bibliographical categories of the arts and sciences. If we add to this strongly secularized but legally approved book production the totally secular, even critical, prohibited books, it is clear that readers of the last three decades of the Old Regime had available a full range of new printed works in which the old equilibrium had been completely shattered—works that relied on scientific and political writings as their basic frames of reference for the description of nature or the organization of the polis. As Alphonse Dupront said: "It is certain that during the final decades of the eighteenth century the centuries-long development of a process of secularization or 'civilization' (a word of the age) reached its peak. [Its] basic tendency was to exhaust all sacral myths, to eliminate all mysteries, in order to manifest a 'civil' society, perfectly homogeneous, in which the quintessential social act was to make public."[20] Dupront designated the exact point at which changing behavior connected with changes in reading matter. Widespread circulation, at once disseminating and vulgarizing texts that undermined or ignored the Christian organization of reality and shattered the foundations of tradition, was accompanied, among the reading elites (the same milieux that had made the most radical break with the old habits and prohibitions), by a new way of envisaging communitarian ties and individual existence. In their divergence from inherited forms, these new ways of thinking perhaps constituted a "prerevolutionary sensibility."[21]

The Reasons for Disengagement

Although certainly one of its signs and among its mainstays, the proliferating diffusion of new ideas does not in itself reveal the fundamental reasons behind a disengagement from tradition that was unheard of for its brutality, its massiveness, and its systematic thoroughness. Let us attempt a few explanations, with the aid of hypotheses formulated by Michel de Certeau and Dominique Julia.[22]

The first important point is the division in the church. After the emergence and consolidation of the various forms of Protestantism that shattered the time-honored unity of Western Christendom, conflict moved to within the Catholic church. Hence the doubly dechristianizing effect of Jansenism among parish priests in various parts of the kingdom (Champagne, Burgundy, the Loire Valley, the Paris region, Paris itself, and Normandy). By their rigor where the sacraments were concerned—that is, by allowing the faithful access to Holy Communion and absolution only after a stringent inner preparation and by demanding of them both knowledge of the mysteries of the faith and profound contrition—the Jansenist curés doubtless turned a number of penitents away from the confessional and the Eucharist when they were unable or unwilling to effect the true conversion demanded of them. Furthermore, when secular powers were mobilized in support of one of the contending parties (the Parlement on the side of the Jansenists, the king and his council on the side of the anti-Jansenist prelates and the Jesuits), a doctrinal and pastoral conflict became a directly political struggle.[23] This meant that it was inevitable that both the authority of the clergy and the certitude of belief were gravely shaken. Jansenist curés and Jesuit missioners engaged in acrimonious combats, with each aiming to destroy the religious legitimacy of the other, and each pronouncing the other heretical. Politicized, manipulated, and disputed between irreconcilable antagonists, the absoluteness of belief was transformed into a simple opinion that, since it was disputable, could be rejected. Unity of doctrine and discipline was lost once and for all, opening the way to incertitude, retreat, and disengagement.

By its particular brand of intransigence, the pastoral Jansenism of a fraction of the French clergy doubtless expressed (and radicalized) the essential dichotomy set up by the Counter-Reformation between a model of the institutional church directed to the imperative task of acculturation and a totally different way of experiencing the sacred that was henceforth devalued and stigmatized. In 1731 a Jansenist parish priest from the diocese of Nantes declared in a letter to a colleague: "Remember, my very dear and venerable colleague, the beautiful words of our divine master *Ecce mitto vos sicut oves in medio luporum* [Behold, I send you as lambs among wolves (Luke 10:3)]: let us regard ourselves, you and I, in these cantons as if we were in China or in Turkey, even though we are in the middle of Christianity, where one sees practically nought but pagans."[24] This letter clearly expresses the unbreachable gap between the Christianity of the clergy and the religion of the people, or, more accurately, the movement by means of which "a culture of the church, mistress, it would seem, of its intellectual and spiritual coherence, cut into the living experience of a broader religious complex that it esteemed necessary to purify."[25] When it established a strict distinction between the sacred and the secular orders at the precise point where their identities were tested existentially; when it instituted the obligation of ecclesiastical mediation in place of direct participation in divine immanence; and when it imposed discipline and controls on elementary religious impulses, invested with irrationality and anxiety, the christianization of the clergy—perhaps paradoxically—turned the faithful away from a religious apprehension of the world.

The ecclesiastical venture that aimed at inducing all Christians to share the clerical definition of Christianity was freighted with unbearable tension. Between the faithful and their Counter-Reformation parish priests—men endowed with a strong theological culture by years in the seminary, conscious of forming a society apart, and traditionally from more fashionable social milieux than their parishioners—mutual incomprehension was unavoidable. On occasion (concerning pilgrimages, confraternities, or exorcisms) the venture even generated open conflict, and everywhere it opposed two ways of experiencing the relation with God.[26] These tensions occurred throughout Europe wherever bishops and parish priests denounced the abuses and superstitions of a religion irreducible to their canons. If in France such tensions led, earlier than elsewhere, to the abandonment of acts that made a public show of obedience to church requirements, it is probably because the French version of Tridentine Catholicism, imbued with Augustinianism even outside Jansenist spheres, set up the most uncompromising cleavage between "popular" experience of the sacred and an institutional definition of licit practices and obligatory rules. The christianizing campaign, mobilizing all its resources (missions, preaching, catechism, schools), had at one time been able to impose acceptance of its norms, but the gap between popular and institutional religion became intolerable when authority was divided and the dynamic of conversion had run its course.

A second basic cause of dechristianization lay in the decline of the parish as the vital framework of people's lives. The latter half of the eighteenth century saw an increase in population migration—both definitive, when people left rural areas for the towns and cities, and temporary, when they left the village to seek employment, customers, or aid. Population movements of this sort had two results. First, they ensured a larger circulation for printed matter, news, and fashions, and hence they introduced new thoughts and new behavior patterns to communities that were formerly closed to the outside. Second, they destroyed the discipline and strained the ties of dependence formerly guaranteed by parish constraint and the authority of the clergy. In general, departure for the big city meant the conquest of a liberty and autonomy that made quick work of the old teachings and inculcated modes of behavior. Even for those who subsequently returned to the village, travel and familiarity with the urban scene were experiences that could easily undermine habits and weaken conformity. It is hardly surprising that the cities were in the avant-garde in the process of secularization and were first to abandon the prescriptions and prohibitions of the church, nor that the most highly dechristianized regions and milieux were those most affected by migrant culture.

Obviously, the trend toward secularization during the eighteenth century needs to be viewed, as Michel de Certeau reminded us, within a long-term process of change from a religious organization of society to a political or economic ethic. The most fundamental change that took place between the sixteenth and eighteenth centuries was, in fact, the substitution of politics—the politics of the reason of state and of absolutism—for religion as the organizing principle and frame of reference for French society. Religious structures and practices appeared unscathed by this shift; in reality, they were reused and newly articulated in accordance with new formal principles that were commanded by the requirements of the king, the state, and social order. "Political institutions *use* religious institutions, infusing them with their own criteria, dominating them with their protection, aiming them toward their goals."[27] The breach effected between spiritual experience—exiled from worldly affairs, relegated to inner life, mystical in the first meaning of the term— and public Christian behavior, henceforth subjected to the secular demands of "politicization," was the cornerstone of secularization, and it lodged at the very heart of the triumphs of the Counter-Reformation church. Instances of abandonment and detachment from the church in the latter half of the eighteenth century can thus be seen as signs of debilitation in practices that had become useless to an autonomous ethic built uniquely on social utility or the imperious demands of conscience.

Catholic Reformation, Dechristianization, and Transfer of Sacrality

By its scope, the dechristianization of the age of the Enlightenment constituted one of the most original and most striking phases of French cultural history. In their own fashion, the ruptures brought on by the Revolution reveal the impact of dechristianization in a variety of ways; for example, the geographical distribution of the clergy's oath in support of the Civil Constitution, which was demanded of all priests in the spring of 1791 and sworn by 54 percent of the parish priests, vicars, and parish assistants.[28] There is a clear contrast between the France of "constitutional" priests who agreed to become "public ecclesiastical functionaries" and that of the refractory priests who refused to swear allegiance to the new constitution. The first group held two bastions: the Paris basin, reaching out to include Picardy, Champagne, Berry, the Bourbonnais, and part of Guyenne; and the left bank of the Saône and the Rhône, including Bresse, Bugey, Dauphiné, and Provence. The second encircled the vast Parisian triangle on three sides: on the west (western Normandy, Brittany, Anjou, and lower Poitou), on the north (Flanders, Artois, and Hainaut), and on the east (from Alsace to Franche-Comté), penetrating like a wedge between the two "constitutional" blocks, since rejection of the oath was high at the heart of the Massif Central and in Languedoc. Thus the geographical distribution of the oath was complex. It was durable, however, and was perpetuated into the twentieth century in religious practice that remained stronger in areas where refractory priests were in the majority and weaker where priests who took the oath dominated.

Constraints imposed by the community were inextricably combined with the agonizing decision that events placed before the clergy. In that respect their choice can be seen as a reflection of the people's relations with both the institutional church before the Revolution and with an entire series of acts and beliefs of which the church was the guardian. Refusal to sign the Ecclesiastical Oath was more pronounced in regions in which Protestantism, consolidated by the Edict of Toleration of 1787, was stronger (for example, in Languedoc and Alsace); in regions joined to the kingdom at a relatively late date, which found it difficult to accept the Gallicanism of the church of France (such as the provinces of the north of France and Franche-Comté); and, above all, in regions in which a dense network of priests of local origin and rural background, seconded by vicars and substitute priests who lived close to the parish priest, projected a solid awareness of clerical identity and clerical particularity (as was the case in the west of France).

To the contrary, where the oath carried the day (in particular in the greater Paris Basin), priests were outsiders and townspeople, and since they were isolated from one another by a more diffuse parish network, they were more immediately subject to pressure from their parishioners. Their acceptance of the Civil Constitution, and, by that token, of the Revolution and its departure from Tridentine and Roman Catholicism, can be legitimately interpreted as the expression of a secularization already in progress and already widely shared, even beyond the limited world of the elites, who, as we have seen, were the first to break with traditional ways.

Approximately the same cleavages pertained in the radical dechristianization of the year II, which peaked between September 1793 and August 1794 and was effected by the *représentants-en-mission*, the *armées révolutionnaires*, and the popular societies. A map of revolutionary toponomy showing the communes that had changed names superimposed on a map showing the rate of priestly defections would place the most radical changes precisely where the number of priests taking the oath was highest—in areas bordering the Massif Central (the epicenter of resignations from the priesthood) and in the Paris region, the Dauphiné, the Rhône Valley, and Provence.[29] This differentiation can be seen as establishing a long-term division between a France that remained Christian and a France that was no longer Christian; it was a division that left observable traces in practice as late as the mid-twentieth century. But if the break was lasting and profound, it is doubtless because it revealed and exacerbated, in a moment of crisis, fractures that had been masked by obligatory conformity in the pre-1789 Christian state.

Thus the two waves of dechristianization in France—the one that brought changes to a number of fundamental attitudes during the three last decades of the Old Regime, and the one that rent the clergy asunder during the Revolution—return us to variations in how deeply the Catholic Reformation penetrated the kingdom. Resistance to secularization was strongest in the regions in which a numerous and mutually supportive clerical society—parish priests, but also vicars, chaplains, and curates' *locum tenentes*—accepted and maintained the "equilibrium, sometimes fragile but always necessary, between the emergent fundamental culture of popular religion, an anthropological reality, and the ecclesiastical culture born of a prodigious history and the bearer of a cosmogony and an eschatology— that is to say, of a conscience and a sense of existing."[30] Conversely, defections came sooner and at a more rapid rate wherever a more widely scattered parish clergy had developed a pastoral policy of brutal acculturation, attempting to instill a purified Christianity with no concession given to experience of the sacred, which it judged to be superstitious and condemned as incompatible with the true faith. The west of France is the classic example of the first case: it had a powerful "clerocracy" of priests native to the area and a vital missionary religion, external and even "baroque" in its emphasis on public devotions and collective acts, and integrationist in its attempts to accommodate deep-rooted rites.[31] The dioceses of the greater Paris area offer a good illustration of the second case. There the rigid Augustinianism of some members of the clergy who strove to convert the inner lives of the faithful was accompanied by weaker clerical control. Thus, by reading the process of secularization unique to French culture of the mid-eighteenth century in reverse, we discern what was singular about the Counter-Reformation in France: it arrived in France later than elsewhere (except in the dioceses of southeastern France); it faced a Protestantism that soon affected only a small minority; it was divided between two views of how to institute the renewed Christianity manifested and symbolized by a tenacious opposition between the devotional compromises of the Jesuits and the sacramentarian intransigence of the Jansenists.

Massive and profound, for all its anomalies and contrasts, the secularization that transformed France during the last third of the eighteenth century should not be understood as a desacralization. Although it marked a distance taken—or imposed—from acts that manifested the submission of behavior to the norms and injunctions of reformed Catholicism, secularization did not, by that same token, signify that all reference to religion was eliminated, not even outside the bastions of traditional faith. Violently dechristianizing in the short term, on a deeper level the Revolution doubtless constituted the manifest culmination of a "transfer of sacrality" that, even before it rose to the surface, had silently shifted to new family-oriented, civic, and patriotic values the affect and emotion formerly invested in Christian representations.[32] Not unparadoxically, if the replenished Christianity of the Catholic Reformation fostered disengagement and defection during the dechristianization of the Enlightenment, the Revolution, through its declared hostility toward the old religion, revealed to all eyes the reality of a transformation in belief that had already occurred.

Tocqueville's dual analysis therefore appears valid. On the one hand, it is certain that eighteenth-century France underwent a process of abandonment of Christian practices unequaled in Europe. Should this be imputed, as in Tocqueville, to the Philosophes' furious attacks on the church guided by an antireligious passion that became "all-prevailing . . . fierce, intolerant, and predatory"? Probably not, if we admit that books did not always have the efficacy that has been attributed to them and if we agree that the most profound changes in ways of being were not the direct result of clear and distinct thoughts. More than the "enlightened" denunciations of Voltaire and the materialists, it was religious discourse, turned inside out by the faithful in their inability to live up to its demands, that produced the most massive abandonment of Christianity. It is also clear, however, that universal incredulity (understood as the ability to set up a distance between oneself and the teachings and commandments of the church) did not imply rejection of all belief in a new set of values that, like the older values they replaced, transcended the particular, expressed the universal, and belonged to the order of the sacred. Thus the process of secularization of belief and practice that began long before the Revolution operated through a process of disengagement and transfer. Was the same true of the changing relationship between the people and its king?

6

A DESACRALIZED KING

I N 1789 THE LOVE OF THE FRENCH PEOPLE FOR THEIR KING
seemed unimpaired. The *cahiers de doléances*—statements of
grievances forwarded to the Estates General—are imbued with
"a state of mind of fervor and monarchic epic."[1] Their reverential,
enthusiastic preambles render thanks to the sovereign, promise him
continued loyalty, and affirm the certitude of a new and felicitous
order of things made possible by his goodness. In the *cahiers* the king
is portrayed as an attentive father coming to the aid of his weakest
children. The commune of Saint-Jean-de-Cauquessac in Gascony
addressed the king in praise of "the paternal love deeply graven in
your achievements by the ineffable deeds that you have [performed]
for your faithful subjects and that have given you the reputation of
the greatest king in Europe." The commune of Lauris, in Provence,
pictured the Estates General as a family reunion: "The dignity of man
and of citizens, abased until this day, will, we feel quite sure, be
raised in this august assembly, in which a just and beneficent king,
surrounded by his subjects like a father amid his children, consulting
them on the interests of his large family, will moderate the avidity of
some, withhold satisfaction of the demands of others, heed the
laments of the oppressed, dry their tears, and shatter their fetters."
As the protector and dispenser of justice, the reigning monarch
revived the merits of the good kings of the past and erased the errors
of the bad ones: "O Louis XVI, heir to the scepter and to the virtues
of Louis IX, Louis XII, and Henry IV, you have, since your first steps

onto the throne, established [good] social habits [*les moeurs*], and, even more to your glory, you have provided an example of them in the midst of a French court" (*cahier* of Lauris). "If Louis XII, if Henry IV are still today the idols of the French because of their good deeds, Louis XVI *le bienfaisant* is the god of the French. History will propose him as a model for kings of all lands and all centuries" (*cahier* of the Third Estate of Barcelonnette).

The *cahiers* thus insisted on restoring and reforging a link that, as the dictionary definitions state, bound a respectful and grateful people to a king whose chief concern was his subjects' happiness. The inhabitants of Sèvres, in the *bailliage* of Versailles, wanted to solemnize the king's accession to the throne in words both spoken and graven in stone:

> We beseech Your Majesty to deign to receive from the nation a title that is worthy of the eminent qualities of such a great monarch and particularly describes [your] patriotic virtues, namely, "Father of the people and regenerator of France." May this act of patriotism and the love of a sovereign for his subjects be transmitted to posterity by a monument adequate to eternalizing the importance of this event, and [may it] impress in the hearts of Frenchmen and even [in those] of foreign nations the unanimity of the sentiments of respect for its sovereign that fills this assembly.

The images traditionally associated with the figure of the king (father, judge, protector) thus appear to have been intact on the eve of the Revolution, deployed all the more forcefully for their contrast between the king's benevolence and the exactions of the seigneurs. As the citizens of Toutry, in Burgundy, put it:

> Having a perfect awareness of His Majesty's beneficent views toward his people and of the excessive vexations perpetrated upon us day after day by the nobility and the clergy, in that they deprive us, one might say, of our subsistence by the daily exactions with which they crush us, we thus implore the aid of His Majesty and beseech him to have the goodness to turn a kindly and favorable regard upon us in the moment of distress in which we today find ourselves.

The inhabitants of Lauris addressed the king in the following terms: "O great king! Perfect your works, support the weak against the strong, destroy the remains of feudal slavery. . . . Complete [the task of] making us happy; your peoples, at the mercy of despots, throng to take refuge at the foot of your throne and come to you seeking their tutelary god, their father, and their champion."[2] Far from diminishing the mystique of the monarchy, the passion for regeneration that seized the kingdom in the spring of 1789 invested it with new expectations and a new tension.

Still, even though the *cahiers* forcefully and fervently proclaim the loyalty and love that bound the orders of society (or the nation) to the monarch, the king as we see him presented in the *cahiers* was no longer fully the traditional king. The adjective *sacré* was still often attached to his name, but the term was already weak semantically. For one thing, the king was no longer the only "sanctified" element in the political order, since the nation, the deputies, and individual rights were also held to be *sacrés*. For another, the king's "sacrality" was no longer necessarily held to be divinely instituted and was often conceived as having been conferred by the nation. This shrinkage in the sacred nature of the person of the king is evident in all the *cahiers généraux* on the level of the *bailliage*, both of the nobility and the Third Estate, independent of their monarchic zeal.[3] Even when the king is praised as a force for regeneration, the representation of the monarchy shows signs of deterioration. Unwittingly, and in the heat of their arguments, the 1789 *cahiers* betray something of the "symbolic disenchantment" that, by separating the king from divinity, made possible (because conceivable) the revolutionary profanations that held him up to ridicule and opprobrium (by portraying him, in words and pictures, as drunk, insane, or a pig), and ultimately the unprecedented act of the execution of the deposed sovereign, which destroyed him in both his physical and his political body.[4] A full grasp of this process requires a look at several chronologies.

Mauvais Discours

The first chronology is short and Parisian. It traces the proliferation, after the 1750s, of statements hostile to the king, denouncing both his person and his authority. The first signs of this hostility could perhaps be found in May 1750, when riots occurred in Paris to protest the arrest of children by the forces of order, in execution of a decree of the preceding year that required that "all beggars and vagabonds who may be found either in the streets of Paris, in the churches, at the doors of the churches, or in the countryside and the neighborhood of Paris, whatever their age or their sex, be taken to *maisons de force*." The immediate cause of the revolt was the excessive zeal of the arresting officers (the *exempts*), who, either in an attempt to humor Nicolas Berryer (the lieutenant general of police) or to exact bribes from the families, picked up not only the preadolescent sons and daughters of vagabonds and *gens sans aveu* (vagrants), but also those of merchants, artisans, and workers. Although the Parisians' wrath was directed primarily at the police force—in particular at the inspectors and their agents, who, since the establishment of the posts at the beginning of the century had undermined the familiar and respected authority of the neighborhood *commissaires des quartiers*—it did not spare the sovereign.

"It is rumored that the king is a leper and bathes in blood like a new Herod," the marquis d'Argenson noted in his journal. The rumor suggested an explanation for the roundup: if the king was indeed the indolent and capricious slave to his depraved pleasures pictured in the *mauvais discours* reported by police informers, it was because he had leprosy; and if children were disappearing, it was because their blood was needed to cure him. This rumor completed the rupture between the city of Paris and a moody and cruel king who neglected the duties of his office. *Vive le roi sans étape! Vive le roi sans maltôtes! Vive le roi sans gabelle!* (Long live the king without army provisionment levies . . . without special taxes . . . without the salt tax). These were the catchphrases that resounded during seventeenth-century revolts, where hostility to those who violated traditional privileges and the rights of the sovereign (who was held to be deceived, led astray, and robbed by evil advisers) was based on a bond between the king, conceived as the dispenser of justice, and the customary rights that he guaranteed.[5] A century later, in a Paris that had experienced the Jansenists' denunciation of an impure and impious king, that bond no longer held. The monarch himself was accused and became the target of increasingly violent threats. Thus in a tavern conversation one police informant overheard someone say that "our market women will all band together; they will go to Versailles to dethrone the king [and] pluck his eyes out of his head, and when they get back to Paris, they will assassinate the *lieutenant criminel* and the *lieutenant de police*."[6]

Robert Damiens's attempted assassination of Louis XV on 5 January 1757 and his execution on 28 March combined to provide at once the most spectacular (and last) exhibition of the sovereign's power to punish and a clear indication of the rift between the king and his people. This dual event—the attempted assassination and the execution—generated two reactions. Newspapers (even those published outside France, which were not subject to royal censorship) drew no connection between the attempted regicide and such contemporary events as the crisis prompted by refusal of the sacraments to priests of Jansenist leanings and the conflict between the king and the Parlement of Paris, a majority of whose members resigned after the king's *lit de justice* of 13 December 1756. The newspapers took the tack of denying any meaning to Damiens's statements and presenting his act as that of an isolated fanatic or a monster working irrationally and without an accomplice. Readers were offered the portrayal of a complex ritual of expiation and reparation, reestablishing the bond between the monarch and his subjects.[7] As Michel Foucault wrote, Damiens's punishment was above all "a ceremonial by which a momentarily injured sovereignty was reconstituted."[8]

But the *mauvais discours* picked up by the police, and the *placards séditieux* they confiscated, express another level of awareness of this event. These denounce a conspiracy: a conspiracy covered up by the judicial interrogation held behind closed doors; a conspiracy in which Damiens served merely as the agent. The Jansenist party, for its part, had no doubts that the attempted regicide had been organized by the archbishop of Paris, the Jesuits, and those members of the Parlement who had remained loyal to the king. In the view of the "devout" party, on the other hand, it was the rebellious members of the Parlement, linked with the Jansenists, who were operating behind the scene. Above all, the word circulating in the streets and the writings spontaneously posted on walls teemed with statements violently hostile to the king, who was held responsible for all the woes of the state and the people and deemed the fair target for a just punishment.[9]

A year and a half after Damiens's execution, Emond Barbier, a lawyer, recorded the following event in his journal:

> Sieur Moriceau de la Motte, bailiff of the *requêtes de l'hôtel* [a court that handled complaints concerning royal secretaries, etc.], a hot-head, fanatic, and a captious critic of the government—a man at least fifty-five, and who married his mistress eight months ago—took it into his head, a month or two ago, to go dine in an inn on the rue Saint-Germain-l'Auxerrois at a *table d'hôte* for twelve. There, having turned the conversation to the terrible Damiens affair, he spoke heatedly about the way in which the trial had been conducted, against the government, and even against the king and the ministers.[10]

Denounced "either by the court of appeals people or by someone at the *table d'hôte* who was nervous about the possible consequences of such a statement," Moriceau de la Motte was arrested, imprisoned in the Bastille, interrogated under torture, and convicted of having written posters hostile to the king and the loyalist members of the Parlement: "It is rumored that *placards* were found among his papers that were posted at the gates of public gardens and other [places] before and after the attempted assassination of the king. He was asked where he had gotten the posters, to which he replied that he had torn them down, but the posters were neither glued nor pierced with holes from having been torn off."

His cause lost by a weak defense, Moriceau de la Motte was sentenced to "make honorable amends before the door of the church of Paris, bare-headed, in his *chemise*, a rope around his neck, with a lighted torch, [and] having signboards before and behind [saying] 'author of seditious statements attacking royal authority,' then to be hanged in the Place de Grève [and have] his goods confiscated." The public ritual of expiation and punishment thus took place according to the usual form. Reiterated proclamation of the crime (by the public crier's announcement of the sentence, by the confession and the honorable amends of the convicted man, by the signs he carried) and the spectacle of exemplary punishment were intended to manifest the restored authority of the king and strengthen respect for the king's inviolable person in all his subjects. The fact that the convicted man was an official of the king and a *bourgeois* of Paris merely added force to the demonstration.

Nevertheless, in September 1758, when the sentence was to be carried out, things did not go smoothly: "There was a great crowd of people assembled along his route and at La Grève. Some were saying that you don't put people to death for words and simple writings; others were hoping he would have his pardon; but they wanted to make an example using a *bourgeois* of Paris—a man who held a [public] office—in order to repress the license of a number of fanatics who are speaking out too boldly about the government." The reactions that Barbier reported show a mixture of the traditional representation of the king as dispenser of justice, who can punish but also must pardon, and a new awareness of a disproportion of the punishment to the crime. Words, whatever they may have been, did not merit death. For the Paris throng, the crime of *lèse-majesté* had lost its traditional impact (even though its meaning had been recalled in the royal declaration of 16 April 1757). In popular opinion, statements attacking the king, whether spoken or written, were no longer considered blasphemous.[11]

The Desacralization of the Monarchy

Barbier's account clearly attests to the dual effects of Damiens's attack. On the one hand, in spite of royal censorship and the prudence of the newspapers, the attempted regicide created a political stage on which the opposing parties accused one another of having wished the death of the king. The *mauvais discours* exchanged in the street or written as *placards* and *libelles* produced a radical politicization in which the monarch was no longer exempt from criticism and aimed at enrolling the common people of Paris in one or the other of the opposing camps. Thus the events of 1757 (perhaps for the first time) implicated the citizenry at large in political strife by creating "popular interest in the politico-ecclesiastical quarrels embroiling the parlements and appellants with the episcopacy and the monarchy of France."[12]

On the other hand, the would-be regicide inspired imitators—in words if not in deeds. In 1757 and 1758 a fair number of men and women of the people, without necessarily grasping the arcane complexities of parlementary or Jesuit politics, deplored the fact that Damiens's blows had missed their target and proclaimed that they would have done better. Accused of being the cause of the people's misery and of neglecting his duties, the king, even more than in 1750, attracted a hatred that did not always spare his family or the monarchy itself. Thus the groundwork for the "desacralization of the monarchy" (to adopt Dale K. Van Kley's expression) was laid in the 1750s, at a time when the *mauvais propos* of the people forthrightly speaking of their hatred of a king unfaithful to his duties joined a politically better-informed discourse of notables opting for either the parlementary-Jansenist party or the "devout" party. The two tiers were connected, since "the refusal of sacraments controversy . . . by desacralizing the monarchical person tended to liberate popular tongues, whatever their particular grievances."[13]

In 1768, at the height of the liberalization of the grain trade, which brought on increased prices,[14] Sartine, the lieutenant general of police, sent out a notice to the *commissaires des quartiers* of Paris: "You are doubtless not unaware that from time to time posters are found posted at the corners of the streets. It is your duty to neglect nothing in seeking to discover the authors in your quarter or at least in making in the breadth of your department exact rounds at the break of day in order to take down those that you find and to bring them to me immediately." *Placards*, in fact, circulated in great numbers in Paris at the time. Some conformed to the traditional model for such protests, denouncing the king's ministers without directly accusing the king. One such was a wall poster found toward the end of September 1768 by the *commissaire* of the rue des Noyers, which demanded that the king "get rid of Mssrs Choiseul and Laverdy, who with a troop of thieves cause grain to be taken outside the Kingdom." The *commissaire* was sure that he could identify the social status of the authors of this poster: "It comes from persons of little means because there is no [proper] spelling and the writing does not at all appear to be dissembled."

Other wall posters attacked the king himself, who was accused of having organized the rise in prices and being the first to profit from it. The bookseller Hardy paraphrased a text of that sort in his journal. According to him, the poster stated that "under Henry IV we suffered a [dearth] of bread occasioned by the wars, but during this time we had a king; under Louis XIV we similarly experienced several other [dearths] of bread, produced sometimes by the wars, sometimes by a real shortage caused by the inclemency of the seasons, but we still had a king; in the present time the [dearth] of bread can be attributed neither to wars nor to a real shortage of grain; but we don't have a king, for the king is a grain merchant."

This *placard*, which alarmed Sartine and the *procureur général* of the Parlement, ended with a mention of Damiens's attempted assassination of the king. It attested to (or aimed at producing) a breach of the implicit contract binding loyal people to a paternal and protective king who provided for his own. "The French people loves its Sovereign," the *Dictionnaire de Trévoux* stated in its 1771 edition to illustrate the use of the word *peuple*, "and the Sovereign is occupied with the happiness of his people; of his peoples. To call a king the father of the people is not so much to praise him as to call him by his name."[15] Paris in the 1760s saw a quite different reality: the king was debauched, venal, and intent on starving the people. He was no longer the king, and a certain number of Parisians were arrested at the time for posting "horrors and imprecations against the king."

In May 1774, during Louis XV's illness, Hardy noted: "Every day a number of people are arrested for having spoken with too much liberty about the king's illness, doubtless to give lessons of circumspection, particularly because the number of malcontents has grown. The rumor was that on rue Saint-Honoré one man said to a friend, 'What difference does that make to me? We cannot be worse off than we are.'"[16] "What difference," indeed; an immeasurable gap had opened up between the lives of ordinary people and the history of the dynasty. On the one hand, the king was no longer anything more than a private person whose physical body, afflicted or radiant, had lost all symbolic value. On the other hand, the man in the street had radically separated his own fate from that represented by the state of the sovereign's person. Humble folk no longer perceived their existence as part of an englobing destiny manifest in the history of the king.

After the death of the king, Hardy remarked, "The people, far from seeming affected by the death of this naturally good but weak king, who, in recent years, had unfortunately become the unhappy prey of an inordinate passion for women encouraged in him by villainous courtiers intent on fanning his distaste for work in order to become more powerful themselves, gave somewhat unseemly evidence of its satisfaction in having changed masters." There is an enlightening contrast here between two reactions. Hardy excused the sovereign by returning to the old theme of the king whose close associates take advantage of him and flatter him into a disorderly life in order to better their own positions. Hardy attributed an attitude to the people, however, that quite brutally expressed the dissolution of the affective ties that had lent meaning to the symbolism of the royal body as an entity manifesting the body politic of the kingdom.

Should we thus conclude that relations between the king of France and his people were radically transformed in the 1750s? Should we concur with Dale K. Van Kley when he states that "the Damiens affair . . . reveals that by 1757 the popular mauvais discours was affecting the monarchy directly," and that "this phenomenon did not long antedate 1757, and that the 1750s were in general decisive in this respect"?[17] It seems certain, in fact, that after the 1750s the authorities (the king's partisans in the Parlement, the *commissaires des quartiers* in Paris, the police inspectors, and their informants) began to pay serious attention to seditious statements, rumored conspiracies, and proffered insults to the king. Does this necessarily mean, however, that the desacralization of the monarchy had inexorably and definitively won over all minds? Perhaps not, and for three reasons.

The Limits of a Rupture

First, Paris was not the entire kingdom. *Mauvais discours* could, of course, be heard everywhere, as proven by the variety of places in which the most violent insults to the monarchy in 1757–58 were registered—in a tavern near Château-Gontier, in another tavern near Gisors, in the city of Clermont-Ferrand, in Mayenne, and in the wineshops of Sézanne in Brie.[18] Still, it was only in the capital, which was racked by political and religious crises, that "bad talk" became "opinions" that prompted fear in the authorities charged with justice and police functions. Opinions fed on the rumors that passed from one street or neighborhood to another and were capable of unleashing a violence that went beyond the merely verbal.

Second, it would be a mistake to see the proliferation of bad talk as a cumulative process that spread ever broader disaffection with the king between 1750 and 1789. After 1774, during the fifteen years before the Revolution, the statements and posters hostile to Louis XVI seem to have been less numerous and less violent than the ones denouncing Louis XV. The sharpest antimonarchical attacks seem to have lost their thrust after the Jansenist conflict subsided and the price of grain stabilized between the Flour War of 1775 (which resulted from a combination of a poor harvest and Turgot's decision to reestablish free trade in grains) and the crisis of high prices in 1788. There was thus a gap in those years between the fury of the *libelles* denouncing the depravity and the weakness of the *late* king[19] and the absence—the relative absence at least—of hostility toward the *reigning* sovereign. This contrast might be seen as support for the hypothesis that texts attacking the royal majesty owed their success more to previously established ruptures than to the introduction of new representations.

Finally, is it so certain that the French of the first half of the eighteenth century were truly persuaded that their monarch was sacred? The question might seem irrelevant if we recall that the French kings and the English kings were alone in manifesting the sacred—one might almost say the sacerdotal—nature of their royalty by a particular thaumaturgic gift, the curing of scrofula (the "king's evil") by the royal touch. The royal miracle was practiced in France to the time of Louis XVI, and it attested that the sovereign's power was supernatural, thanks to his anointment at his coronation and the intercession of Saint Marcoul, a healing saint before whose relics all newly crowned French kings prayed, and that both his authority and his person were sacred. "The sacred character of kings, so often affirmed by the writers of the Middle Ages, remains an obvious truth for modern times."[20]

Still, does this mean that the body of the monarch was indeed considered sanctified or that there was a real belief in a religion of royalty? The fact that many texts speak of the kings as "gods in bodily form" (according to one jurist in 1620)[21] does not by itself prove full belief in the literal sense of such declarations. Some historians find it extremely difficult to see true political sacralization of the person of the monarch in the wholly theoretical and fictional construction of the transcendence of the monarchy or in funeral rituals organized on the basis of the doctrine of the two bodies of the king—the physical body, vulnerable and mortal, and the political body, which never dies. If it is true, as Alain Boureau has written, that "conception of the institution does not infer any belief," the relation of subjects to their king cannot be conceived in the same terms as the relation of the faithful to the sacred as experienced in religious faith.[22] Understood in this manner, this impossible sacrality—whether the problem stems from reticence on the part of the church, which had little inclination to accept an unmediated divine institution of kings,[23] or from the sentiment that all mortal bodies, including those of the kings leading the *danses macabres*, were doomed to a common destiny—counsels prudence in putting a name to the process that weakened the relationship between the king and his people. More than a desacralization (which supposes previous sacrality) we should perhaps speak of an affective rupture; a disenchantment that was probably not completely new in the mid-eighteenth century (Louis XIV had been the object of a similar rejection) but one that accustomed people to dissociate ordinary existence from the destiny of the sovereign.

Monarchical Conformity and Self-Interest

Jacques-Louis Ménétra, a glazier by profession, is a good example of this disenchantment. His journal and his other writings express a totally conventional loyalty to the monarchy—which is not to say that this loyalty was insincere. In 1763 he returned to Paris from Châtillon "to see the inauguration of the equestrian statue at the Place Louis XV." In 1770 he and his wife attended "that fatal marriage of the dauphin," the future Louis XVI, an event marred by a pushing match and a free-for-all that left 132 people dead and several hundred wounded ("It was a night of celebration changed into a night of mourning. . . . All we could do was wait over that fatal celebration which was like a prelude to the misfortune of the French"). In 1781 he wrote a poem to celebrate the birth of the dauphin:

> D'un dauphin nos voeux sont exaucés,
> Amis il vient du bon temps de vendange,
> Vive cet illustre sang de Bourbon.

With a dauphin our wishes have been granted.
Friends, he comes in the good season of the grape harvest;
Long live this illustrious Bourbon blood. [24]

Thus we find in Ménétra none of the bad talk and rude remarks
reported by the police and the chroniclers. Barbier tells us that in
February 1763, on the occasion of the same inauguration of the statue
of Louis XV that Ménétra attended:

> On the 23rd of this month, the equestrian statue of the king was
> placed on the pedestal in the new square across from the Pont-
> Tournant of the Tuileries. It took three days to transport the
> statue from the workshop, which was at Roule. There was a
> great crowd to see the mechanics of this operation, supervised
> by a builder from Saint-Denis, a man of great skill. The gover-
> nor of Paris, the *prévôt des marchands*, and the city fathers were
> under tents [with] Madame la marquise de Pompadour, M. le
> duc de Choiseul, the prince-marshall de Soubise, and others.
> But, as in a crowd there are always trouble-makers and ill-
> intentioned people, it was reported that along the way and in
> the square several persons were arrested for proffering indecent
> remarks about why the statue was advancing so slowly. They
> were saying that the king was going along the way he was led;
> that they would have a hard time getting him past the Hôtel de
> Pompadour; that he had to be held up by four *grues* [cranes;
> prostitutes] to be lowered on the pedestal, along with allusions
> to the ministers and several other *mauvais discours*. [25]

Ménétra wrote nothing of this sort. Even without violently antimonarchical sentiments, however, his political attitudes were imbued with an instinctive mistrust of authority and a fierce yearning
for independence. Where *commissaires du quartier,* police inspectors,
the watch, the militia, the *gardes françaises,* and, in general, all *épétiers*
(men with swords) were concerned, Ménétra was well aware of the
need for wariness and the art of avoidance, and, when the occasion
arose, resistance. His practice, then, confirms a political attitude
governed by self-interest and defense of one's interests. "I have never
liked to be hindered in any way, much less to lose my freedom," he
declared proudly, proclaiming a right to liberty that accepted neither

the consecrated hierarchies of a stratified society nor hindrances on private enjoyments. In Ménétra's "primitive Rousseauism" the king was respected, but he was kept at a distance, as were his agents.[26]

From Political Rituals to Court Society

If we wish to enlarge our angle of vision chronologically, it is tempting to trace the breach between the king and the common man to a major change within the monarchy involving the substitution of court ceremonial for the rites of the state. There is indeed a clear contrast to be drawn between these two modes of presenting monarchical power. This, at least, is the hypothesis suggested by Ralph E. Giesey.[27] The great political rituals organized into a ceremonial system of state rites—royal funerals, coronations, royal entries, the lits de justice—had a dual nature. On the one hand, the public character of the ceremonial authorized a direct relation between the king who was present (whether dead or alive) and all those who attended the event; on the other hand, the exceptionality of the event suspended, for the defined period of its duration, the ordinary course of time. In court society, in contrast, these two elements were reversed. Through the "privatization" of etiquette, the king was confined to a closed space and subjected to a ceremonial without end: he was removed from his subjects and hemmed in by a ritual that excluded any participation on the part of the people. Consequently, the ways in which the king was perceived and imagined were radically altered.

When did this removal, this gulf between the king's "privacy" and his subjects' gaze, begin? One observable break came during the reign of Louis XIV, who abandoned the rites of state—his last royal entry into Paris occurred at his marriage in 1660; he held no lit de justice after 1673—and chose to fix his court at Versailles. We may need to seek even further back in time, however, to 1610, when the system of public ceremonials was dismantled. At that date the young Louis XIII, still a minor, held a lit de justice in the Parlement of Paris even before the late king, Henry IV, had been buried. Indicating by this means that the fullness of his power owed nothing to funeral ritual, the new sovereign destroyed the symbolic significance that had been invested in royal funerals. These funerals had several unusual aspects. First, the reigning king did not participate in any public function connected with the obsequies for his predecessor. Second, an effigy of the late king played a central role in the rites. (This effigy was a wooden, wicker, or leather mannequin with a wax face modeled to resemble the late king's features, and bearing the insignia of sovereignty. Laid out on a processional bed, it was served by the king's household and displayed, at some distance from the corpse of the late king, in the cortège that made its way through Paris.) Third, at the end of the ceremonies at Saint-Denis, the crown, the scepter, and the hand of justice were removed from the effigy to cries of "The King is dead! Long live the king!" and distributed among the late king's suite.

This funeral ritual had a dual meaning. It signified that the royal "dignity" (office, rank, or title) remained attached to the dead king up to the time he was buried, even though sovereign power to make laws passed to his successor at the moment of the preceding monarch's death. The "dignity" of the reigning king was thus considered incomplete until his predecessor had been lowered into his tomb and he himself had been anointed and crowned. The use of an effigy—a solid object that could be exhibited, "nourished," and carried—was more appropriate than using a corruptible corpse (even when embalmed) to support the long and complex ritual dramatizing this political idea, which, by implication, required the concealment of the living king, who was not yet accoutred with full monarchic dignity. On the other hand, the funeral ritual, whose impact was heightened by its exceptionality, gave visible form to the principle of royal sovereignty. The effigy designated and displayed what was ordinarily invisible: the undying political body of the king. Conversely, his natural body, ordinarily visible, was out of sight, sealed up in the coffin. In the funeral procession, the clergy accompanied the king's mortal remains by their presence and their prayers, but it was the magistrates of the Parlement who walked surrounding the wax image, because "justice never ceases."[28]

When, in 1610, Louis XIII confounded the order of rituals, thereby altering their meaning, he dealt a fatal blow to the entire construction that linked the public nature of ceremonies to public display of the mystery of the monarchy. In fact, the entire system fell to pieces. The reigning king was present at the exposition of the effigy (which disappeared from the ceremony after 1610); the anoint-ment and coronation of the new king became a simple confirmation of the full possession of sovereignty rather than a ritual of inaugura-tion; the invention of the new rite of the *roi dormant* (the sleeping king) joined into one the natural body and the political body of the king, which formerly had been dissociated in the king's mortal remains and his effigy. Even before the establishment of the cult of the monarchy within the court society, then, the political body of the king had been absorbed into his physical body, thus making the distinction between the individual person of each sovereign and the royal *dignitas* invisible and even inconceivable. With Louis XIV, the affirmation of the unity of the symbolic body of the monarch (for the obverse of *l'Etat, c'est moi* is *le moi, c'est l'Etat*) was to obliterate the older way of constructing and presenting power and place much greater insistence on the absoluteness of royal power than on the perpetuity of the royal dignity.[29] By eliminating popular participa-tion in ceremonials of sovereignty—thus effecting a profound change in the concept of royalty—the shift from state rituals to court society that had been prepared by innovations introduced into the royal funeral of 1610 would thus become the essential act that distanced the people from the king.

The Court as Public: Ritual without Presence

This analysis is a cogent one, but it requires refinement. First, court ceremonial cannot be considered as belonging to a privatized do-main. Versailles was, in fact, a palace open to "a varied throng, and an enormous, constant, and obsessive one."[30] People had many reasons for going there. They went to visit the palace and the grounds, as recommended by a number of guidebooks printed during the seven-teenth century; they went on administrative business after admin-istrative offices were installed in the château in 1684; they went to see what they could of the important events in court life (royal mar-riages, the reception of extraordinary ambassadors, the ceremony of the "king's touch," or the *Grand Couvert* on Sunday). One medal struck in 1685 bears the legend *Hilaritati Publicae Aperta Regia* (The palace of the king open for the pleasure of the public), solemnizing the fact that the king's house was open to his people.[31] To this first kind of publicness, ensured by the people's physical presence, printed images depicting court pomp and ceremony added a second, more far-reaching one. Engravings and "wall almanacs" (large posters bearing a calendar and a picture) assured wide circulation (to judge by the modest price of the engravings) of depictions of the marriages, births, and funerals celebrated at the court.[32] Court ceremonial was not, therefore, a private cult. Open to attendance by a variety of people and publicized through pictures, it remained in the public sphere.

With regard to the public nature of the acts they involved, then, the difference between court ceremonial and the great rituals of state was not as great as might be thought. Like court activities, state ceremonials were witnessed directly, in an immediate relationship between the king and the people, by only the limited number of spectators present in the cities in which they took place (Paris, Saint-Denis, Reims), and even then the spectators could observe no more than small parts of a long and complex ritual. As in the case of court ceremonies, the efficacy of state ritual was based on a number of media—pictorial, written, and spoken—that separated representation of the sovereign power from the physical presence of the king, be he dead or alive.

Furthermore, it was at the very moment in which the system of state rituals was coming apart—when court society was becoming established and royal entries and *lits de justice* were disappearing— that the monarchy established a new public ritual, the *Te Deum*.[33] This innovation, introduced by Henry III in 1587, accomplished two things. It took the hymn of praise to God that had been part of the ritual of the coronation ceremonies or the king's entry into a city and made it the nucleus of an autonomous ceremony; it combined the song of celebration of God with the reading of a psalm and prayers said for the king. The ceremony of thanksgiving—ordained by royal letter and celebrating the triumphs of the monarch (the birth of a dauphin, a military victory, a peace profitable to the realm)—focused on the sovereign, who bent religious ritual to his glory; it fell into the category of the great rites of state even though it did not require the actual participation of the king. Celebrated simultaneously throughout the kingdom and bringing together all the orders and the bodies of society, the *Te Deum* proliferated the presence of the king even when he was not there in person. Thus the ritual could "render present everywhere that unique personage, the incarnation of the state, at the very moment when, not deigning to show himself to his peoples, he chose absence."[34] This explains the increasing frequency of celebrations of the *Te Deum*: although it was used in Paris to celebrate victories only rarely before 1620, there were eighteen such occasions between 1621 and 1642, twenty-two during the minority of Louis XIV, eighty-nine between 1661 and 1715, and another thirty-nine between 1715 and 1748.[35]

Finally, although the minority of Louis XIV in 1643 and that of Louis XV in 1715 permanently fixed the model of succession invented in 1610, one cannot conclude that coronation at Reims had lost all symbolic impact.[36] First, even though the new king's investiture by the *lit de justice* gave him full sovereignty, only anointment and coronation could confer "sacrality" on him by any definition of the term. Second, the stability of that ritual, which underwent little change between 1484 and 1775, made the *sacre* of the king a privileged occasion for the conservation of dynastic and national memory. It brought together the founding myths of the monarchy (the legend of the Holy Ampulla containing the sacred ointment for the anointment of French sovereigns, carried by a dove descending from heaven) and the legend of Clovis, the first anointed king and the first thaumaturgic ruler. Although the people—even the people of Reims—were not present at the ceremony (at most, they were spectators at the sovereign's entry into the city), the ceremony was a strong force in shaping the popular image of the king. Even at the height of the court society, and even if it had lost something of its constitutional significance, the ritual of the *sacre* continued—as event, representation, and memory—to lend support to the irreducible uniqueness of the royal mystery.

Representation in Evolution

What were the effects of the development that Ralph Giesey has called "the merging of the two bodies, formerly distinct, into one"? That is, what happened when the natural body of the monarch absorbed the political body of the realm, replacing the theoretical fiction manifested in a ritual that distinguished between the mortal body of the flesh-and-blood king and the undying corporative and mystical body of the sovereign? With Louis XIV, the *humanitas* of the ruling king became the embodiment of the monarchical *dignitas*.[37] Even more than the overweening ego of Louis XIV, this change reflects a shift in the very definition of the notion of representation. The representational notion underlying the ritual of royal funerals rested on the principle that an image (in this case the effigy, which was also called *représentation* in Old French) can express symbolically an absent object or an invisible entity (here the perpetuation of the dignity—the office and function—of the king). The representational notion underlying the unity of the body politic and the historical body of the king is a totally different one because it supposes the presence of the thing signified in the sign: a coincidence of the representation and the thing represented. Conceived in this manner as ostentatious exhibition, representation of the monarchy found its model in the Eucharist. The phrase (doubtless apocryphal) *l'Etat, c'est moi* functioned in a way similar to Christ's "This is my body"; it made the body of the king into a sacramental body.

The first consequence was that the portrait of the king functioned just as effectively as the king himself; inversely, the physical person of the sovereign, in flesh and blood, was in itself his representation. If "to represent will always be to present oneself representing something,"[38] the portrait of the king in painted, written, sculpted, or engraved form, but also the immediate presence of the monarch, could be taken as the incarnation of the absoluteness of power. The transposition of the eucharistic model into the political realm endowed the body of the king with the threefold visibility of the body of Jesus: "as sacramental body, it is visibly *really present* in the visual and written currencies; as historical body it is visibly *represented*, absence become presence again in 'image'; as political body it is visible as *symbolic fiction signified* in its name, right, and law."[39]

The new way of conceiving and practicing the representation of the sovereign power had several consequences. The first concerned the way in which the figure of the king was presented. Tradition made broad use of symbolism, drawing from heraldry (the escutcheon bearing the fleur de lis), from allegories based on classical references (the king as a musician-hero—Orpheus, Amphion, or Cadmus—as Hercules, or, under Louis XIII, as Apollo), and from

Christian symbols traditionally connected with Christ (the pelican, the phoenix, and the sun—a symbol with a handsome future). The sun symbol figured among the royal devices as early as the reign of Charles VII. Developed during the reign of Charles IX, it became central in the early Versailles period.[40] The king, still young and still flushed with military success, provided the "body" of his emblem, the "soul" of which was the formula *nec pluribus impar*:

> The sun is chosen for the body: In the rules of this art, it is the noblest of all and, by its uniqueness, by the radiance that surrounds it, by the light that it communicates to the other stars that serve as something like a court, by the equal and just distribution that it makes of that same light to all the various climes of the world, by the good that it does in all places, everywhere ceaselessly producing life, joy, and action, by its unfailing movement (yet ever appearing tranquil), and by the constant and invariable course from which it never deviates nor balks, it is assuredly the most vibrant and the most beautiful image for a great monarch.[41]

The choice of the sun symbol and of Apollo, identified with the sun, commanded the entire symbolic system of the château of Versailles and its park. As Félibien remarked, "As the Sun is the device of the King, and as poets equate the Sun and Apollo, there is nothing in this superb dwelling without relation to that divinity."[42] From Tuby's *Chariot of Apollo,* sculpted for the monumental fountain at the end of the garden facing the palace, to the Grotto of Thetis (a nympheum turned into the workshop of the Sun, decorated by a sculptural group by Girardon of *Apollo Served by the Nymphs* and by two groups by Guérin and the Marsy brothers of *The Horses of the Sun Groomed by the Tritons*), there was a coherent intent to use symbols to magnify the grandeur of the king by combining the images of the Greek god and the heavenly body.[43]

During the 1670s, however, the same symbolic representation that had been given widespread circulation in accounts of royal entries and engravings waned at Versailles. The various stages of the decline of the solar and Apollonian myths are familiar. In 1674 the mythological and cosmic *grande commande* planned for the Parterre d'Eau was abandoned; in 1678 two projects presented by Le Brun and destined for the Galerie des Glaces—a story of Hercules and a story of Apollo—were rejected; in 1684 the Grotto of Thetis was destroyed. The older emblematics was replaced by "real allegory"; that is, by representing the king in his own likeness and illustrating the history of his reign. This is what occurred in 1674 in connection with the decoration of the Grand Degré du Roi (called the Stairs of the Ambassadors), which showed the great deeds of the king since his ascension to the throne. This was also the case in 1678, when a decorative scheme representing the triumphs of the monarch was chosen for the vaulted ceiling of the Galerie des Glaces. By setting the painting of historical events within the allegorical repertory, by showing the sovereign as he was and with his own lineaments, "the history of the king dismissed fable, to become its own fable."[44]

How are we to interpret this important change? First, it should be said that sun symbolism did not totally disappear from all the royal dwellings. At the same time that its use was in decline at Versailles, it was being used in the royal château of Marly and, to a certain extent, in the Trianon de Marbre. Should we conclude that the cosmic and mythological themes still deemed suitable for the decoration of pleasure houses were considered less so for a governmental palace? The pleasure house could employ subtle representations displaying only a visible sign of a concealed referent; the seat of government needed clear, simple images of unambiguous meaning.[45] This hypothesis, which connects the function of the building with its decorative scheme, has a certain pertinence. It should not mask the fact that the abandonment of the symbolic repertory, not only in the decorative schemes of the royal residence but in all print imagery (from engravings for the Cabinet du Roi down to those sold by print merchants), reflected a broader change that was profoundly transforming the meaning attributed to representation of the royal person.

This change had genuine importance in a system of political persuasion in which the "power to effect the recognition of power" directly depended on the efficacy of "instruments for the demonstration of power by public display [monstration]."[46] Lesser use of force to ensure the sovereign's domination implied that his subjects' belief in him and loyalty to him could be captured by other means. Contrasting modes of representation were an essential part of this operation, since it was "the representational framework [that] operate[d] the transformation of force into potential and of force into power."[47] The abandonment of symbolic motifs in favor of a more directly and broadly readable imagery seems to have attained its objective, because the court society and the figuration of the king in his historical role functioned like a well-oiled machine for producing obedience without using brutal constraint. The pacification (the relative pacification, at least) of the social sphere and a lessened need for state violence were rooted in the submission of captured imaginations. Pascal cut to the essence of the mechanism by which the image makes the king:

> The habit of seeing kings accompanied by guards, drums, officers, and all the things which bend the human machine toward respect and awe, causes their countenance, when occasionally seen alone and without such accompaniment, to inspire respect and awe in their subjects, because we cannot in thought separate their persons from the paraphernalia which is generally seen to go with them. And the world, unaware that the effect arises from this habit, thinks that it arises from an innate force; whence the phrase, "the character of divinity is stamped on his visage," etc.[48]

The King's Portrait

By its presence alone, in a system in which the image of the king functioned as well as his person and power was given as sacred, the king's countenance, freed of all symbolic camouflage, constrained the imagination. It was as if the change in the representation of the king from complex allegories to a simple, unambiguous, easily available figuration had taken a lesson from Pascal: "Who hands out reputations? Who apportions respect and veneration to people, to achievements, to laws, to the great, if not this faculty of imagination? All the wealth of the world would be insufficient without its help."[49]

From Louis XIV onward, the portrait of the king, which immediately activated what Pascal called *la faculté imaginante* of his sub-

jects, appeared in all written genres and iconographic media, including some that in appearance had little to do with celebration of the
monarchy. To suggest one example: In seventeenth-century Lyons,
the marriage ritual required that the husband give his wife a nuptial
charter blessed by the priest along with her wedding ring. This paper
contained the words of the vows and the donation spoken by the
husband during the ceremony set into a cartouche surrounded by
pictures (woodcuts; later, copperplate engravings, often colored),
with subjects taken from religious iconography (the Evangelists,
Saints Peter and Paul, the Trinity, or paired scenes of the Temptation
of Eve and the Marriage of the Virgin). These charters were in no way
secular, and even less did they have any political content. They were
printed in large numbers by the *imagiers* of Lyons, and every married
couple owned one (given that the marriage ritual required it) and
kept it in the family home as long as they lived. Even these marriage
charters, however—like wall calendars and broadsheets—contributed to the widespread presence of the king's image. One printed
version of such charters shows the king and the queen on the occasion
of their own marriage. The engraver noted on the border surrounding
the image: "This charter was made in the year of the Marriage of
King Louis XIV in the Year 1660." The motif seems to have met
with success, since Louis and Marie-Thérèse appear on another series
of charters, still in use in the 1680s, that added the Trinity and the
Evangelists to the picture of the royal couple. An engraving of the
monarch was thus installed at the heart of a large number of Lyonnais
homes, pictured engaged in the same act that gave the engraving its
reason for being. The ordinary lives of married couples in Lyons were
thus connected with a dynastic event, which was a way to have
humble folk feel, through a respected image, that they and their king
shared in a common history.[50]

Thus representations of the sovereign figured in a number of print
pieces that common folk encountered in their daily lives. It is quite
possible that these banal and familiar images did more to cement
widespread belief in the legitimate and inviolable authority of the
ruler than the grandiose decorative schemes restricted to a small
number of viewers. This touches the most essential definition of
popular political culture under the Old Regime, which doubtless

depended upon subjecting the mental representations of the king's subjects by means of the figurative representations they were given of the glorious body of their sovereign. How, then, are we to account for the fact that at one given moment—in Paris at least, but in a kingdom as strongly centralized as France, the humors of the capital were decisive—that system of beliefs cracked?

There is no easy answer to this question, as this chapter has shown. Should we date the gap between the king and a people who no longer perceived their sovereign as the incarnation of a common destiny from the 1750s? from the 1670s? perhaps even from 1610? Is it fair to consider the movement that caused certain of the king's subjects to forsake him or to set themselves up against him in word or deed a desacralization in some way parallel to the process of dechristianization? And should one lend more weight to violent and profanatory *mauvais discours* or to a peaceful detachment that used conformist loyalty as a screen behind which to construct an ethic of self-interest untouched by political transcendence? These are not certitudes; each of these questions defines a point at which further research and reflection is needed.

The hypothesis I might risk is the following: although the literal sense of the *cahiers de doléances* of 1789 is ambiguous, juxtaposing an exalted affirmation of the older representations and a new way of looking at the king (still seen as paternal, perhaps, but no longer as sacred in the traditional manner), it is doubtless because for several decades the system of the representation of the monarchy elaborated under Louis XIV had been in crisis. There were several reasons for this. First, the eucharistic model, borrowed to make royal power more easily conceivable and to endow images of the sovereign with a sacramental dimension, lost its efficacy as a consequence of the people's growing detachment from religion. Second, the less frequent presence of the king amid his subjects and the decline in the number of state rituals (mainly due to the simple fact that kings' reigns were longer) weakened the sentiment of participation in a common history. Finally, the progress of critical modes of think-ing—both in the intellectualized forms of a "public opinion" that debated formerly prohibited questions and in the spontaneous reac-tions of a less gullible man in the street—undermined the absolute authority long associated with impenetrable and intimidating mysteries of state. As Pascal put it, "Man is naturally credulous and incredulous, timid and daring."[51] At some point during the eighteenth century, the incredulity of the French in their relationship with representations of the person of the king triumphed over their credulity, and daring triumphed over timidity.

7

A NEW POLITICAL CULTURE

REDULOUS OR INCREDULOUS, TIMID OR BRAVE, THE people's relationship to the king was not all there was to popular politics. Peter Burke, in a broad hypothesis, has described the period between the early sixteenth century and the French Revolution as a time of "the 'politicization' of popular culture."[1] In Burke's view, "in Western Europe at least, between the Reformation and the French Revolution, craftsmen and peasants were taking an increasing interest in the actions of governments and feeling a greater sense of involvement with politics than ever before." Given its connection with the pressing demands of the centralized state, which demanded men for its armies and money for its expenditures, and fueled by the large-scale circulation of songs, images, and pamphlets hostile to the authorities, the people's participation in affairs of state, following Burke's line of thought, grew as the early modern period progressed. It would be a mistake to see this process as linear or cumulative; nevertheless, it produced a growth of political consciousness and moved events in the direction of a long-term change that, in France at least, destroyed the established order.

Was There a Politicization of Popular Culture?

The thesis merits examination and discussion. First, it is not certain that an increase in the number of printed texts that took sides regarding affairs of state in and of itself implies that the buyers and readers of such texts were of the people. Grenoble during the Fronde offers an instructive example. Thanks to the ledger of sales on credit kept by the bookseller Nicolas, we can isolate the urban milieux most eager for *libelles* and pamphlets. While merchants and tradespeople made up 13 percent of Nicolas's customers in general, they accounted for only 5 percent of buyers of *mazarinades* (political satires). Conversely, officeholders in the court system and the state financial offices figured more prominently among buyers of *libelles* (58 percent) than among his clientele as a whole (30 percent). Thus, rather than reaching the more "popular" readers, political pieces were primarily bought by those—as potential actors in a movement of resistance to royal power or the possible victims of political change—whose social status directly depended on events.

The same holds true concerning the circulation of *La Gazette*, the periodical published by Théophraste Renaudot from 1631 onward. In Grenoble it was primarily the elites of the sword and of the robe who figured more prominently among buyers of the journal than among the buying public in general; the reverse was true of craftsmen and the merchant classes. The *Gazette* was read above all by those who, because of their rank or office, were connected with the monarchy, and who therefore had a direct interest in affairs of state.[2] In the eighteenth century, *cabinets de lecture* and cafés undoubtedly enlarged the readership of periodicals. Nonetheless, their relatively high subscription price and their limited pressruns lead us to suppose that they had few readers among the common townspeople and even fewer among peasants.

To look at the question of pamphlet readership from another viewpoint, political literature seems notably absent from the corpus of print titles destined for a wide range of readers, urban and rural. The Bibliothèque bleue, for example, depended on low production costs to provide inexpensive versions of texts that had already been published in more elegant forms for a wealthier clientele. Set in type that was often worn and mismatched, illustrated with woodcuts that had already seen long service, sewn and covered with the familiar blue paper (though black, red, or marbled papers were also used), and sold by peddlers in town and country alike, these cheap editions were the invention of provincial bookseller-printers of the latter sixteenth century—men like Benoît Rigaud, who worked in Lyons between 1555 and 1597, and Claude Garnier, whose warehouse in Troyes in

1589 contained almanacs and prognostication books, primers and civility books, saints' lives and songbooks (*noëls*) between blue or black paper covers. From the early seventeenth century onward, first in Troyes, then in Rouen, and later in several provincial cities and in Avignon, there were bookseller-printers who specialized in this trade (continuing to offer the more classical titles) and provided new readers with texts that had had a smaller circulation and a more select readership in their original editions.[3]

In the repertory of titles thus destined for the broader public only three texts—or rather, three genres—can be identified as more or less directly political. The first is exemplified by a *mazarinade* entitled *La conférence agréable de deux paysans de Saint Ouen et de Montmorency sur les affaires du temps. Réduit en sept discours, dressés exprès pour divertir les esprits mélancoliques*, which was put out several times during the seventeenth century by publishers in Troyes and reprinted by Jacques Oudot (active 1680–1711) and later by his widow and their son Jean under a permission granted in 1724. Published and circulated in a place and time remote from the events that gave the text its meaning—the strife of the Fronde—the text doubtless lost much or all of its political pertinence and became perceived (as were many other texts of the Bibliothèque bleue that parodied language and literary genres) simply as an amusing piece that played on the patois of its two peasant actors.[4]

The second traditional political genre included accounts of the "misery" of journeymen and apprentices. One such publication was *La misère des garçons boulangers de la ville et fauxbourgs de Paris*, published on six different occasions during the century (under a permission of 1715) by Troyes publishing firms; another was *La peine et misère des garçons chirurgiens, autrement appelés Fratres. Représentés dans un entretien joyeux et spirituel d'un garçon chirurgien et d'un clerc*, printed five times under a permission of 1715. Texts of this sort, which belonged to the repertory of joking, burlesque accounts of apprenticeship, were in no way virulent social or political criticism, and they were doubtless received by their readers as picturesque and amusing tales, thus neutralizing any possibility of a subversive reading.

Was the same thing true of the third genre—the various texts devoted to the two "social bandits," Cartouche and Mandrin, that figured in the peddlers' catalogues of literature? The answer is less categorical. On the one hand, while respecting the motifs and the conventions of a strongly coded genre (the literature of roguery and its representations of the counterkingdom of false beggars and real thieves in *L'histoire de la vie et du procès du fameux Louis-Dominique Cartouche. Et plusieurs de ses complices* and *L'histoire de Louis Mandrin. Depuis sa naissance jusqu'à sa mort. Avec un détail de ses cruautés, de ses brigandages et de ses supplices*; burlesque and its parodies of learned forms of literature in *Le dialogue entre Cartouche et Mandrin. Où l'on voit Proserpine se promener en cabriolet dans les Enfers*), these texts aimed at countering any identification the popular reader might feel with the brigand adversary of the authorities. On the other hand, despite the censors' vigilance and the authors' emphasis on the bandits' cruel deeds, guilt, and final repentance, they nonetheless offered a representation of the noble bandit redressing the scales of justice, which tended to increase the popularity of heroes whose targets were the wealthy and the tax collectors. To this extent, then, in their own way, the works in the Bibliothèque bleue played a part in the "growing politicization" that invaded the descriptions of crime and portrayals of criminal figures in the eighteenth century.[5]

Narrations of the lives of Cartouche and Mandrin, however, constitute only an infinitely small part of a catalogue dominated by works of religious instruction and devotion, works of fiction (chivalric romances, short stories, farcical tales), works on apprenticeship, and technical "how-to" books. If their presence—albeit tenuous—within the repertory of the books published for the commonality indicates that this repertory was not totally out of touch with its times, it must not lead us to forget that by obligation, taste, or habit, the readers of the little blue books massively consumed traditional, conformistic texts in which any hint of political preoccupations was glossed over.

The statements sent (between 1790 and 1792) in response to Abbé Grégoire's questionnaire concerning "the patois and the mores of country people" support this conclusion. In answering question 37, "What sort of books are most commonly found in their homes?" (that is, the homes of country folk), Grégoire's respondents presented an inventory of the works in French most commonly owned by peasants before 1789. They mentioned books of hours, works of piety, almanacs, books on sorcery, and the Bibliothèque bleue, but they never mentioned political works of any sort. In the view of these observers—who stood somewhat apart from the peasant world but were familiar with the rural scene as judges, parish priests, and travelers—the sudden appearance of political texts in country areas was a direct result of the Revolution. Grégoire himself spoke sarcastically in his report to the Convention of Prairial, year II, of the "puerile tales of the Bibliothèque bleue, old wives' tales, and [tales] of the Sabbath"; it was only with the Revolution that politics arrived in the rural world to sweep away the unchanging, archaic traditional library and make room for a constantly changing and polemical literature that brought the conflicts dividing the nation to the heart of the village.[6]

Furthermore, even if we admit that collective political consciousness had grown, at least in the cities, that does not mean that the challenge to state power grew progressively as time went on. Quite the contrary. Affairs of state became the stakes in open, multiple, and violent conflicts before the mid-seventeenth century, first with the Ligue, then with the Fronde. But the stabilization of the modern state, realized by the (at least partial) achievement of a double monopolization—that of the power to tax, centralized to the sovereign's advantage, and that of legitimate violence, which gave him military force, thus making him the master and guarantor of the pacification of social space[7]—prevented for nearly a century and a half the recurrence of crises similar to those earlier ones that had set the kingdom ablaze and twice shaken the authority of the king.

More than a politicization of popular culture, then, there was the institution of a separation between the practices and motivations of the culture of the village or town square (henceforth disqualified, hemmed in, and divested of any political charge) and a politics whose stakes, actors, and actions were circumscribed within the narrow limits of rivalries that racked the royal court or confrontations dividing the restricted society of the holders of public power. Between the reigns of Louis XIV and Louis XVI, the kingdom saw nothing to compare with the broad-scale use of the resources of carnivalesque culture (scatology, role inversion, animalization) during the Wars of Religion and the wars of the Ligue to deride and attack political and religious enemies. There was a defolklorization of politics that echoed the depoliticization of folklore. Does this mean, however, reversing Peter Burke's view, that the rupture brought on by the

Revolution occurred in a society less preoccupied with its common
destiny than that of the first period of modernity, between the mid-
sixteenth century and the mid-seventeenth? Probably not. It is
certain, however, that the way this preoccupation was expressed had
profoundly changed, as the changes in forms of resistance to power
amply demonstrate.

From Tax Revolts to Antiseigneurial Lawsuits

Rebellions against authority long took the form of armed revolts that
comprised either a certain number of uprisings of some duration,
involving several communities or spread over several provinces, or
riots of lesser importance, more limited in both scope and aims.[8] The
chronology of such uprisings is clearly circumscribed, at one end of
the time scale by the revolt of the Pitauds of Aquitaine in 1548, and
at the other by the revolts of the Bonnets Rouges of Brittany in 1675
and the Tard-Avisés of Quercy in 1707. Incontestably, revolts peaked
during the second quarter of the seventeenth century, with its many
peasant disturbances (in Quercy in 1624, in several provinces of
southwest France in 1636–37, in Normandy in 1639 with the revolt
of the Nu-Pieds, and in a number of provinces in 1643–45), as well
as urban uprisings.[9]

The major target of these revolts was nearly always state fiscal
exactions in one or another of their varied forms: the obligation to
lodge soldiers, stricter controls on tax collection that resulted in
heavier payments of the taille, the introduction (real or imaginary) of
new rights to tax the circulation of merchandise or the sale of wine
and salt. The basically antifiscal nature of these rebellions is clear
from the brutal names given to the people who bore the brunt of the
uprisings—court officials and soldiers, commissioners or sergeants at
arms—who were indiscriminately called *gabeleurs* or *maltôtiers* (tax
collectors, extortionists). Antitax sentiment also explains the geography of the revolts. By and large they spared "the king's France" (Paris
and the Capetian domains), where the proximity of the sovereign's
rule kept obedience firm and the people submissive. They were rare
in the France of "pays d'états," which enjoyed fiscal protection thanks
to compromises won in the past between the assemblies of the
provincial estates and the monarch. They were repeated and vig-

orous, on the other hand, in a third France that included the regions surrounding the Paris Basin (Normandy, Poitou, especially the Massif Central, which saw repeated uprisings, Quercy, Rouerge, and Périgord), Brittany, Guyenne, and Gascony. In this France of village *communes* and seigneurs, of freedoms and immunities (authentically certified or proclaimed by tradition), the fiscal demands of the financial state, considerably augmented under Richelieu's ministry, were seen as intolerable acts of aggression that destroyed "public liberties."[10] Although the central power was not at stake in these conflicts (unlike the Ligue and Fronde conflicts), the revolts of the early seventeenth century show every appearance of direct political strife, in that villages and provinces stood firm to oppose agents of the king who were responsible for enforcement, on the local level, of monarchical fiscal exactions.

Other characteristics of these uprisings follow logically. Seventeenth-century revolts can be called "popular" to the extent that they mobilized whole communities and were based on local solidarities, excluding no social group. Gentlemen, priests, and local officials shared in them and played their parts at the side of the peasants and the lesser townspeople, all united against a threat to rights they considered ancestral and inalienable. Reference to custom thus lent legitimacy to rebellions that claimed to be in defense of justly acquired and longstanding privileges against iniquitous encroachments. The revolts were carried on in the name of the king against officials who deceived him and served him ill; they were justified by an appeal to a traditional and tacit right, guaranteed by the sovereign, authorizing the people to rise up against new developments that unduly (and unbeknownst to the king) menaced the contract establishing that right.

The uprisings also borrowed ritual forms from the culture of custom: they used masks, disguises, and role inversion; they dealt their spontaneous and often murderous justice in the language of festive practices resembling carnival parodic trials, charivari rites, or popular penalties deriding the victim. In this they fully belonged within the universe of popular culture, provided the latter is defined not as the culture of the common people (rural and urban) as opposed to that of the notables, but as a repertory of themes and acts ready for use by people of a variety of social levels (not necessarily in like fashion) and available to express what the communities refused, and what they hoped for, in their relations with the state and its agents.

When antitax revolts disappeared, after a last upsurge in 1660–75 (in the Boulonnais, Béarn, Roussillon, the Vivarais, then in Brittany), rural protest was not exhausted, but its forms were radically transformed. Seventeenth-century rebellions directed against state encroachments were followed in the eighteenth century by a type of contestation that "had changed soul, tactics, and strategy."[11] First, the targets were no longer the same. The peasants' hatred shifted from the royal tax collector to the local lord, the parish priest and his tithes, and the enterprising tax farmer. Methods changed as well, and recourse to administrative procedures or to the royal courts replaced open violence and brutal vengeance. Finally, the geography of resistance was reversed, in that antiseigneurial struggles were most bitter in eastern France, where few rebellions had taken place earlier, and they seemed least vigorous in the provinces of the center and the south that had been the site of so many great popular revolts from 1624 to 1648.

Burgundy was the site of a good example of a tenacious and stubborn struggle that used the judiciary system to reach its ends.[12] After 1750, rural communities brought more and more lawsuits against the seigneurs before the royal courts (the local *bailliages* and, if necessary on appeal, the Parlement of Dijon) to obtain the suppression of seigneurial rights they considered unjust. The chief targets of the communities' tenacious lawsuits were the *guet et garde* collected for the repair of the seigneurial castle, the right of *triage* that guaranteed the lord one-third of the village forest for his own use, and the right of *four banal* that obligated the peasants to bake their bread in the oven owned by the lord and pay for the privilege. Even when their recourse to justice was thwarted, the villages refused to give up. They had resources from the sale of firewood from the communal forests and rental fees from their communal pasturelands to back them up, and they were encouraged by the royal intendant, who, in order to put an arrogant lord in his place, gave them liberal authorization to institute further lawsuits. Although such suits had limited objectives, the peasants' causes were soon transformed by the rhetoric of the lawyers who pleaded them and who took each specific case as an opportunity to attack the very foundation of seigneurial claims. They agreed that seigneurial dues were the contractual counterparts of a protection that the lords no longer ensured and that rights that were not uniform throughout the province were null and void, and they asserted that monarchical legislation took precedence over clauses in the land rolls that contradicted the royal law. As they expressed, but also fashioned, peasant protest, the men who defended village community rights shattered the authority of custom and tradition.

This raises a problem, however. It is as if the revolts of the seventeenth century—with their nostalgia for the Golden Age, their myth of the abolition of the *impôt*, their millenarian thrust, and their communitarian unanimity—really existed outside the sphere of politics, which supposes the existence of realistic stakes, a controlled expression of conflicting interests, and the peaceful settlement of differences through the arbitration of recognized institutions. This later conflict, on the other hand, which we would have to call the "politicization of the village," no longer had the early phases of the modern state as its adversary, but the seigneurial system. Throughout the eighteenth century it was this sort of apprenticeship in politics that occurred in the rural communities, at least in some parts of the kingdom, when they turned their hostility away from state taxes, which they finally accepted, and took as their target a seigneury that had become unbearable both for its archaic and arbitrary privileges and for its capitalistic dynamism. Antiseigneurial protest did indeed focus on exactions, but also at issue were the taking over of common lands, the fencing in of meadows, and the constitution of large farms. This contest had limited aims, but it was carried on by a more literate peasantry better acquainted with the city (thanks to exchanges and migration), and it was expressed in a reforming judicial rhetoric that did more to undermine the foundations of the exercise of power than the earlier flare-ups of violence. Paradoxically perhaps, it was when brutal rebellions against the holders of public power had calmed and the conflict directed at the government of the kingdom had disappeared that a prudent, day-by-day, and unspectacular politicization at the village level accustomed the French to perceiving their relationship with the authorities in a new manner. That the monarchy did not fall victim to this challenge to the established order earlier than 1789, and that, to the contrary, it even encouraged challenge by supporting the demands of the rural communities, matters less than the result of that attitude, in that henceforth people were less inclined to accept traditional dependencies without examination and more apt to subject to review and criticism what had long seemed to belong to the immutable order of things.

1614–1789: The Shift in Peasants' Expectations

One possible way to measure the profound transformation in the relationship between the rural world and authority that occurred between the period of open revolt and that of legal and procedural conflicts is to compare, for a given locality, the grievances submitted at the two last convocations of the Estates General, in 1614 and in 1789. The *bailliage* of Troyes, for instance, provides an ample documentation, available in published form: for 1789, 250 *cahiers de doléances* of parishes have been preserved; for 1614 there are 11 *cahiers de châtellenie* (royal districts smaller than a *prévôté*) and 54 books of minutes from the primary assemblies. (At the earlier date, the Third Estate was convoked on the three geographical levels of parish, *châtellenie*, and *bailliage*, whereas in 1789 the divisions were only two: parish and *bailliage*).[13] Differences between one corpus and another, analyzed by the same criteria, may show shifts in the expectations of the peasants in Champagne; that is, changes in what they rejected and, beyond that, the evolution of their representation of the social world and the political state.[14]

In 1614, peasants' expectations crystallized around three sorts of complaints: remonstrances concerning the functioning of justice and the status of offices; a desire for religious reform; and protests against royal fiscal policy. In the parishes these three headings account, respectively, for 10, 17, and 48.5 percent of all *doléances* (grievances). These percentages change somewhat in the *cahiers de châtellenie* drawn up by an assembly grouping together representatives of the villages in the district and inhabitants of the town or small city that was its seat (22, 22, and 28.5 percent). The proportion of antifiscal grievances—which account for 60 percent of all grievances at the primary assemblies, since to explicit complaints against taxation must also be added those lamentations against calamities and unjust distribution of lands that were offered as reasons for finding the tax burden insupportable—therefore diminished at the higher stage of the convocations. The difficulties of daily life seem to have been less severe for the inhabitants of the *châtellenies*, thus permitting them to grant more room in their grievances to religious concerns and the reform of the judicial system. In comparison with the three preoccupations of fiscal policy, the Christian religion, and the judicial system, other grievances were minor; in particular, complaints about the seigneurial system account for only 3.2 percent of grievances at the parish level and 3.9 percent of those of the *châtellenies*.

In 1789, sixty years later, the equilibrium among causes for protest had changed notably. Fiscal grievances, of course, still occupied first place with 33 percent of all complaints. Above all, they were nearly ubiquitous in the *bailliage*: 99 percent of parishes complained of direct taxes, and 95 percent complained of indirect taxation. Next in importance, however, comes an unprecedented incidence of antiseigneurial complaints, which appear in eight out of ten *cahiers* and account for 11 percent of all grievances (12.5 percent if we add complaints against the tithe). Next in order come complaints concerning justice and offices (10 percent), then those regarding the clergy, which have declined to 6 percent. From the earlier convocation to the later one, complaints against matters referring most directly to the king—taxes and justice—remained approximately equal. Religious concerns, on the other hand, gave way to recriminations aimed at the seigneur or the tithe collector.

How are we to understand these differences, first among them the lower rate of religious complaint? In 1614, parishes and *châtellenies* both expressed a concern that they had been spiritually abandoned. Their disquiet, rooted in strong anxieties—that of dying without receiving last rites, for instance—led them to demand that parish priests reside in their parishes, that the number of vicars be increased, that Mass be celebrated more regularly, and that preaching and teaching of the catechism be intensified. An awareness of the moral and intellectual mediocrity of the clergy after the Wars of Religion is also apparent. In a time of religious fragmentation and uncertainty,[15] the village communities looked to the clergy to reestablish order and unity. To this end, they emphasized that the man of God needed to be different from the laity, and that his difference should be immediately visible in his dress (cassock and *bonnet carré*), mores (sexual abstinence in particular), and education.

The Catholic Reformation fashioned this new-style priest, who was prepared in theology and pastoral care by the seminaries and whose mores were generally irreproachable. The *cahiers* recognize this fact: complaints about the behavior of the clergy were as much as 9.5 percent of all complaints in the *châtellenies* and 7 percent in the parishes in 1614; in 1789 they accounted for less than 1 percent. The faithful no longer had any cause to complain of their clergy, though the inverse was true. The negative judgment leveled by seventeenth-century parishioners at their priests had, by the end of the Old Regime, become the verdict of curés concerning their flocks. The same traits—vulgarity, drunkenness, immorality—recur in these transposed judgments, showing that the gap between the two groups, which the people themselves had wanted in 1614, had been so firmly established that the parish priests—even though they were inceasingly recruited from among peasants' sons during the last two decades before the Revolution—had become largely estranged from the rural world they denounced. [16]

As for the material conditions of the clergy, 1789 brought new and pressing complaints against the tithe (*la dîme*). In 1614 the *cahiers* of Champagne kept to two principal points: the church must live on its own resources (which led to a demand for a better administration of the church's temporal holdings); and the church must live on the exaction instituted by the Bible (which explains the absence of complaints against the tithe at that time). The village communities' hostility focused on the priests' demands to be paid for sacraments and burials and on the clergy's pressure on the dying to persuade them to leave their wealth to the church (custom in Champagne authorized priests to receive bequests). In 1789, to the contrary, refusal to pay the tithe as it was then collected was widely proclaimed. This grievance admittedly accounts for only 1.7 percent of the total, but it is encountered in one out of every two *cahiers*. Criticism of the tithe did not signify a demand for its simple abolition, however: only fifteen *cahiers* make this demand. Others complain of the misdeeds of the tithe collectors or of quotas considered too large; they propose that the sums collected be used for different purposes (generally for the benefit of the parish priests); they demand the elimination of particular sorts of tithes (those that had become the property of laymen through intendation; those levied on newly cultivated lands; or other extraordinary tithes) added to the principal one. More than anticlerical sentiment, what the *cahiers* from the *bailliage* of Troyes reveal here is the people's desire to participate in decisions that immediately concerned their own existence. In the vast majority of parishes, the principle of the tithe was not challenged; what the communities wanted was to be able to set (or at least to negotiate) the sums involved, the conditions of collection, and the use to which the money would be put. Burdensome though it was, the tithe was accepted in 1614 because the need for a more immediately present and more exemplary church was what mattered most. In 1789, while the clergy was no longer the target of a large number of complaints, the tithe was considered ripe for reform.

The same thing was true of seigneurial rights. At the beginning of the seventeenth century, the *cahiers* from each parish in the *bailliage* paid relatively little attention to the institution of the seigneury and attacked neither the principle nor the extent of seigneurial exactions. What the village communities did object to were hunting parties that destroyed the crops, the usurpation of communal lands, and the constraints that went along with levies of seigneurial dues. Even allowing for the seigneurial officials' role in the consultation procedures (which put them in a position to direct peasant complaints toward royal taxation, which was in competition with seigneurial exactions), the essential feature was the strength of a representation of the society of orders and estates that recognized the legitimacy of the rights and privileges of the seigneur as the corollary of his responsibility to provide defense and protection.

The situation was very different in 1789. At that date, 82 percent of the parishes stated complaints against the institution of seigneury. The prerogatives most decried were those pertaining to seigneurial justice (16 percent of all complaints in the category); next came hostility to seigneurial rights in general, denounced either as unfounded or as unfairly imposed (11 percent), opposition to feudal lawyers (*feudistes*) and to revision of land rolls (11 percent); complaints against the head tax (the *cens*; 9 percent), against exclusive hunting rights and the right to keep a dovecote (7 percent), against *banalités*, or seigneurial monopolies (bake oven, mill, etc.; 6 percent), against the *corvée* (obligatory labor service; 6 percent), and against *lods et ventes* (the lord's percentage of the sale when peasant lands changed hands; 4 percent). When these grievances are recast in order of frequency of appearance, justice heads the list (mentioned by one-half of all parishes), followed by the *cens* (41 percent of parishes), the *corvée* (25 percent), hunting rights (24 percent), land rolls (23 percent), and seigneurial monopolies (22 percent).

Three attitudes toward seigneurial rights predominated in the villages. The first and most widespread favored reform. In 45 percent of the grievances, the *cahiers* speak of "regaining," "transferring," "reforming," "diminishing," or "simplifying" seigneurial exactions. In a lower key, 32 percent of the grievances simply express complaints without suggesting any remedy; in a higher key, 21 percent express a desire to see such rights abolished outright. This desire for abolition appears frequently only in the case of three seigneurial dues: the *corvée* (more than half the protests against this feudal right demand its abolition), hunting rights, and seigneurial rights and monopolies. This may well be a good indication of the true hierarchy of peasant dissatisfactions in Champagne on the eve of the Revolution. Apart from these instances, however, the antiseigneurial contestation expressed in 1789 involved no sweeping desire for abolitionist revolt. It consisted rather in a solid and obstinate will for reform that was ready to examine, criticize, and reformulate the various privileges of the masters of the land. There too, where formerly there had been an expectation of a needed protection—the lord's protection against marauding soldiers or royal tax collectors—that required the inhabitants' sacrifice and submission, there was now a desire to use the king and the Estates General to negotiate a more just division of responsibilities and rights.

The principal enemy, both in 1614 and in 1789, was royal taxation. Both in sheer number of complaints and in unanimity among the various groups, taxes headed all lists of grievances. Almost all parishes at both dates had something to say about the tax burden. This is easily explained by the nature and circumstances of the convocations, in that the primary mission of the Estates General was to consent to royal taxation, and this latter was the only exaction that the king, to whom the grievances were addressed, could modify by his will alone. In 1789, direct taxes came in for the most criticism, and the chief demand was that they be more equally distributed. This demand took two forms: a refusal of fiscal privileges (encountered in

74 percent of the *cahiers*) and a demand for the equal application of fiscal burdens (demanded by 97 percent of *cahiers*). In 1614, protest turned instead against increases in the taille, against tax-collection procedures (with a demand for verification of the accounts), and against the proliferating exemptions granted to cities, self-proclaimed nobles, and officeholders. At the earlier date, grievances were not ultrasensitive to unbearable inequalities between commoners and nobles but were primarily directed at the undue extension of (or the usurpation by people who had no right to) privileges held to be legitimate when they were matched by a service rendered to the community. One hundred seventy-five years later, the parishes of Champagne had replaced this hostility toward illegitimate exemptions (in no way incompatible with respect for justified privilege) with a new demand for the equal distribution of fiscal obligations.

Can we say, though, that a comparison of grievances expressed in 1614 and 1789 in the *bailliage* of Troyes gives us the key to transformations in the political culture of the mass of Frenchmen (here represented by peasant village communities)? Prudence reminds us that Champagne was not the entire kingdom of France and that the discourse of grievances was filtered through texts written by others than the illiterate or semiliterate people who first expressed them. Nonetheless, comparisons between the earlier and later corpuses clearly show a difference between two ways of thinking and experiencing society's relationship with institutions. In 1614, the effects of the Wars of Religion were still being felt and, in an economic conjuncture of reconstruction, the village communities were protesting against the harsh demands of the financial state. A sharp sense of moral and spiritual abandonment accompanied despair—real or exaggerated—based in genuine distress. This explains the respect for protective institutions (the seigneury, for one) and the desire for a christianization, hence a clericalization, of society. The ideal that the 1614 *cahiers* express is that the authorities, secular and spiritual, should take charge of the body social and enjoy, in return for their promise of safeguard—here below and in the afterworld—privileges and rights held to be perfectly legitimate.

In 1789, expectations were quite different, tending to question what earlier had been taken for granted and to demand that the authorities respond to the opinions and aspirations of the people. In two centuries, the church of the Catholic Reformation and the judicial and administrative state had brought the desired security, but at the high price of notable financial and cultural sacrifices. It was thus a protected and sheltered society—an ordered and pacified society—that debated measures that might harmonize its desires with the order that reigned in the world. The reform of seigneurial and ecclesiastical exactions in the name of social utility and the move for fiscal equality in the name of justice were the two chief points expressing a desire for control over, or at least participation in, decisions that governed common existence. Thus understood, the politicization of the village that turned its attention to "particular" and "nearby" objects, as Tocqueville called them,[17] appears as the inverse of the process by which the monarchical state established its monopoly of violence. By loosening the enforced ties that had subjected the weaker to the authority of their immediate protectors, instituting regular procedures for resolving conflicts, and reducing the savagery of the social sphere, the consolidation of the modern state created the very conditions that eventually made dependencies formerly accepted as self-evident come to be perceived as intolerable. This development perhaps underlay the widespread mind-set that came to view as desirable and necessary that profound recasting of the body social and the body politic that was effected, under conditions of urgency, in 1789.

The Urban Scene: Work Conflicts and Political Apprenticeship

In the cities and towns, politicization arose out of an increasing number of conflicts between journeymen and masters, and, thanks to interest in objects "near" and "particular," it transformed the relation to authority. Just as antiseigneurial contestation followed the great antitax revolts in rural areas, the disappearance of urban uprisings (which had been particularly intense between 1623 and 1647)[18] was followed in the cities by confrontations within the trades over conditions of the workplace. Although it is as yet impossible to draw up full statistics concerning workers' *cabales* and strikes during the eighteenth century, the examples of Nantes and Lyons warrant two conclusions. First, both communal archives and police records attest that conflicts occurred in almost all the trades (twenty out of twenty-seven in Nantes; all sixteen in Lyons). Second, the same records show an incontestable increase in worker agitation after 1760. In Nantes, strife broke out on thirty-six occasions between 1761 and 1789, as against only eighteen times during the first sixty years of the century (major encounters account for nineteen and ten of these, respectively). In Lyons, the three decades preceding the Revolution were marked by eighteen conflicts, while only seven occurred between 1701 and 1760 (but nine had occurred during the seventeenth century).[19] The rise in worker insubordination, a theme dear to Restif de la Bretonne and Louis-Sébastien Mercier, was more than a literary motif to express nostalgia for a lost harmony; it was a reality expressing journeymen's and urban workers' new representation of the social world.

There was, in fact, a close connection between the *cabales* that aimed at forcing the masters to give ground and the strengthening of worker sociability. In all cities and towns and in every trade, workers had similar reasons to protest: they refused to accept guild control of hiring and, conversely, they demanded free job placement; they demanded higher pay and more frequent payment along with better living and working conditions; they repudiated hindrances to leaving a workshop (in particular, obligatory registration—*certificats de congé* that demonstrated permission to quit a job and the personal *livret* that workers were obliged to carry). They showed an ardent desire for independence. The proliferation of conflicts—characterized by concerted work stoppage, the "damnation" (boycotting) of masters who turned a deaf ear to the journeymen's demands, and the pressure put on *compagnons* who refused to join work actions or demonstrations of force—implies the development of a broad range of modes of worker association, from the totally spontaneous to the most thoroughly institutionalized. Within the *compagnonnages*, the *confréries*, and the tavern assemblies, urban workers could be found engaged in a form of politics that, although it did not attack public power, nonetheless accustomed people to organizing collective action, often led them to create a common purse, and always incited them to debate the defense of shared interests.[20]

Defense of common interests did not necessarily or uniquely imply recourse to strikes. As with the rural communities, the urban journeymen's groups used juridical codes and lawsuits to gain recognition of their rights. Throughout the eighteenth century they bombarded the Parlement with appeals to abolish new and unfavorable regulations promulgated by the guilds and confirmed by the lieutenant general of the police, the city governments, or the Parlement itself. If it is true that "the 'typical form of protest' in the eighteenth century trades was neither the food riot nor the strike but . . . the lawsuit," the collective action of the *compagnons*, far from being detached from public life, found in the formalities and the vocabulary of judicial procedure a means for joining the major political debates.[21] The arguments developed by the attorneys and *procureurs* engaged by the *compagnons* were certainly not couched in the journeymen's own language, but these arguments accustomed workers to think of their disputes with the masters according to mental categories—those of civil law and natural law—that universalized and politicized every individual lawsuit.

This apprenticeship in politics on the part of journeymen was doubtless accelerated by Turgot's abortive reform, which caused disillusionment and disappointment.[22] The edict of February 1776 abolishing the guilds had, in fact, given rise to great hopes among the workers, who interpreted it as giving them the right to leave, freely and immediately, the master under whom they worked and to hire themselves out as they wished. Even more, a number of them understood the measure as a chance to establish themselves independently, thereby abandoning the dependent condition of paid workers. The authorities' restrictions on the application of the edict, swiftly followed by the reestablishment of the guilds in August 1776, put a quick stop to their enthusiasm. The increase in the number of conflicts within the trades and the workplaces during the twelve last years of the Old Regime (at least thirty-five of them in Paris between 1781 and 1789)[23] was doubtless due to strife between the journeymen, by now bitter and disenchanted, and the masters, who were determined to restore their prerogatives. The crisis of 1776 established an immediate connection between the many scattered and swiftly changing confrontations throughout the working world and politics on the governmental scale, which tended to draw together isolated instances of tension. For the journeymen, the disputes that had set them against their masters had taken on meaning within a conflict in which the authority of the king himself was at stake. Thus the politicization that had sprung from work-related concerns and daily life was linked to affairs of state.

The same was true, but in the defense of contrary interests, where the masters of the guilds were concerned. In the lawsuits they instituted against the journeymen to ensure application of the new regulations, in their struggle against the *faux ouvriers* who set up shop out of the reach of guild control in their rooms or in certain privileged places (such as the faubourg Saint-Antoine),[24] and in their protests—in salvos of lawyers' memoirs—against the edict of February 1776, the masters, in their fashion, associated safeguard of their domination over the journeymen and participation in the public sphere. The "metaphor of the sans-culotte" of the year II, which forged the ideal image of "an independent producer, living and working under the same roof as a small number of journeymen, having with them familiar and intimate relations and sharing the same preoccupations and the same interests," should not mislead us.[25] It does not correspond either to the structures of artisanal production (characterized, at least in Paris, by big workshops, a high degree of division of labor, and high mobility among journeymen, who had little lasting attachment to their masters) or to the vocabulary of the many and varied disputes that set masters and workers against one another throughout the eighteenth century, especially after 1760. The politicization of the trade world doubtless owed more to the repeated expression of these antagonisms, formulated both in physical confrontations in the workplace and in judicial battles, than to any perception of a common condition.

The Public Literary Sphere: The Salons

In the world of the social and intellectual elites, lesser dependence on state authority was marked by the emergence of an autonomous cultural sphere with two salient traits: first, the constitution of a public whose critical judgments and literary practices were not governed uniquely by either the court's decrees in the realm of taste or the authority of the academies; second, the affirmation of a market for cultural goods with its own logic working within, and often counter to, the hierarchies of value and persons imposed by older forms of patronage. Some have proposed that a first sign of this change occurred during the period of the Regency, when the royal court lost its exclusive prerogative to regulate aesthetic norms. The "public literary sphere" created at that time was based on institutions that produced a new legitimacy, such as the cafés, the salons, and the journals. That legitimacy rested on new principles: the free exercise of the critical faculties, the monopoly of which was removed from the ecclesiastical, academic, and administrative institutions that claimed it; the equality of all persons engaged in comparing opinions and ideas, despite differences of estate and condition that separated them in the social world; and the intent to both represent and form the judgment of a new public of which the fashionable and literary elite considered themselves the spokesmen and teachers. Thus, with a thirty- or forty-year lag in respect to England, France made room for intellectual practices founded on the public use of reason by private persons whose critical competence was not tied to their membership in an official body or to the world of the court, but to their quality as readers and spectators brought together by the pleasures of convivial conversation.[26] It is this hypothesis that we need to examine now.

The salons were the primary form of conviviality, bringing together in an organized manner people from the worlds of fashion and literature who met to share pastimes such as gaming, conversation, reading, and the pleasures of the table. There were subtle filiations and rivalries between the various social sets, each of which was dominated by a woman (though not always: Baron d'Holbach had his salon). Thus, during the first three decades of the eighteenth century, the salon of the marquise de Lambert at the Hôtel de Nevers was contrasted to the "court" at Sceaux grouped around the duchesse du Maine, where the old etiquette was perpetuated. Beginning in the 1750s there was a sharper rivalry between the society of Madame Geoffrin, who had formerly been a habituée of the salon of Madame de Tencin, and the group that frequented the apartments of Madame du Deffand, formerly an intimate of the marquise de Lambert. Later, after 1764, the salon of Mademoiselle de Lespinasse, rue Saint-Dominique, vied for the company of men of letters and foreign visitors with the salon of the lady's aunt and former protectress, Madame du Deffand. A fierce rivalry for the highest distinction thus reigned in the society of the Parisian salons. In the last analysis, what was at stake was control of an intellectual life that had been emancipated from the tutelage of the monarchy and the court.

The salon assured writers an entry into the world of the powerful. In the salon of the marquise du Deffand in the 1750s, for example, such friends of the mistress of the house as Charles Hénault, the president of the Parlement of Paris, Jean-Baptiste Formont, heir of a family of wealthy merchants and bankers from Rouen, or the comte de Pont-de-Veyle, Madame de Tencin's nephew and an amateur author, could meet Philosophes like Turgot, Marmontel, La Harpe, Condorcet, and Grimm, as well as the great ladies of the Parisian aristocracy such as the duchesse de Luxembourg and the comtesse de Boufflers (each of whom had her own circle), the duchesse de Mirepoix, the duchesse d'Aiguillon, the marquise de Forcalquier, and the comtesse de Rochefort.[27]

The small group of regulars who made up d'Holbach's coterie on the rue Saint-Honoré included aristocrats of ancient families (the chevalier de Chastellux and the marquis de Saint-Lambert), nobles of more recent date (d'Holbach himself; the physician and chemist Darcet; Le Roy, who had the post of *lieutenant des chasses* at Versailles; or the *fermier général* Helvétius), foreigners established in Paris (Abbé Galiani and Melchior Grimm), the sons of good bourgeois families from Paris and the provinces (Diderot, Abbé Raynal, Morellet, Suard), and intellectuals of more humble origins (Naigeon, Marmontel, and Doctor Roux). This knot of regulars, bound by friendship, love of a fine table, and philosophical connivance (and not so much by their atheism, which not all of them shared), met a larger circle of occasional guests that included travelers, diplomats, literary personalities, and aristocrats.[28] By this mixture of people whose differences were forgotten for such moments of pleasure and discussion, the salons gave support and reality to one of the themes dearest to philosophic texts after the middle of the century: the mingling of *hommes de plume* (professional writers; "as much at ease in society as in their study," as Voltaire wrote in the article "Gens de lettres," of the *Encyclopédie*) and the great, not uniquely as protectors or patrons but also as genuine men of letters.

Participation in the society of the salons was thus a necessity for anyone who wanted to get ahead. It was there that protection, pensions, employment, and subsidies could be obtained; it was there that elections to the Académie française were secured. "Hardly does one of the forty [members] draw his last breath than ten candidates present themselves. . . . They rush post-haste to Versailles; they get all the women talking; they stir up all the intriguers; they pull all the strings."[29] The factions that formed, in and out of literary circles, were first organized in the salons, guided by the preferences of the women who were their hostesses. Thus in 1754 d'Alembert, after three unsuccessful attempts, was elected to the Académie française thanks to the solicitous intervention of the marquise du Deffand, which proved more powerful than Madame de Chaulnes's efforts in favor of her candidate.[30] In the seventeenth century, elections to the Académie primarily reflected the wishes of the important figure who lent his protection to that body (first Richelieu, then Chancellor Séguier, then the king); in the following century, candidacies were decided in Paris, as the outcome of battles between coteries that were ideological confrontations as well. The election of d'Alembert, for instance, marked the beginning of the philosophical party's conquest of the Académie française, and it guided that bastion of intellectual legitimacy during the 1760s. In that same decade, the salon of Mademoiselle de Lespinasse, exiled from the salon of Madame du Deffand, from whom she robbed the new-fledged academician, became a haven for the victorious Philosophes, welcoming Condorcet, Malesherbes, Turgot, Suard, Abbé Morellet, Marmontel, and the marquis de Chastellux. As places where the aristocracy and the writers met and where a certain measure of social mixing occurred, and as places where works and cultural actors could find independent intellectual consecration outside rule-bound institutions and established cultural bodies, the salons were the first to encourage the new public literary sphere born in the early eighteenth century and emancipated from the tutelage of the court and the Académie française.

The Faculty of Judgment: Literary and Artistic Criticism

The journals, which devoted a large amount of space to aesthetic criticism, were the second support of the public literary sphere. For French periodicals, which were often printed outside the kingdom of France, the years 1720–50 were important ones. The number of new periodicals grew notably (forty-eight new periodicals were created between 1720 and 1729; seventy between 1730 and 1739; ninety between 1740 and 1749). The great learned reviews of the late seventeenth century were followed by periodicals dominated by literary authors and devoted to a critical examination of new books.[31] The titles of the periodicals created during this thirty-year period clearly show this by their inclusion of such terms as *Bibliothèque* (featured in thirteen new reviews), *Spectateur* (including Marivaux's *Spectateur français*) and *Spectatrice* (eleven new reviews on the model of *The Tatler* and *The Spectator* of Addison and Steele), and *Nouvelles littéraires* (six new reviews, including the one founded by Raynal in 1747), to which *Le Pour et le Contre*, the periodical of Abbé Prévost, founded in 1733, should be added. The new periodicals of the second quarter of the eighteenth century proclaimed and shared the aims of listing recently published works, subjecting them to "disinterested criticism," to "critical examination," to "observations," "reflections," or "judgments" (according to the vocabulary of the journals' titles), providing extracts, and communicating news of the Republic of Letters.[32] In doing so, they both gave expression to and fueled the free and literary sociability of the cafés and clubs that were spreading throughout France, in imitation of the English model.

The press rapidly adapted its publishing formulas and the content of its production to the expectations of a public avid for information and opinions on new works. This had several results. First, journals came out more frequently: in 1734, nearly half of the literary periodicals were monthlies (only one-fourth of them appeared more often); thirty years later, in 1761, more than half of all literary periodicals were weeklies or bimonthlies. Furthermore, long articles or copious extracts increasingly gave way to shorter notices, which permitted more books to be called to the attention of the readers, whose curiosity was thus better satisfied.[33]

Finally, and most important, the periodical gave a more generous account of the new genres than it did of traditional works. During the first three decades of the eighteenth century, this was not yet the case. The thematic distribution of 1,309 works reviewed in the twenty or so periodicals published in 1734 does not differ notably from a similar distribution of requests for publishing permissions, both *privilèges* and *permissions simples*. Although overall proportions are similar for the two, the journals show somewhat less theology (one-fourth of the titles mentioned, as opposed to one-third for the registries of *privilèges*) and more belles-lettres and history (twice as frequently mentioned in the journals).[34] If we follow the evolution of two periodicals that showed little fondness for novelty—the very academic *Journal des Savants* and the *Mémoires de Trévoux* , an organ of the Jesuits—we see that as early as the 1750s an important difference had set in between the total production of authorized books and the works that the journals chose to review. The shift in categories is spectacular. The number of religious books reviewed in the journals dropped precipitously (they accounted for less than 10 percent of reviews at a time when they still represented one-fourth of all public permissions), while the number of works on the arts and sciences increased to nearly one-half of all books reviewed (40 percent in the *Mémoires de Trévoux* and 45 percent in the *Journal des Savants*.[35]

Thus there were more periodicals, they appeared with greater frequency, and they were increasingly more open to the newest intellectual interests, all of which created a market for evaluations henceforth freed from the exclusive guidance of the official periodicals and founded on the opportunity to compare opinions. Even though the various journals used similar techniques of analysis relying on the same procedures (summaries, quotations, extracts, references, and commentaries),[36] and even though they vied with one another to dictate, through their choices and decrees, the "correct" interpretation of works, the very fact that there were a number of periodicals in circulation fueled critical debate and lively discussion. By claiming to speak in their readers' name and by setting up their readers as arbiters of taste liberated from fixed norms and ossified authorities, the literary periodicals brought a new, autonomous, and sovereign entity into being: the public.

After 1737, the date from which it was organized on a regular basis, the biennial exposition in the Salon carré of the Louvre promoted by the Royal Academy of Painting and Sculpture produced a similar effect.[37] The Salon considerably enlarged the number of viewers in a position to view art. In addition to the limited number of connoisseurs (made up, as in the musical realm, of patrons and theoreticians),[38] throngs of the general public crowded the Louvre during the four or five weeks of the expositions. If we suppose that the booklet put out by the academy on the occasion of each Salon (giving the artists' names, the subject of the paintings, and, when necessary, an "explanation" for each work) was bought by one out of every two visitors, we can estimate that fifteen thousand people came to the salons toward the end of the 1750s, and more than twice that number did so in 1780.[39] These salons were fashionable events, and they prompted a flood of publications—articles in the journals, *libelles* and pamphlets (often anonymous and printed with false addresses), and critiques inserted in *nouvelles à la main* (subscription newsletters) such as those written by Diderot between 1759 and 1771 for Grimm's (later, Meister's) *Correspondance littéraire*, which was distributed to some fifteen highborn subscribers scattered through Europe. A space was opened up in which, on the one hand, divergent aesthetic conceptions could be compared, and, on the other hand, the public's judgment (or a judgment given as being that of the public) could stand as the primary authority for evaluation of works of art. The exposition, which was presented under the patronage of the *directeur des bâtiments du roi* and organized by an officer of the academy (and which took great care to respect the hierarchy both of the academic ranks and in pictorial genres) thus led—somewhat paradoxically, given its initial intentions—to the launching of polemical debate on the ends and means of painting.

When the public at large had an opportunity to compare works and form judgments, the traditional authorities risked losing their monopoly to dictate taste, thus threatening established reputations and the accepted hierarchies. This led the academy to attempt closer surveillance of the Salon carré exhibitions. In 1748 it instituted a jury composed of its own officers and professors from among its ranks, who were charged with choosing works by academicians and others whose pieces were deemed worthy of inclusion. The control was severe, for at the end of the Old Regime fewer than fifty artists were admitted to the Salons, and the number of works shown rarely rose above two hundred. The jury's conservatism translated into nervousness on the part of the artists who enjoyed the highest number of commissions, and who viewed an institution that aimed at dictating their clients' preferences, thus perhaps depriving them of their market, with some anxiety. It was in vain, however, that Charles-Nicolas Cochin, the secretary of the Academy of Painting and Sculpture, attempted in 1767 to discourage criticism by insisting that critiques be signed. In spite of its hesitations, the Salon carré nonetheless imposed a new principle of artistic consecration, removing the process from behind the closed doors of the academy and bringing it out into the open and into the arena of contradictory criticism and free appreciation.

The Politicization of the Public Literary Sphere

In the long run, the constitution among the elites of a public literary sphere based on the various institutions that provided intellectual sociability and on the emergence of a market for artistic judgment and works of art produced a profound change in the cultural practices that it brought into the public sphere, eventually strongly politicizing them. As outlined in chapter 1, there are two ways of understanding that politicization. The first, which owes much to the work of Augustin Cochin, holds that the voluntary associations of the eighteenth century (clubs, literary societies, Masonic lodges) were laboratories in which a "democratic" sociability prefiguring that of Jacobinism, though not defined explicitly, was invented and tried out. Outside the traditional corporate society of the Old Regime, without communication with that society and in competition with it, there emerged a political sphere based on principles totally different from those structuring the monarchical state:

> Yet real society did reconstruct, in other ways and other places, beyond the monarchy, a world of political sociability. This new world was based on individuals, and no longer on the institutional groups to which they belonged; it was founded on the confused notion called "opinion" and came into being in cafés, salons, Masonic lodges and the so-called *sociétés de pensée*, or "philosophical societies." One can call it democratic sociability—even though its network did not extend to all of the people—simply to express the idea that its lines of communication were formed "below," and ran horizontally in a disjointed society, where all individuals were equal.[40]

Even when they stated their respect for the sovereign and their conformity with traditional values, as they usually did, the new forms of intellectual sociability tended in practice to deny the foundations of the traditional order.

But the process of politicization can be understood in another way: as the application, beyond the literary domain alone, of a critical judgment unconstrained by limits on its empire or by obligatory subjection to instituted authority. By giving support and regular application to the public exercise of reason, both the increased circulation of printed written matter and the greater opportunities for the use of aesthetic judgment led individuals to think for themselves—to evaluate works and ideas freely and to construct a common opinion from the clash of competing viewpoints. This meant that there was no longer a clear division between obligatory beliefs and loyalties, on the one hand, and opinions that could legitimately be challenged, on the other. When a critical approach had become habit, no domain of thought or action could be protected from free examination, not even the mysteries of religion or those of the state. "Our age is, in especial degree, the age of criticism, and to criticism everything must submit. Religion through its sanctity, and lawgiving through its majesty, may seek to exempt themselves from it. But then they awaken just suspicion, and cannot claim the sincere respect which reason accords only that which has been able to sustain the test of free and open examination."[41] This remark, which Kant offered in the preface to the first edition of his *Critique of Pure Reason* in 1781, forcefully describes the gradual submission of political authority to the jurisdiction of judgment and the verdict of reason. In France, as elsewhere in Europe, the shift that annulled the radical dichotomy (instituted by absolutism) between the individual's inner judgment, regulated by his individual conscience, and the reason of state, commanded by principles that owed nothing to common morality, had in large part been effected by the progress of two major social bodies: the Republic of Letters and Freemasonry.

Liberty in Secret and the Secret of Liberty:
Freemasonry

Masonic society merits particular attention because it was the largest of the new groups providing intellectual sociability. In 1789 Masons numbered at least fifty thousand in France, or one man out of every twenty among those classes of the urban population likely to have been admitted into a lodge.[42] From the foundation of the first lodge in Paris in 1725 (by a group of English emigrés), Freemasonry spread rapidly. Its growth peaked twice: first during the 1760s, as an institutional crisis was shaking the Grande Loge de France (which eventually led to the constitution of the Grand Orient de France in 1773); and then in the 1780s, when between 20 and 40 new lodges were created annually. The expansion of Freemasonry (there were 635 lodges of the Grand Orient alone on the eve of the Revolution) could not be stopped either by internal dissent or by competition from the more immediately political societies that flourished in the 1780s.[43]

The spread of Freemasonry cannot be measured by the same standards used to evaluate the other Enlightenment societies like salons, clubs, or academies. It was singular in its continuity, its massive numbers, and its broad distribution. After 1750, lodges proliferated throughout the kingdom. They were particularly strong along the main routes, the rivers, and the coast, as well as in the provinces of the south of France; they were less numerous in Alsace and the western provinces, areas more hesitant to welcome a society that had been condemned by papal bulls in 1738 and 1751. Furthermore, although Freemasonry was an exclusively urban cultural phenomenon, it reached cities and towns of all types and sizes, even the smallest. In 1789, eighty-one towns of fewer than two thousand inhabitants had a lodge. This spread did not follow the usual pattern, moving from the bigger cities toward the smaller towns; lodges existed in cities and towns of all varieties as early as 1750. Nor was implantation the work of the recruitment policies of the Grand Orient, as lodges flourished even before 1773 in cities with populations under ten thousand. Obviously, the spread of Freemasonry responded to a wide demand that persisted throughout the century. How are we to understand this phenomenon?

Perhaps it can be explained—in an approach inspired by Augustin Cochin's thesis—as the expression of an impulse toward egalitarianism that cleared new space within a society of orders and estates, a space where individuals were not distinguished by their juridical condition and merit was the only legitimate basis for attaining higher ranks and dignities. In this view, Freemasonry set up an area of "democratic sociability" within a society that was far from democratic, showing by its example that social ties could be forged not on the basis of obligatory membership in separate and stratified bodies but on that of the essential equality that exists between all individuals.

This ideal, clear as it is, nonetheless contrasts with the realities of an inegalitarian society—realities often reflected within Freemasonry itself. For example, until the foundation of the Grand Orient, which insisted on election to the higher ranks, high-ranking posts tended to become "traditional" offices that were considered the property of those who held them. Furthermore, the abstract and universal equality upon which Masonic association rested had to compromise with the exclusions and specializations that governed recruitment to the lodges on the practical level.

Freemasonry was, of course, much more open to membership than the other institutions of intellectual sociability of the age. Members of the Third Estate formed the great majority, comprising 74 percent of the members in Paris and 80 percent among the members of the lodges established in the thirty-two cities in the provinces that also had an academy. In those same cities, only 38 percent of the *académiciens ordinaires* were members of the Third Estate. The lodges also welcomed members from social categories that were generally not represented in the literary societies or other intellectual associations—merchants, shopkeepers, and craftsmen, for instance. In the lodges of Paris, men in wholesale commerce and manufacturing represented 17.5 percent of lodge members from the Third Estate, and those from trade milieux and shopkeepers another 12 percent. In provincial cities that boasted an academy, the two categories accounted, respectively, for 36 percent and 13 percent of Masonic recruitment, whereas only 4.5 percent of academy members from the Third Estate were merchants (appearing in notable numbers in only a few places), and no craftsmen or shopkeepers appeared on their lists.[44]

Freemasonry nonetheless had its rejects—all those whose "vile and mechanical" trade deprived them of the leisure indispensable for entry and the means required for contribution to the works of charity that were among its fraternal obligations. There are a great many statements justifying such exclusions, particularly when lodges founded by people of modest means requested recognition by the

Grand Orient. In 1779, for instance, the Clermont Lodge in Toulouse wrote: "Although Freemasonry levels all estates, it is nonetheless true that one must expect more from men who all occupy a distinguished estate in civil society than one can expect from the plebeian." In 1786, the *vénérable* of a lodge in Nancy wrote to inform his correspondent of the refusal of the Chambre des Provinces of the Grand Orient "to multiply Masons of a class little apt to do good, or who, as soon as they do so, always turn to the detriment of their families. Secondly, since these Masons have not by their estate been in a position to receive a good education, it is disagreeable for the entire body of Masonry to be obliged to fraternize with them." In 1788 a dignitary of the same Chambre des Provinces stated in a letter: "Our goal in seeking to give Masonry back its ancient luster has been to admit to participation in our Regime only those persons who are masters of their time and whose fortunes permit them to participate without inconvenience in the relief of humanity."[45]

This explains the deliberate exclusion from Masonic society of those who had neither education nor wealth; it also explains the strict social specialization of the Masonic lodges, which grouped together men who already had connections outside Masonic society, whether through membership in the urban elite, a shared profession (the law, the liberal professions, or commerce), or their common subalternate social status. As the *vénérable* of a lodge in Amiens wrote in 1785: "When it is not feasible to frequent others in civil society it is impossible to do so as a Mason."[46]

Although the juridical hierarchy separating social bodies and social estates disappeared for the time that members worked together in their lodge, that does not mean that Freemasonry occasioned any profound social mixing. The equality it boasted was more aristocratic than democratic, as it based putative parity among men on their holding identical social properties.[47] Far from holding an abstract and absolute concept of equality, Masonic sociability attempted to consider individuals independently of their differing social condition and, in the tensions and conflicts it underwent, to produce a cross between egalitarian principles and exclusivity, between a respect for social difference (detached from the distinctions of social order) and the constitution of a separate society. Its success can thus be seen as the result of dual and contradictory impulses: on the one hand, the diffusion among the social elites (reaching well below the aristocracy) of a practice of equality among people of wealth, education, and leisure; on the other hand, the appropriation, by milieux usually excluded from the most literate forms of cultural sociability, of a less intellectually demanding mode of association that secularized traditional values and traditionally Christian activities.

Freemasonry's formidable power of attraction in eighteenth-century France resulted from this conjunction of socially contrary aspirations unified by a common critical function. Masonic society was in principle governed by morality and regulated by freedom of conscience, but by that very fact it set itself up as a judge of the reason of state. Although they swore an unfailing political loyalty, the lodges, cut off from society by the secrecy that was demanded of all brothers, nonetheless undermined the monarchical order by proposing a new system of values, founded on ethics, that was necessarily a negative judgment of the principles of absolutism.

The old distinction between individual conscience and state authority was thus turned counter to its founding intent: "What the burghers, seeming not even to touch the State, created in their lodges—in that secret inner space within the state—was a space in which, protected by secrecy, civil freedom was already being realised. Freedom in secret became the secret of freedom."[48] The actions of the ruler, the principles of his government, and reasons of state thus came to be measured by a morality that, although it was formed in a retreat from society, nonetheless became "the world's better conscience." More than the invention of a modern concept of equality, democratic in the manner of the Revolution, it was doubtless this new formulation of the relationship between morality and politics that gave Freemasonry its power, at once secret and critical.

This reverse politicization, born of an awareness of the distance between the ethical demands underlying Freemasonry and the specific principles, detached from all moral ends, that governed the practices of power, combined with another form of politicization based in the set of cultural practices emancipated from state tutelage in the early eighteenth century. Thanks to the constitution of a public whose judgments were not necessarily those of academic authority or the princely patron, thanks to the emergence of a market for cultural products that permitted at least a partial autonomy to those who created those products, and thanks to the widespread diffusion of skills that made possible a larger circulation of the written word, people acquired habits of free judgment and contradictory criticism. The new political culture that arose after 1750 was the direct heir of these transformations in that it substituted for an all-powerful authority, which decided in secret and without appeal, the public manifestation of individual opinions and the will to examine freely all established institutions. Thus a public was formed that, more sovereign than the sovereign, obliged the king to confront contrary opinions.[49]

However, the constitution of this new public space must not obscure the differences in the ways in which the various groups in society forged a connection between their daily concerns and affairs of state. The definition of politics in the Old Regime was no more unanimous than it is in the twentieth century. Several definitions coexisted: politics could be seen as participation in the rational order of critical judgment and political debate; as having a formal structure regulated by judicial procedure; or as a statement in the traditional language, sensitive to premonitory signs and secret correspondences. These various "modes of production of opinion,"[50] which it would be crippling to characterize too hastily in strictly social terms (thus setting up a dichotomy between the politics of the lettered and the politics of the people), relate back to different ways of constructing what is politically conceivable. For all those opposed to it, the new field of discourse that emerged toward the middle of the eighteenth century circumscribed a common space of possible statements and actions; but it in no way eliminated other sorts of "political" culture that were not necessarily apprehended as political and that articulated in other terms the relationship between the concerns of ordinary life and the claims of state power.

As the peasant protest movements and the recriminations of city journeymen show, however, the "politics" situated outside politics was by no means inert: its forms of expression and its fundamental aspirations changed as the century progressed. The public space of the Revolution can be characterized as "a modern political space created in a largely traditional cultural and mental environment."[51] In saying this, however, we should not forget that before the revolutionary event, the various ways of experiencing politics were not mutually exclusive or noncommunicating. Even though the public was not the people, the people, through chosen spokesmen, learned to mobilize the resources of juridical and Enlightenment rhetoric to make its wants known. Conversely, the public political sphere, bourgeois in its base, was haunted by the figure of an anonymous, worrisome, and dreaded "people," excluded yet always invoked. The new political culture of the eighteenth century resulted from these different modes of politicization which—each in its own way— profoundly stirred the traditional order.

8

DO REVOLUTIONS HAVE CULTURAL ORIGINS?

ATRUE REVOLUTION NEEDS IDEAS TO FUEL IT—WITH-
out them there is only a rebellion or a *coup d'état*—and the
intellectual and ideological underpinnings of the opposition to the government are therefore of the first importance."[1] Lawrence Stone's affirmation serves as the point of departure for this
chapter, which will focus on a comparison of preconditions for
revolution in England and France.

My question is, if we follow Lawrence Stone's analysis and consider
all revolutions (the English Revolution in the seventeenth century or
the French Revolution in the eighteenth century) as neither pure
accidents produced by chance circumstances nor absolute necessities
whose moment and modalities were logically inscribed in their very
causes, what place should we accord to cultural factors within revolutions' preconditions that make a radical rupture of this sort both
conceivable and desired? My intent in sketching a parallel between
these two revolutions that occurred a century and a half apart is not so
much to point to similarities that might warrant the construction of
an overall model of interpretation as it is to use the English precedent
to suggest new questions (or to revive old ones) to put to the situation
in France.

First, however, it may be useful to recall the five decisive factors in
Stone's examination of the intellectual and cultural preconditions of
the English Revolution. In the chapter of his book titled "New Ideas
and Values" he stated that the elements undermining adherence to
the old political and religious order were (1) religious aspiration

(Puritanism), (2) a juridical reference (English common law), (3) a cultural ideal (the ideology of the "country," as opposed to the royal court), (4) a mental attitude (the development of skepticism), and (5) an intellectual frustration linked to the "growing realization that the numbers of the leisured class equipped with higher education were increasing faster than the suitable job opportunities."[2] My purpose is not to establish whether or not this analysis is pertinent to the origins of the English Revolution (a much-debated topic) but rather to investigate whether identical or analogous traits can be found in France during the decades immediately preceding the French Revolution.

Religion and Politics

At first sight there is one evident difference between the two countries. In seventeenth-century England a Christian reference justified taking a stance different from that of the instituted authorities. By asserting the superior rights of conscience and individual judgment, by legitimizing opposition to established powers that were betraying divine commandments, and by introducing a millenarian certitude that a new order was imminent, the preaching and teaching of Puritanism furnished both structure and leaders to the English Revolution and, even more, inaugurated a widely shared manner of basing dissent and the hopes of present times in a literal reading of the Bible. Stone concluded: "It is as safe as any broad generalization of history can be to say that without the ideas, the organization and the leadership supplied by Puritanism there would have been no revolution at all."[3]

In eighteenth-century France, to the contrary, a profound detachment from the teachings, prohibitions, and institutions of Christianity prepared the Revolution. In chapter 5 I attempted to pinpoint the chronology and modalities of, and the reasons behind, this process of dechristianization, which, under the cover of a conformist respect for obligatory practices, in fact distanced entire segments of the population of the kingdom from religion. Does this, however, invalidate any possible parallel with the situation in England?

Perhaps not, and for two reasons. The first has to do with the importance of Jansenism in the political debates that shook France after the bull *Unigenitus* in 1713 and, even more, with the crisis of the refusal of the sacraments to the Jansenists halfway through the century. I have no intention of drawing up a list of possible connections between Jansenism and Puritanism (even though they exist, for instance, in obsessive reference to the Bible and emphasis on individual salvation); I mean only to stress the political importance of a movement that combined, first, a theology of grace; second, a Gallican ecclesiology influenced by Edmond Richer in which the church's infallibility resided not in the decisions of its hierarchy but in the unanimous consent of the entire community of the faithful; and, third, a parlementary constitutionalism that considered the court of justice—the parlement—the depository and guardian of the fundamental and ancient laws of the kingdom and that deemed the exercise of sovereign authority as a mandate simply delegated to the king.

It is true that after 1770, and in particular after the "coup" of Chancellor Maupeou against the parlements, the Jansenist movement lost its unity and coherence: "Long an ideological compound, it now tended to dissolve into its constituent elements which were then free to recombine with others."[4] This explains the separation between the constitutional demands of the parlements (which were close to the ecclesiastical hierarchy) and the Jansenist causes during the two decades immediately preceding the French Revolution. It also explains why a number of the Jansenists joined the "patriot" party, which was imbued with Enlightenment ideas. Thus it would be an error to exaggerate the impact of Jansenism by holding it to be comparable to Puritanism. Still, like Puritanism, Jansenism used religion as a basis for a radical critique of both ecclesiastical and ministerial despotism that, at least in some places (Paris for one), accustomed people to mistrusting instituted authorities.

Furthermore, and this is a second reason to investigate the religious parallel between England and France, dechristianization does not necessarily mean desacralization. Several traits associated with Puritanism—the Puritans' certitude that the cause they defended was just, the primacy they accorded independent moral judgment over the pronouncements of authority, the expectation of social regeneration—had correspondences in the movement that, even before 1789, invested new values (familial, patriotic, and civic) with the affective and spiritual intensity traditionally reserved to Christian belief. References to Roman and Greek antiquity replaced biblical citations, furnishing both a lexicon and an aesthetic to this transfer of sacrality. For example, the new paradigm of painting (as asserted in David's masterpieces presented in the Salon carré—the *Bélisaire* [1781], the *Serment des Horaces* [1784], the *Mort de Socrate* [1787], and the *Brutus* [1789]) reflected a conception of representation inspired by Diderot ("If when one makes a painting, one supposes beholders, everything is lost") put to the service of the celebration of civic virtue.[5] By the choice of classical, patriotic, and political subjects, but even more by a manner that thrust aside academic rules and conventions, David's painting in the last decade of the Old Regime aimed at producing an emotion, an enthusiasm, and a loss of self in the spectator that brought something of religious experience into aesthetic experience. The warm reception given to such works by the public who frequented the Salons contrasted sharply with the reticence of academic critics (who concentrated on pointing out the painter's shortcomings), indicating that for many, the sacred could henceforth be experienced outside the formal settings of the institutional church.[6] Thus it is undeniable that an upsurge of feeling comparable in intensity, if not in content, to the aspirations of Puritanism contributed to the break that occurred with the French Revolution.

The Language of Law

The second matrix of the English Revolution of the seventeenth century was the juridical ideology of English customary law—the common law. The common law did more than provide a foundation for the demands of the opposition (in such matters as limitation of royal prerogatives in the name of the time-honored English Constitution or the defense of individual rights against the encroachments of the state): it furnished a language and a repertory of references by which political issues could be formulated. "This intensive legalism was as pervasive as Puritanism in its effect on the mental set of the early seventeenth century."[7] To what extent was this also true in France in the eighteenth century? As we have seen, in France the linguistic resources of the law and of juridical procedure helped to turn single, localized conflicts of a private nature into general and public causes. Such was the case, for instance, in the lawsuits instituted by rural communities against their seigneurs or by journeymen in the trades against their masters, or in the strategies used in juridical memoirs to invoke—and to constitute—public opinion. The procedures for the convocation of the primary assemblies preparatory to the calling of the Estates General and the process of writing up the *cahiers de doléances* offer the clearest picture of the enormous influence of juridical reference in the waning years of the Old Regime.[8] One social group—officeholders representing the king or the seigneurs and men of the law, attorneys, notaries, and *procureurs*—played a prominent role in this process. It was these men who usually presided over the assemblies of the rural communities, in conformity with article 25 of the electoral law of 24 January 1789, which stipulated that the primary assemblies must have as their presiding officer the judge of the district in question or, failing that, a public official. In some places the communities ignored the injunction and designated their own *syndic* or *consul* as presiding officer, but in general the rule was respected and the presidency was entrusted to a seigneurial official or a man of the law, who often came from the city, as a number of seigneurial judges, *procureurs fiscaux*, *baillis*, or *châtelains* were city-dwelling attorneys or notaries. The position of presiding officer gave these men notable influence on the drafting of the *cahiers de doléances* from the primary assemblies, and this was even more true when one man held multiple presidencies within the seigneurial district he controlled. This meant that certain "rural intellectuals" (as Georges Lefebvre called them) played a major part in the writing of the grievances, as did the presiding officers—men of the law—of assemblies in circulating model *cahiers*.

The jurists' appropriation of the consultation is also evident in their overwhelming presence in the assemblies on the *bailliage* level. Rural communities often chose such men as their representatives to the assemblies of the Third Estate. In the *bailliage* of Troyes, for instance, officeholders, men of the law, and members of the liberal professions, who accounted for 7 percent of all inhabitants of the *bailliage* present at the primary assemblies, made up 28 percent of rural deputies. In the *sénéchaussée* of Draguignan, the same percentages were, respectively, 4 percent and 45 percent. At the assemblies of the entire *bailliage* these rural deputies met deputies from the cities, who also tended to come from the same milieux: 40 percent of city deputies in Rouen were officeholders, men of the legal professions, and (in lesser proportion) members of the liberal professions, and the same was true of 42 percent of city deputies in Troyes and 67 percent in Nancy.

Thus it is hardly surprising that men of the robe dominated the committees charged with writing up the *cahiers* of the largest *bailliages*. They furnished twelve redactors out of twenty in Orleans, fifteen out of twenty-four in Troyes, and thirteen out of fourteen in Draguignan. This preponderance can also be found in the committees charged with writing the *cahiers* of the *grands bailliages*, which met after the sessions of the principal and secondary *bailliages*. In Orleans, eleven out of sixteen committee members were officeholders or lawyers; in Troyes, three out of ten were seigneurial officeholders, two were lawyers, and four were mayors or members of city councils. Moreover, the *cahiers* on the *bailliage* level were often based on the *cahier* from the largest city in the district, which was drawn up by a committee in which officeholders and jurists were either in the majority (in Orleans, Toulouse, and Besançon) or in equal numbers with wholesale merchants (Rouen and Troyes).

Thus it is clear that on all levels the consultation was kept firmly in hand by the world of the robe. The assembly that was elected at the end of the electoral process reflected this firm hold: of the 648 deputies of the Third Estate to the Estates General, 151 were lawyers (23 percent of Third Estate deputies) and 218 were judicial officeholders (34 percent), to whom we might add 14 notaries and 33 deputies who held municipal posts.[9] All in all, then, nearly two-thirds of the future members of the Constituent Assembly came from the milieux that had the greatest influence over electoral procedures and the writing of the *cahiers*.

The *cahiers* bear a clear imprint of juridical and administrative culture. First, in their very form: the majority of the *cahiers* from the primary assemblies organize their grievances by articles (more rarely, under headings). The *bailliage principal* of Montbrison can stand as an example: 60 percent of the *cahiers* from that district organize their grievances under explicit categories. A majority of the *cahiers* organized in this way limit themselves to numbering their grievances, usually in rudimentary fashion (*premièrement* or *primo*, 2°, 3°, and so on), sometimes more emphatically (*première doléance, seconde doléance, troisième doléance*, and so forth). A minority of *cahiers* make the organization by articles more explicit, using *item* or *article*, often abbreviated as *art.* or *1er art.*, etc.). This is also the mode of presentation of 150 out of 154 *cahiers* in the *bailliage principal* of Rouen and of 116 out of 133 *cahiers* from Semur-en-Auxois. The *cahiers* that fail to follow these patterns are of two quite different sorts. Some express the peasants' complaints in a manner that approaches the spontaneous flow of speech, without paragraphs or order of priority; others, written by local intellectuals, break out of the mold of presentation by articles to use a rhetoric full of reforming zeal and Enlightenment influences.

Two traditions stood behind the strong predominance of composition by articles. The first, the notarial tradition, was accustomed to enumeration, to the ordered description of goods, and to putting a testator's last wishes into order. The second, the administrative tradition, took inspiration from the style of edicts and decrees and was reinforced in the eighteenth century by more frequent surveys and censuses. Comparison of the form of the 1614 and the 1789 *cahiers* clearly attests to the diffusion, in a century and a half, of a written style based on analysis, classification, and prioritization. Even when they appear to be broken up into articles, the *cahiers* of 1614 are poorly organized; the articulation is weak in their presentation of grievances and they lack the explicit ordinal indications that make the majority of the 1789 *cahiers* so easy to grasp. The difference between the two sets of *cahiers* is a clear measure of the advances in a juridical and bureaucratic mode of thought and writing in the men who held the pen at the convocation of the Estates General.

The vocabulary of the *cahiers* is another sign of the influence of juristic culture. The lexicon of the Enlightenment is rarely apparent in them. In a sample of eight *cahiers* from the *bailliage* of Semur-en-Auxois, the word *instruction* appears only eight times, as does *raison*; *luxe* and *préjugé* appear three times, *éducation* twice, and *lumières*, *bonheur*, and *progrès* only once.[10] In three *cahiers* from *communautés de métier* (trade associations) in Reims, although the word *lumières* appears seven times in the *cahier* of the mirror makers and upholsterers, *bonheur* appears only five times, *instruction* only four times, *humanité* twice, and *progrès* not even once.[11] Furthermore, certain words that seem new tend to be used in an older meaning, as with *constitution* or *liberté*. The conclusion is clear: "Massively, the vocabulary of the Enlightenment, in full ferment for thirty years, had not reached the world of minor jurists, judges, men of middle status in the liberal professions, regents and professors, or even the bourgeois of the smaller towns (which were as rural as they were urban) who held the pen or gave form" to the grievances. [12]

The vocabulary that sprang spontaneously to mind to express the communities' grievances was one "of juridical structure and skeleton, elaborated during at least the past two centuries within the framework of the institutions of the French monarchy." [13] Taken as a whole, it offers a traditional view of administrative districts, social status, the formal aspects of the consultation, and institutions. In the *cahiers* of the towns of the *bailliage* of Semur-en-Auxois, the ten nouns most frequently encountered are, in order: *article(s)* (226 occurrences), *état(s)* (139), *droit(s)* (62), *impôt* (59), *ordre(s)* (51), *députés* (44), *majesté* (42), *assemblée(s)* (38), *juges* (33), and *province* (29). Even the vocabulary of denunciation and reform belongs to traditional language, as with the word *abus*, already frequent in 1614, and with terms designating the body social and politic. In Burgundy *cahiers*, *habitants* is used more often than *citoyens*; *royaume* more often than *nation*. In Reims, *nation* is frequent in the *cahiers* of the trade corporations—except in those of the poorest trades, which prefer the older *peuple(s)*—but the word is used passively: rather than implying any demand for power, the term signifies only the traditional relation of subordination to royal authority. The term *citoyen* was also slow to take hold: often it competed with its apparent opposite, *sujets*, or it was absorbed into the vocabulary of a society of orders and estates, as in the seeming oxymoron *ordre de citoyens*.

Juristic modes of presentation and legal vocabulary in the *cahiers* served for the formulation of concrete grievance, leaving little room for demands more directly inspired by philosophic literature. Denunciations of arbitrary abuses of power, demands for individual rights, calls for a declaration of rights guaranteeing the sovereignty of the nation, civic equality among citizens, individual liberties, and the right to property together account for no more than 5 percent of grievances in any body of *cahiers*—rural or urban, primary, or on the *bailliage* level. In the *bailliage* of Troyes, such general demands account for 0.8 percent of the grievances in the *cahiers* from the rural communities, 2.4 percent of those of urban associations and communities, 1.2 percent of those of the largest city in the district, and 0.4 percent of the *cahier* of the *bailliage*. For the *bailliage* of Rouen the percentages are, respectively, 2.4 percent, 3.5 percent, 3.5 percent, and 2.9 percent; in the *bailliage* of Orléans they are 0.8 percent, 2.4 percent, 1.2 percent, and 2 percent. Scrutiny of the grievances thus fully confirms Daniel Mornet's evaluation of the *cahiers*: "To tell the truth, ideas hold little place in them, and, all the less, philosophical ideas."[14]

The *cahiers de doléances* were by no means the only form of political expression in France at the end of the eighteenth century. Their mass should not lead us to conclude that the language of jurisprudence was the only idiom available for the expression of criticism and expectations. The defense of individual liberties and the demand for a new equilibrium between the monarchy and society found support in two other sources besides the ancient juridical tradition of customary law: in the philosophical definitions of the rights of man, as elaborated by the Enlightenment, and in competing absolutist, parlementary, and administrative theories of political representation. The mid-century public debate between the monarchy and its opposition constructed a sphere of autonomous discourse apart from juridical reference.

Nonetheless, as the *cahiers* amply show, at the end of the Old Regime the language of the law continued to provide a fundamental resource for the formulation of both the antagonisms that were tearing society asunder and the hopes for reform addressed to the sovereign. The intellectual hegemony of the Enlightenment thus failed to destroy the juridical culture borne along by a host of men who held public office and practiced jurisprudence, whose language both expressed and distorted the aspirations of those who attended the primary assemblies in 1789. The new public space launched by the Revolution was not destructive of this juridical culture, as shown by the fact that in 1789 and 1790, political argument, as practiced by a large number of lawyers, tended to cast juridical rhetoric into the consecrated form of the catechism as it heralded the new order.[15]

The Court and the City

The third cultural origin of the Revolution of 1642 noted by Lawrence Stone is "the ideology of the 'Country' ": "Spread by poets and
preachers, and stimulated by the news letters about the goings-on at
Court, it defined itself most clearly as the antithesis to this negative
reference group."[16] Was there an equivalent in France to this court/
country antithesis, which in England discredited both the court and
the city (London) in the name of a moral and Puritan ideal, a
traditional and patriarchal way of life, and a fierce attachment to local
political institutions?

  If we consider the diminished role of the court after the death of
Louis XIV, the answer might seem to be no. Three developments
contributed to the court's loss of importance. First, with Louis XV
and Louis XVI, Versailles became merely one royal residence among
many. The sovereigns' incessant moves between the capital, the
palace at Versailles, and one château or another deprived the court of
the geographical stability that it had known since 1682, and, by that
token, severely weakened the identification of a form of ceremonial
(the ceremonial of court etiquette) with the installation of power in
one place, Versailles.[17]

  Second, court ritual had also been attenuated by the increased
"privatization" of royalty. It would, of course, be a mistake to
exaggerate the contrast with the previous reign: Louis XIV built not
only the grand reception rooms in the palace of Versailles but also a
number of *petits cabinets* for the enjoyment of more intimate pleasures.
Conversely, although Louis XV remodeled the palace and its gardens
to satisfy his private passions (for drawing, botany, agronomy, and
turning decorative wood objects), it was on his initiative that the
"palatial work" undertaken by his predecessor was completed (the
Chapel and the Opera, the inauguration of the Salon of Hercules in
the grand apartments, the finishing of the sculptural decoration of
the Fountain of Neptune, and the installation of the ministries
outside the palace, in separate buildings better adapted to their
functions).[18] Nonetheless, Louis XV's understanding of his profession as king, and, later, Marie-Antoinette's understanding of her
tasks as queen were felt to break with a public, ritualized representation of the monarchy. The retreat of the sovereigns into an intimate

sphere of family and friends, free of the rigors of etiquette and far from the sight of both the court and the people, was experienced as a destructive break with the ritual of the embodiment of the monarchy.

As the century ran its course, the court lost its role of aesthetic guidance. As early as the Regency, leadership in criticism and judgment had shifted to the city—that is, to the various forms of sociability (salons, clubs, journals) that made up the public literary sphere in Paris. Paris was where works were evaluated, reputations were made or unmade, and the world of the arts and letters was governed. At the end of the century, Louis-Sébastien Mercier recorded this fact, seemingly without displeasure:

> The word *court* no longer inspires awe among us as in the time of Louis XIV. Reigning opinions are no longer received from the court; it no longer decides on reputations of any sort; no one says now, with ridiculous pomposity, "The court has pronounced thus." The court's judgments are countermanded; one says openly that it understands nothing; it has no ideas on the subject [and] could have none; it is not in the know. . . . The court has thus lost the ascendancy that it had regarding the fine arts, letters, and everything pertaining to them today. In the last century, the preferences of a man of the court or a prince were quoted and no one dared contradict them. Expertise [*le coup d'oeil*] was not as prompt then, nor as well formed: people had to depend on the judgment of the court. Philosophy (here is another of its crimes) enlarged the horizon, and Versailles, which forms only one point in this picture, is included.

Mercier concluded by shifting from a comparison between the court and the city of Paris to one between the capital and the provinces: "It is from the city that the approbation or disapprobation adopted in the rest of the kingdom comes."[19]

The court's diminished role as a visible site of power, a theater for public ceremonial, and an aesthetic lawgiver might thus invalidate any comparison with England, where the ideology of the "country" was brandished against a powerful political and cultural model. Nonetheless, even stripped of part of its former attributes, the French court remained a powerful force in fixing the collective imagination or instilling rejection in it. Newsletters and libels spread the negative image of a court that was both destructive and depraved. Among the best-selling "prohibited books" sold in Troyes by Bruzard de Mauvelain between 1783 and 1785 were four titles criticizing the court: *Les Fastes de Louis XV*, by Buffonidor (Villefranche, 1782), the work Mauvelain ordered most often from the Société typographique de Neuchâtel (eleven times) and in the greatest number of copies (eighty-four); *L'Espion dévalisé*, by Baudoin de Guémadeuc (Neuchâtel, 1782), with ten orders and thirty-seven copies ordered; *La Vie privée, ou, apologie de Mgr. le duc de Chartres*, by Théveneau de Morande (London, 1784), ordered five times for a total of seven copies; and *La Vie privée de Louis XV*, by Mouffle d'Angerville (London, 1781), ordered only three times but for a total of eighteen copies.[20]

These works, written by pamphleteers who specialized in the genre, and avidly sought after throughout the kingdom, used denunciation of the late monarch and his favorite (Louis XV, who died in 1774, and Du Barry) to brand the court of that age as equally guilty of prodigality and turpitude, as abundantly illustrated in anecdotes concerning the great personages of the kingdom. Explicitly or implicitly, these texts all drew a connection between the corruption of the sovereign and the courtiers, the degeneration of the monarchy into an oriental despotism, the waste of public funds, and the misery of the people. *Les Fastes de Louis XV*, for example, states: "Louis XV was ever the same—that is, he always remained plunged into debauchery and dissolute living. Despite the miseries of the people and public calamities, his mistress's prodigality and depredation increased so much that in a few years she would have engulfed the kingdom if the death of the Sultan had not put a stop to it."[21]

Financial and political scandals during the 1780s lent a contemporary reality to denunciations of the late king. In February 1781 the publication of Necker's *Compte rendu au Roi*, which listed the beneficiaries of royal pensions and subsidies, unleashed its readers' fury and fueled polemics against the court. The text was a veritable best-seller. Published by the Imprimerie royale, it went through seventeen editions (including one by the Société typographique de Neuchâtel) and received twenty-nine reviews or analyses in current periodicals. *La Gazette des Gazettes*, published by the Société typographique de Bouillon, estimated the number of copies of the *Compte rendu* at forty thousand, a figure that is doubtless smaller than the real figure and would have been inadequate to satisfy the enormous demand.[22]

In 1785 and 1786 the group of pamphleteers subsidized by the banker Clavière, which included Brissot, Dupont de Nemours, and Gorsas (and which often concealed its identify behind the prestigious signature of the Comte de Mirabeau), excoriated the court's stock speculations as a way to strike at Calonne, the *controleur général*. A close connection was thus established between the defense of special interests (those of the Geneva banker, who played the stock market short) and a radical critique of the court and the government (Calonne first among them), who were accused, in a Rousseauistic and moralizing rhetoric, of raising stock prices, thus placing stocks out of the reach of the general public. Through their pamphlet wars, rival factions in the Exchange thus had an immediate political impact, which worked against Calonne, whom they denounced as a manipulator working for his own enrichment (incidentally not far from the truth) just when he was posing as a reformer of state finances.[23] Finally, it was during these same two years that the diamond necklace affair irremediably compromised the queen and, with her, the court.[24] Enflamed by the pamphleteers, the entire country rose up in eighteenth-century France—as in seventeenth-century England—against a court rendered detestable by what was glimpsed and imagined there.

The Capital and the Provinces

There are other ways to describe the French version of this antithesis, however. The first brings us back to Tocqueville and his central thesis: "How administrative centralization was an institution of the Old Regime and not, as is often thought, a creation of the Revolution or the Napoleonic period."[25] Tocqueville included among the consequences of this important change (which brought on the destruction of all intermediary powers, the disappearance of local liberties, and the equalization of social conditions) the breach that opened up between the capital and the provinces. A new antithesis replaced the old opposition of city and court: "How in France, more than in any other European country, the provinces had come under the thrall of the metropolis, which attracted to itself all that was most vital in the nation."[26] Because it was the seat of the central government, which occupied the entire sphere of public authority, the capital became omnipotent and appropriated to itself all intellectual activity ("by then Paris had absorbed the intellectual life of the whole country at the expense of the provinces") and all economic activity ("besides being at once a business and commercial center, a city of pleasure seekers and consumers, Paris had now developed into a manufacturing city").[27]

The validity of Tocqueville's analysis is less important here than the opposition of capital to province, which pictures the capital as inexorably attractive and desperately destructive. From the mid-eighteenth century onward, a good many essays, novels, and theatrical pieces gave literary expression to the cultural dyad formed by Paris and the provinces, usually using comparison of their differences to satirize the customs and fashions of the capital.[28]

Two texts, published twenty years apart, can serve as examples of these. In *La Capitale des Gaules, ou, la Nouvelle Babylone* (1759), Fougeret de Monbron, a fine exemplar of the "low-life of literature," joined the attack on luxury that had been popular among writers since the 1730s. To prove (against the apologists for luxury, Voltaire primarily) that "luxury is the gangrene of all political bodies," he showed the provincial freshly arrived in Paris with the aim of frequenting bohemian literary circles, and the baneful role of a capital perverted by gambling, theatrical spectacles, and debauchery:

> One must admit that in reality Paris owes its splendor and its riches uniquely to the scarcities and the exhaustion of the provinces starved by their inhabitants themselves. How many [people] do we see every day who, enticed by the attractions offering pleasure and licentiousness, come to Paris to dissipate in two or three evenings of crapulous living what used to suffice to maintain them at home with honor for years at a stretch! How many dehumanized fathers consume their children's patrimony there! How many children, lost in debauchery, devour their fathers' inheritance there! How many young people destined to fill distinguished posts in the provinces and on whom their families have pinned their fondest hopes have come to this

dangerous Babylon to consume their entire fortunes as well as their innocence and their good name![29]

Although this literary exercise and its conventional rhetoric do not necessarily imply sincerity of opinion (even if the journals of the age took *La Capitale des Gaules* seriously and answered it accordingly), they do betray a commonplace that was equally present among political statisticians hostile to overpopulated capital cities and that can be seen, in its own way, as an "ideology of the 'Country.' "

The tone is similar in Mercier's *Tableau de Paris*, published in 1782: "Formerly, routes between the capital and the provinces were neither open nor frequented. Each city kept the younger generation of its children, who lived within the walls that had seen their birth and lent support to their parents in their old age. Today the young man sells his inheritance in order to spend his portion far from his family's eyes: he pumps it dry so he can shine for one instant in the seat of license."

The imagined seductions of the capital had just as strong an effect on young females from the provinces: "She is avid for news of that city. She is the first to exclaim, 'He comes from Paris! He arrives straight from the court!' She no longer finds grace, wit, or opulence around her. The adolescents listening to these tales imagine, exaggerating all [the city's] traits, what experience must cruelly contradict one day; they hasten to obey this epidemic that precipitates all the youth of the provinces toward the abyss of corruption."[30]

Throughout, Mercier's *Tableau de Paris* opposes Paris and the provinces (by now a literary cliché), using the hackneyed theme of the Parisian in the provinces as a way to ridicule his sense of superiority: "When a Parisian leaves Paris, he never stops talking about the capital in the provinces. He compares everything he sees with its habits and customs; he pretends that he finds ridiculous anything that differs from them; he wants everyone to change his ideas to please him and amuse him. . . . He imagines that he stands out by praising nothing but Paris and the court."[31] Mercier also turned the theme around to show the provincial man of letters who has come to the capital, thus remarking on the cultural differences between Paris and the other cities of the kingdom:

Paris has furnished literature with nearly as many great men as all the rest of the kingdom. . . . If one takes into account that there has never been a famous man born in the provinces who has not come to Paris to form himself, who has not lived there by choice, and who has not died there, no longer able to leave this great city despite his great love for his birthplace, this race of enlightened men, all concentrated in the same place while the other cities of the kingdom offer barren heaths of an incredible sterility, becomes an object of profound meditation on the true and underlying causes that precipitate all men of letters to the capital and keep them there as if by enchantment.[32]

Le Tableau de Paris, one of the most broadly circulated of the prohibited books, nourished provincial imaginations with a representation of the capital as both attractive and insatiable. This representation strengthened a defense of the provinces that was expressed in various ways during the eighteenth century, from local histories sponsored by the provincial academies (fully half of which had a project of this sort) to "natural histories" written by geographers, and from administrative inventories of the wealth and resources of the various regions to physical and nosologic descriptions of medical topographies.[33]

A second way to understand the opposition of country and court in its French context during the late eighteenth century consists, following Norbert Elias, in a description of the process that brought on the Revolution as the exhaustion of a "balance of tension" that, by establishing the court as a necessary counterweight to the power of the holders of judicial and financial offices, made possible the domination of an absolute king.[34] Seen in this manner, sovereign power depended directly upon the equilibrium that made two dominant groups—the court aristocracy and the bourgeoisie de la robe (the magistrature)—sufficiently interdependent to keep them from being tempted to imperil the order that ensured their social power, yet sufficiently in competition with one another to make unity against the monarch impossible. The court was an institution essential to this arrangement. On the one hand, it subjected the king's oldest and most immediate rivals to his direct control; on the other, through the giving and withholding of royal subsidies it permitted the consolidation of noble fortunes that were sorely tried by an economic ethic that made expenditures proportional not to revenues but to the demands of social status. This explains the central role of the court in the monarchical strategy of the reproduction of social tension: "The tension and equilibrium between the various social groups, and the resulting highly ambivalent attitude of all these groups to the central ruler himself, was certainly not created by any king. But once this constellation had been established, it [was] vitally important for the ruler to preserve it in all its precariousness."[35]

In the eighteenth century, however, this structure of tensions, frozen into a definition inherited from the reign of Louis XIV, was no longer capable of absorbing new social partners and could only repeat the conflicts that had existed among the old partners: the king, the aristocracy, and the parlements. The reinforcement of the social power of groups who had formerly been easily removed from the mechanisms of domination instituted a decisive rupture between the self-perpetuating distribution of power, henceforth taken over by rival but interconnected "monopoly elites," and the reality of the new equilibrium between forces that was favorable to the "privileged strata." This is why it was impossible to conserve, but also impossible to reform, the court society—defined, following Elias, as a social formation in which the relations and patterns of domination were organized on the basis of the existence of a court:

> Even if it often happened, particularly in the various power struggles at the court in the last decades of the monarchy, that representatives of one of these main cadres attempted to limit the privileges and so the power of another, the means of power were really too evenly distributed, and the common interest in maintaining traditional privileges against the growing pressure from unprivileged strata was too great, to allow one side a decisive increase in power over the other. The even distribution of power between monopoly elites, the maintenance of which Louis XIV had consciously striven for as a condition for strengthening his own power position, now regulated itself. All parties kept watch with Argus-eyes to ensure that their own privileges, their own power, were not curtailed. And as every reform of the regime threatened the existing privileges and

power of one elite in relation to another, no reform was possible. The privileged monopoly elites were frozen in the equilibrium consolidated by Louis XIV.[36]

Once again, my intention is not to test the pertinence of this explanatory model, which has the signal merit of not reducing the social process culminating in the Revolution to an overly simplified opposition between the aristocracy and the bourgeoisie—oversimplified because at least some groups within the aristocracy and the bourgeoisie constituted privileged monopoly elites and were, by that token, as much bound to one another as they were in competition (perhaps even more so). Of course, we still need to identify more accurately the unprivileged strata whose new power brought the old balance of tensions to the breaking point (avoiding, however, the pitfall of characterizing the bourgeoisie excluded from this alliance as immediately "capitalist"). In any event, this perspective permits a better comprehension of the deeper meaning of the attacks against the court found in manuscript newsletters and printed pamphlets. Beyond the denunciation of real persons or the profanation of the symbols of the monarchy through defamation of the court, they attempted to destroy one of the three fundamental supports of absolute monarchy (the others were fiscal monopoly and monopoly of the legitimate uses of force) and, with it, the social configuration that had authorized and perpetuated it.

The Erosion of Authority

Lawrence Stone mentioned a fourth factor in his reflections on the ideological origins of the English Revolution: the erosion of authority. In the family, the state, and the church, "the spread of scepticism, which was slowly eroding belief in traditional values and traditional hierarchies," caused "a real crisis of confidence."[37] Several chapters in the present volume (touching on the circulation of "philosophical" books, changes in Christian behavior, and shifts in perceptions of the royal person) have attempted to measure the importance and significance in eighteenth-century France of the most obvious instances of disengagement from traditional beliefs. Even if some reservations need to be stated, exceptions and deviations need ex-

plicit mention, and, on occasion, overly abrupt statements of relationships (for example, between the book, reading, and belief) call
for revision, the overall picture seems clear: after 1750, and perhaps
even before, a critical attitude came into being among a large segment of the population of France. Although not necessarily expressed
explicitly in clear thought or organized discourse, this new attitude
induced people to abandon their traditional actions, reject inculcated
obedience, and perceive sources of power formerly viewed as objects
of awe and reverence in a more detached, ironical, or suspicious
manner. In this sense, it is legitimate to recognize an erosion of
authority in the decades preceding the French Revolution as well. Its
modalities, its language, and the ways in which it was translated into
action were not the same as in seventeenth-century England—far
from it—but its effects were of the same order. That is, it prepared
people's minds for the sudden and radical collapse of an order that had
already been emptied of its powers of persuasion.

Frustrated Intellectuals and Political Radicalism

Lawrence Stone added one last factor to his set of causes of the English
Revolution: "educational over-expansion." The psychological and
political effects of this phenomenon were considerable:

> The extraordinary expansion of enrolments in Oxford and
> Cambridge meant the creation of a small army of unemployed
> or under-employed gentry whose training had equipped them
> for positions of responsibility, but for whom the avenues of
> opportunity were clogged. Neither the central bureaucracy, nor
> the army, nor colonial expansion in Ireland, nor even the law
> could absorb them all. The result was frustration and resent-
> ment among large numbers of nobles, squires and gentry.
> Second, the Universities were turning out degree-holding
> clergy in numbers well in excess of the capacity of the Church to
> absorb them. They flooded into low-paid curacies with little
> prospects of promotion. . . . Many other graduates filled lec-
> tureships in the towns, and a few got themselves taken on as
> private chaplains in noble households. All were resentful of a
> society which had over-trained them and could not employ

them, and many naturally drifted into religious and political radicalism.[38]

There was thus a close connection between the constitution of a large population of "alienated intellectuals" (to borrow Mark Curtis's term)[39] and the rise of an ideology critical of the state and the church.

Could this same state of affairs be found in France a century and a half later? Or, to put the question in different terms, did France in the final decades of the eighteenth century experience a like imbalance between the number of students granted diplomas by the universities and the number of posts available to them? The answer to the question obviously depends on the gap between the subjective aspirations of all who hoped that the degree they had obtained would assure them the position to which that degree traditionally gave access, on the one hand, and, on the other, on their objective chances of success, given the changed state of the job market. Strictly speaking, a response to the question supposes that it is possible to compare two conjunctural phenomena—the number of university students working toward a degree and the market of posts and benefices to which they aspired. Unfortunately, neither is easy to determine.

The difficulty derives primarily from the special characteristics of the university system in France. There were a good many universities (twenty-eight in the late eighteenth century), there was no strong hierarchy among them, and they were extremely heterogeneous, with some faculties offering instruction only and others offering degrees, some drawing students from afar and others with a more local recruitment. Such differences in function and prestige among individual universities make it difficult to aggregate data drawn from them, the more so because French university archives permit the construction only of discontinuous data series and only relatively late in the period.[40]

Still, one conclusion clearly emerges from a comparison of the figures on the number of degrees granted: there was an enormous increase in the number of graduates from the law faculties during the three final decades of the Old Regime. This holds true for the whole century. In the eleven universities for which data are available, if we take as base 100 the number of bachelors' degrees in law per decade for 1680–89, the index stood at only 126 in the 1750s, but after that date it rose to 141 during the 1760s, 164 during the 1770s, and 176 during the 1780s. This spectacular growth, which constituted a high point for the century in all universities, also surpassed the highest levels reached at the end of the seventeenth century (where data are available), after the reform of law studies in 1679. Thus whatever our scale of observation—within the century or from one century to the next—it is clear that the last thirty years of the Old Regime saw a hitherto unheard-of production of graduates in law. The average number of bachelors' degrees in law, which stood at 680 in 1680–89 and between 800 and 900 from 1710 to 1750, rose to 1,200 during the 1780s.

The pattern is not the same in theology and medicine. In theology, in fact, the number of degrees granted declined, rose, then declined again during the eighteenth century. For bachelors in theology, the turning point came during the 1750s in Paris, the 1720s in Avignon, and the 1690s in Toulouse, where a second dip followed a small rise during the 1740s. The same tendency proves true for holders of the *licence*, whose average number per decade declined in Paris beginning in the 1750s. In their manner, then, serial data on university enroll-ments anticipate and reflect the disengagement from the institutions of the church that weakened recruitment to the clergy and opened the way for newcomers—the sons of merchants and peasants—to careers in the church.

Doctorates in medicine show great variety from one university to another. In some, the doctoral degrees granted rose (as in Montpellier beginning in the 1730s or in Strasbourg from 1760 onward); others declined (as in Aix-en-Provence or Avignon, where the number of new doctors per decade sank to a level lower than in the seventeenth century). Overall, however, there was a clear rise, with an annual average of 160 doctoral degrees in medicine during the 1780s, as opposed to only 75 per year between 1700 and 1709. Nonetheless, the proportion of doctors of medicine to bachelors of law, which stood at one to eight at the end of the eighteenth century (as compared to one to four in the United Provinces in the same epoch) emphasizes the high preponderance of jurists in the French university system during the Old Regime.

Can we then conclude that there was an overproduction of jurists? An exhaustive study of the market for positions to which law graduates could aspire is, of course, an impossible task at this point, but several regional examples attest to an imbalance created by the increased number of bachelors of law. In Toulouse at the end of the Old Regime, the list of *avocats* ballooned (with 215 *avocats* in the Parlement, as opposed to 87 in 1740), newcomers thronged (on average 7.5 per year between 1764 and 1789 against 3.8 per year during the first half of the century), and the corps grew younger (more than half of the *avocats* of Toulouse had not reached forty in 1789). One result was an increased number of lawyers who never pleaded a case: this was true of 160 out of 300 men on the rolls of the bar between 1760 and 1790, and of 173 out of the 215 *avocats* in the Parlement surveyed in 1788.[41]

The same holds true for Besançon and Franche-Comté in general. A higher number (too high a number) of lawyers meant that some had no cases to plead or were without access to the Parlement, where positions were monopolized by the families who already held them. Nor could they acquire positions of secretary to the king (which conferred noble status); its price was too high for their means. Frustrated in their hopes for social promotion, deprived of a clientele, held at bay by the officials of the sovereign law courts, the lawyers of the end of the Old Regime were ill-treated by their times. Thus it is hardly surprising that they argued the rights of talent against inherited privilege, or that (in Franche-Comté and elsewhere) they boldly joined the patriots' party.[42]

At the end of the Old Regime, then, there was a striking contrast between the chances for employment offered the holders of doctors' degrees in medicine and bachelors of law. Newly fledged physicians who wanted to set up practice in the largest cities, where positions were controlled either by the corps of *docteurs-régents* (if the city had a university) or by the *collège des médecins*, did not always find a situation in keeping with their hopes. Nevertheless, the low density of doctors in the kingdom (one physician for every twelve thousand inhabitants, as opposed to one per every three thousand in the United Provinces) offered them possibilities. The same was not true of bachelors of law, who, even though they were free to adopt the title of *avocat* (which was not an office), risked finding that it brought them little profit.

The tension between available posts and expectations found specific and particularly acute expression in the world of letters.[43] After

1760, in fact, a great number of writers found themselves excluded from positions and revenues to which they aspired, whether these were academic positions, "gratifications" and pensions granted by the monarchy, or sinecures connected with official institutions. The latter, like appointments to the sovereign law courts, were monopolized by the generation of authors born during the 1720s and 1730s, who tenaciously fended off newcomers. There were important consequences to this gulf created between the "haves" of the world of letters (often of the Philosophes' party) and the jobless "have-nots." For one thing, increasing numbers of authors with no social situation or employment were forced to create institutions of their own that were not those of the literary world (the cafés, literary societies, "museums," and lyceums) and to accept whatever minor jobs the publishing world of the Enlightenment offered them in order to earn a living.

Second, the gulf between the two groups encouraged reciprocal hostility, prompting both scorn of the *canaille de la littérature* on the part of established authors (as in certain passages in Voltaire and Mercier or in Rivarol's *Petit almanach de nos grands-hommes* [1788]), and bitter resentment on the part of the "gutter Rousseaus" when others occupied places they considered rightfully their own. Even when it was paid and in the service of a party or a coterie, pamphleteering was a fine way to denounce the "establishment" of the Enlightenment, the leaders of cultural institutions, or the holders of state power who had shattered dreams of a brilliant and profitable career. By a mechanism (common during the Old Regime) that imputed all social ills to politics, frustrated writers came to hold the king, his court, and his ministers responsible for their failed lives. This doubtless explains the fierce hatred of the old order often present in commissioned pamphlets, whose authors believed themselves the victims of an intolerable injustice.

Thus eighteenth-century France also had its "alienated intellectuals." Lawyers with no cases and writers with no jobs had organized their futures on the basis of an outdated representation of the value of a university degree or of the evidence of talent. In a saturated market where a number of posts were monopolized, the positions to which these people aspired proved out of their reach, forcing them to accept less prestigious and worse-paid employment and even (for the writers) tasks without honor. Both groups played a decisive role in the prerevolutionary process—the writers by the increasing number of pamphlets and *libelles* they wrote; the lawyers by providing leadership for the campaigns of the patriot party and the consultation preparatory to the Estates General. To say this does not imply any return to an old interpretation that sees the unsuccessful intellectuals' desire for revenge as a cause of the Revolution; it simply emphasizes that in a large segment of the groups most intensely engaged in criticism of the authorities, a wounded awareness of an unhappy fate may have brought a radical disengagement from a society held responsible for their woes. The collapse of an order so contrary to the just recompense of merit and talent was easily accepted and even ardently desired.

The intellectual and cultural preconditions of revolution in early seventeenth-century England and in France in the late eighteenth century thus have certain points in common. The references are, of course, not the same in the two different times and places, and the expectation of a new order is not expressed in identical terms. Nonetheless, these two historical situations show a similar configuration, combining the disappointment of a large segment of the intellectual classes, the erosion of an all-powerful authority, the imputation of social ills to the person who held sovereign power, and a widely shared hope for a new era. This complex of thought and affect, of objective reality and subjective perception, perhaps constitutes the necessary condition that brings all revolutions within the order of the possible. In any event, it was clearly evident, with its particular modalities, in the kingdom that was to produce the Revolution of 1789.

CONCLUSION

THE SPECIFIC FORMS THAT THE FRENCH REVOLUTION took seem anything but necessary when they are viewed within the long-term course of the cultural shifts that transformed the acts and the thoughts of the French of the Old Regime. A first paradox is that the Revolution reintroduced large-scale violence in a land in which, for more than a century, the "process of civilization" (to use Norbert Elias's term) had made notable advances, radically reducing and circumscribing violence. There seems to have been a clear break between revolutionary behavior, which made broad use of both the spontaneous violence of riots and the institutionalized violence of the Terror, and the pacification in the social sphere that a state monopoly on recourse to force had made possible.

Brutality had not been completely eliminated—far from it, as proved by the aggressive behavior typical of relations among neighbors, in the working world, and within the family in rural and urban areas alike. Nonetheless, after the mid-seventeenth century, by obliging individuals to keep a tighter control over their impulses, censor their emotions, and rein in spontaneous acts, the judicial and administrative state considerably lowered the threshold of violence that the body social would tolerate. There are a number of signs of this all-important evolution: blood crimes and violence against persons declined among cases of "legal" criminality (crimes, that is, that were known and punished by the courts of justice, which were increasingly absorbed by crimes against property). The older sort of revolt characterized by merciless fury disappeared and was replaced by confrontations that used the more peaceful means of recourse to the law courts or the expression of political grievances. Private recourse to force to settle personal and familial differences declined. Where violence persisted (ingrained as it was in patterns of popular behavior), the authorities paid scant attention to it, given that it did not threaten the established order and was seldom aimed at society's notables.

Even though the French Revolution is far from being reducible to the violence that it employed or authorized, the event brought to the surface behavior patterns that had apparently been eradicated and forgotten. This is not the proper place to measure or interpret revolutionary violence, whether in the riots, the Terror, or in military campaigns, but only to reflect on the possible connections between such contradictory phenomena as the (at least relative) pacification of Old Regime society and the massive use of force during the Revolution. To recognize a total discontinuity between these two facts would be to postulate that in one of its concrete and fundamental aspects the Revolution had no origins, and that, far from being rooted in its century, it broke with its times, and for the worse.

The notion merits discussion. On the one hand, the more spontaneous forms of revolutionary violence clearly show the limits of the effort to eradicate brutality. At the end of the eighteenth century, the civilizing process had not transformed all the inhabitants of the kingdom. The personality structure that instilled in individuals stable and rigorous mechanisms of self-constraint, substituting self-imposed prohibition and repression for exterior constraints, was not yet universal. The rough ways of both peasants and townspeople clearly attest to the persistence of another mode of being with a greater freedom in expressing emotion. With the Revolution, the mechanisms that had kept this half-stifled popular violence within the bounds of the private sphere collapsed, giving ancient habits of punitive behavior a chance to reemerge in the sphere of relations with authority.

On the other hand, in its institutional forms, revolutionary violence brought to its logical completion the movement giving the state a monopoly on the legitimate exercise of force. In this sense, neither obligatory conscription nor the mechanisms of the Terror were in contradiction with the monarchy's long-standing attempt to reserve the use of arms to public power alone. They had two original features, however: they used force to oblige all citizens to use force against the enemies of the nation, and they instituted an administrative violence whose purpose was protection of the civil community, but which became available for political solutions to conflicts in the individual sphere. Just as the courts of the Inquisition had given a form, language, and legitimacy to denunciations inspired by totally secular interests, the revolutionary courts made it possible to mobilize state violence to settle (often expeditiously) a large number of private tensions fueled by accumulated bitterness, inexpiable hatred, and rivalries that originally had little connection with the destiny of the republic.

Once the Terror had passed (and whether it was necessary to the Revolution or a derailment of it is beside the point here), the long-term evolution continued, and the state was assigned the essential task of using its powers of coercion and persuasion to constrain individual behavior. Momentarily interrupted by a return to archaic behavior patterns and massive use of state violence, the civilizing process returned to the course it had taken since the mid-seventeenth century, instilling everywhere a form of psychic economy that, before 1789, was not yet that of all French men and women. The discontinuity between revolutionary violence and the pacification of social relations that preceded it was thus perhaps less pronounced than it might appear. Precisely because appropriation of force by the monarchical state was both well advanced and still incomplete, it permitted a simultaneous return to older behavior patterns and the institution of political violence on a broad scale and according to carefully regulated forms.

It is also paradoxical that the long process of the invention of the private sphere culminated with the institution of the full dominance of the public sphere. As it entered into the Revolution, France seemed to throw itself into politics, henceforth conceding no room for the pleasures and passions of the individual. An entire set of practices that before 1789 were left to personal preference and lay out of the reach of monarchical authority were invaded and devoured by state decrees. These included fashions in dress, the setting and the objects of daily life, the conventions of family cohabitation, and even language. In its determination to establish an absolute transparency and a unanimous enthusiasm, the Revolution intended to place all aspects of life under public scrutiny. By doing so it hoped to exorcise the dangers of the private sphere—the domain of contradictory interests, egoistical enjoyments, and secret undertakings. The public nature of all acts became the condition and token of the new order.

Here too there was an abrupt break with two earlier tendencies supporting the emergence of the private. On the one hand, there was the process of the privatization of behavior, which set up a strict division between conduct that was allowed or required to be public and conduct that had to be removed from the community's sight, either because civility demanded it or because personal happiness made it preferable. On the other hand, there was the process of the deprivatization of public authority that, by detaching state power from individual interests, created another sphere in which those interests could take refuge. The Revolution and its exclusive passion for publicness thus seems incongruous in an age that delighted in a new and more intimate organization of ordinary life. The joys of free conviviality, the comforts of family life, and the pleasures of solitude seem a poor preparation for the imperious political demands that seized the kingdom in 1788 and gripped it for a decade.

Still, beneath the level of open opposition, a strong continuity existed between the new public culture and the sphere of the individual. Indeed, it was the constitution of the private as a form of experience and a set of values that made possible the emergence of a space both autonomous of state authority and critical of it. By taking for themselves the ethical imperatives denied by the reason of state, practicing free exercise of the faculty of judgment, and annulling obligatory obedience to a society of orders and corps, the institutions and forms of sociability founded on the rights of private persons created a sphere of discourse within the fabric of the absolute monarchy that undermined its principles.

This new public space, built on intellectual practices belonging to the order of the private individual, fed on conflicts proper to the private sphere in two ways. First, it assigned political significance to simple familial or conjugal strife (a strategy of the *mémoires judiciaires*); second, it stigmatized the monarch and his close associates by revealing their corrupt mores (a favorite procedure of the clandestine *libelles*). Even beyond the small number of persons who participated directly in the new political sociability, people became accustomed to seeing individual affairs transformed into general causes. This procedure was not restricted to pamphlet literature but also lay behind the lawsuits instituted by rural communities against their seigneurs or by journeymen workers against their masters. The omnipresence of politics imposed by the Revolution was thus not contradictory to the privatization of conduct and thought that preceded it. Quite the contrary: it was precisely the construction of a space for liberty of action, removed from state authority and reliant on the individual, that permitted the rise of the new public space that was at once inherited from and transformed by the creative energy of revolutionary politics.

Thus the French Revolution had roots in the century that it brought to an end, even where it most spectacularly seemed to run counter to the old evolution. Is this to say that it thus had cultural origins and that those origins can be designated with total certainty? A view of that sort supposes, in principle, that the event and its origin belong to distinctly different, clearly separated, sets of facts connected by a causal relation. Daniel Mornet's classic work thinks in these terms, which are also the ones that this volume has perforce accepted as a working hypothesis. But it should not be allowed to overshadow two other perspectives that shift the terms of the question. The first holds that the revolutionary event had a momentum and dynamic of its own that were not contained in any of its conditions of possibility. In this sense, the Revolution had no origins, properly speaking. Its absolute belief that it represented a new beginning had a performative value: by announcing a radical break with the past, it instituted one.

But the side of human actions based on reflection and will does not necessarily tell us the meaning of historical processes. Both Tocqueville and Cochin emphasized that in reality the participants in the Revolution did exactly the opposite of what they said and thought they were doing. The revolutionaries proclaimed an absolute break with the Old Regime, but in fact they strengthened and completed its work of centralization. The enlightened elites claimed they were contributing to the common good in peaceful *sociétés de pensée* loyal to their king, but in fact they were inventing the mechanisms of the

Terror and Jacobin democracy. The pertinence of Tocqueville's and Cochin's analyses is not at issue here; I cite them for the warning they offer any historian overly eager to think of the Revolution in accordance with the categories it gave itself—a belief in the radical discontinuity between the new political era and the old society being foremost among them. The origins of the revolutionary event and its intelligibility cannot be determined by its own actors' awareness of it. That the revolutionaries believed in the absolute efficacy of politics—which they thought capable of both recasting the body social and regenerating the individual—does not oblige us to share their illusion of a new advent.

Hence my preference for a second perspective that considers the periods of the Revolution and the Enlightenment as inscribed together in a long-term process that both included and extended beyond them, and as sharing, in different ways, the same ends and similar expectations. Alphonse Dupront expressed this notion well:

> The world of the Enlightenment and the French Revolution stand like two manifestations (or epiphenomena) of a greater process—that of the definition of a society of independent men without myths or religions (in the traditional sense of the term); a "modern" society; a society with no past and no traditions; [a society] of the present, wholly open toward the future. The true connections of cause and effect between the one and the other are those of this common dependence on a broader and more whole historical phenomenon than their own. [1]

This view offers a different way to reformulate the problem of origins, which entails a different consideration of the conditions that made the revolutionary event possible—an event that was, indissolubly, both emancipation from an old order defined and guaranteed by its transcendences and a way of turning back against the state, and its reason of state, the freedom of conscience and the high ethical demands that the same state had abandoned to the individual sphere at least two centuries before.

NOTES

1. ENLIGHTENMENT AND REVOLUTION; REVOLUTION AND ENLIGHTENMENT

1. Daniel Mornet, *Les Origines intellectuelles de la Révolution française 1715–1787* (Paris: Armand Colin, 1933, 1967). This work was written roughly at the midpoint of Mornet's career; he was a faithful disciple of Gustave Lanson, professor of letters at the Sorbonne. Before World War I Mornet published *Le Sentiment de la nature en France. De Jean-Jacques Rousseau à Bernardin de Saint-Pierre* (Paris: Hachette, 1907); "Les enseignements des bibliothèques privées (1750–1780)," *Revue d'Histoire Littéraire de la France* (July–September 1910): 449–96; and *Les Sciences de la nature en France au XVIIIe siècle* (Paris: Armand Colin, 1911). Three requirements, strongly expressed in his *Origines intellectuelles*, underlay Mornet's approach and distanced him from aesthetically inclined and ahistorical literary criticism: the demand to grasp the literary production of an epoch in its totality rather than limiting study to the "great" authors and "great" texts of tradition and the literary canon; the need to investigate not only the texts but the literary institutions, the works' circulation, and their audience (which led Mornet in his 1910 article to a pioneering interest in library inventories); the importance of using counts and percentages to measure circulation ("what matters just as much as the number is the proportion of the number," *Origines intellectuelles*, p. 457). In his later works—the *Histoire de la littérature française classique, 1600–1700, ses caractères véritables et ses aspects inconnus* (Paris: Armand Colin, 1940), for example—Mornet shifted away from Lanson's perspective, which earned him a biting critique from Lucien Febvre in "De Lanson à Daniel Mornet. Un renoncement?" *Annales d'Histoire Sociale* 3 (1941), an article reprinted in Febvre's collected essays in *Combats pour l'histoire* (Paris: Armand Colin, 1953).

2. Mornet, *Origines intellectuelles*, p. 2.

3. Ibid., p. 3.

4. Ibid., p. 477.

5. Michel Foucault, "Nietzsche, la Généalogie, l'Histoire," in his *Hommage à Jean Hyppolite* (Paris: Presses Universitaires de France, 1971), pp. 145–72, available

in English as "Nietzsche, Genealogy, History," in Foucault, *Language, Counter-Memory, Practice: Selected Essays and Interviews*, trans. Donald F. Bouchard and Sherry Simon (Ithaca: Cornell University Press, 1977), pp. 139–64.

6. Foucault, "Nietzsche," p. 161; *Language*, p. 154.

7. Foucault, "Réponse au Cercle d'Epistémologie," *Cahiers pour l'Analyse* 9, Généalogie des Sciences (Eté 1968): 9–40, quotation p. 11.

8. Jean Marie Goulemot, "Pouvoirs et savoirs provinciaux au XVIIIe siècle," *Critique* 397–398 (1980): 603–13.

9. Thomas Schleich, *Aufklärung und Revolution. Die Wirkungsgeschichte Gabriel Bonnot de Mablys in Frankreich (1740–1914)* (Stuttgart: Klett-Cotta, 1981), p. 210; Hans Ulrich Gumbrecht and Rolf Reichardt, "Philosophe, Philosophie," in *Handbuch politisch-sozialer Grundbegriffe in Frankreich 1680–1820*, 10 vols., ed. Rolf Reichardt and Eberhard Schmitt (Munich: R. Oldenbourg Verlag, 1985–), 3:7–88. See also Jeremy Popkin, "Recent Western German Work on the French Revolution," *Journal of Modern History* 59 (December 1987): 737–50.

10. Edgar Quinet, *La Révolution* (Paris: A. Lacroix, Verboeckhoven et cie, 1865; reprint, Paris: Belin, Littérature politique, 1987), "Timidité d'esprit des hommes de la Révolution," pp. 185–90, and "Du Tempérament des hommes de la Révolution et de celui des hommes des révolutions religieuses," pp. 513–15.

11. Norbert Elias, *Über den Prozess der Zivilisation. Soziogenetische und psychogenetische Untersuchungen* (1939; Frankfurt-am-Main: Suhrkamp, 1969); available in French as *La Civilisation des moeurs* (Paris: Calmann-Lévy, 1973), and *La Dynamique de l'Occident* (Paris: Calmann-Lévy, 1975), and in English as *The Civilizing Process: Sociogenetic and Psychogenetic Investigations*, trans. Edmund Jephcott (Oxford: Basil Blackwell, 1978, 1982; New York: Pantheon Books, 1982).

12. François Furet, *Penser la Révolution française* (Paris: Gallimard, 1978), p. 35, quoted from *Interpreting the French Revolution*, trans. Elborg Forster (Cambridge: Cambridge University Press, Paris: Editions de la Maison des sciences de l'homme, 1981), p. 19.

13. Gustave Lanson, "Programme d'études sur l'histoire provinciale de la vie littéraire en France," *Revue d'Histoire Moderne et Contemporaine* (1903): 445–53; "L'Histoire littéraire et la sociologie," *Revue de Métaphysique et de Morale* (1904): 621–42.

14. Mornet, *Origines intellectuelles*, p. 471.

15. Furet, *Penser la Révolution*, pp. 38–39; *Interpreting the French Revolution*, pp. 17–28.

16. Hippolyte Taine, *Les Origines de la France contemporaine* (1876; Paris: Robert Laffont, 1986), vol. 1, *L'Ancien Régime*. The letter to Boutmy of 31 July 1874 is cited in the introduction by François Léger, "Taine et les *Origines de la France contemporaine*," p. xxxi.

17. Ibid., p. 187. Taine is quoted from *The Ancient Regime*, new rev. ed., trans. John Durand (New York: H. Holt, 1896), pp. 191, 250–51.

18. Erich Auerbach, *Mimesis. Dargestelte Wirklicht in der abendlärdischen literatur* (Bern: Francke AG Verlag, 1946), chap. 15, available in French as *Mimésis. La représentation de la réalité de la littérature occidentale* (Paris: Gallimard, 1968), pp. 365–94, quote p. 388, quoted from *Mimesis, the Representation of Reality in*

Western Literature, trans. Willard R. Trask (Princeton: Princeton University Press, 1953), p. 387.

19. Alexis de Tocqueville, *L'Ancien Régime et la Révolution* (Paris: Gallimard, 1967), p. 81, quoted from *The Old Régime and the French Revolution*, trans. Stuart Gilbert (Garden City, N.Y.: Doubleday, 1955), p. 20.

20. The quotations from Tocqueville in this paragraph and the following come from *L'Ancien Régime et la Révolution*, book 3, chap. 1, pp. 229–41, quoted from *The Old Régime*, pp. 138–48.

21. Ibid.: *L'Ancien Régime*, p. 158; *The Old Régime*, p. 81.

22. Ibid.: *L'Ancien Régime*, p. 43; *The Old Régime*, p. vii.

23. Keith Michael Baker, "On the Problem of the Ideological Origins of the French Revolution," in *Modern European Intellectual History: Reappraisals and New Perspectives*, ed. Dominick LaCapra and Steven L. Kaplan (Ithaca: Cornell University Press, 1982), pp. 197–219, quotation p. 212; Baker, *Inventing the French Revolution: Essays on French Political Culture in the Eighteenth Century* (Cambridge: Cambridge University Press, 1990), pp. 12–27.

24. Baker, "On the Problem of the Ideological Origins," pp. 213–16.

25. Augustin Cochin, *Les Sociétés de Pensée et la démocratie moderne* (Paris: Plon-Nourrit et cie, 1921; Paris: Copernic, 1978); Augustin Cochin, *Les Sociétés de Pensée et la Révolution en Bretagne (1787–1788)* (Paris: H. Champion, 1925); François Furet, "Augustin Cochin: la théorie du jacobinisme," in his *Penser la Révolution française*, pp. 212–59, available in English as "Augustin Cochin: The Theory of Jacobinism," in Furet, *Interpreting the French Revolution*, pp. 164–204; Ran Halévi, "L'Idée et l'événement. Sur les origines intellectuelles de la Révolution française," *Le Débat* 38 (1986): 145–63.

26. Jürgen Habermas, *Strukturwandel der Öffentlichkeit, Untersuchungen zu einer Kategorie der bürgerlichen Gesellschaft* (Neuwied: Hermann Luchterhand Verlag, 1962), available in French as *L'Espace public. Archéologie de la publicité comme dimension constitutive de la société bourgeoise*, trans. Marc B. de Launay (Paris: Payot, 1978), and in English as *The Structural Transformation of the Public Sphere: An Inquiry into a Category of Bourgeois Society*, trans. Thomas Burger and Frederick Lawrence (Cambridge: Polity Press, Cambridge, Mass.: MIT Press, 1989).

27. Michel de Certeau, "La Formalité des pratiques. Du système religieux à l'éthique des Lumières (XVIIe–XVIIIe)," in his *L'Ecriture de l'histoire* (Paris: Gallimard, 1975), pp. 153–212, available in English as "The Formality of Practices: From Religious Systems to the Ethics of the Enlightenment (the Seventeenth and Eighteenth Centuries)," in his *The Writing of History*, trans. Tom Conley (New York: Columbia University Press, 1988), pp. 153–212.

28. Michel Foucault, *Surveiller et punir: Naissance de la prison* (Paris: Gallimard, 1975), available in English as *Discipline and Punish: The Birth of the Prison*, trans. Alan Sheridan (New York: Pantheon Books, 1977).

2. THE PUBLIC SPHERE AND PUBLIC OPINION

1. Jürgen Habermas, *Strukturwandel der Öffentlichkeit, Untersuchungen zu einer Kategorie der bürgerlichen Gesellschaft* (Neuwied: Hermann Luchterhand Verlag, 1962), available in French as *L'Espace public. Archéologie de la publicité comme dimension constitutive de la société bourgeoise*, trans. Marc B. de Launay (Paris:

202   Notes

Payot, 1978), and in English as *The Structural Transformation of the Public Sphere: An Inquiry into a Category of Bourgeois Society*, trans. Thomas Burger and Frederick Lawrence (Cambridge: Polity Press, Cambridge, Mass.: MIT Press, 1989). See also Peter Hohendahl, "Jürgen Habermas: 'The Public Sphere' (1964)," *New German Critique* 1, 3 (1974): 45–48, and Jürgen Habermas, "The Public Sphere: An Encyclopedia Article (1964)," *New German Critique* 1, 3 (1974): 49–55.

2. Habermas, *L'Espace public*, p. 38; *The Structural Transformation*, p. 27.
3. René Descartes, *Discours de la Méthode*, in his *Oeuvres complètes* (Paris: Gallimard, Bibliothèque de la Pléiade, 1953), pt. 3, p. 141, quoted from *Descartes's Discourse on Method*, trans. Laurence J. Lafleur (Indianapolis: Bobbs-Merrill, Liberal Arts Press, 1960), p. 18.
4. Ibid.: *Discours de la Méthode*, p. 144; *Discourse on Method*, p. 22.
5. Habermas, *Structural Transformation*, p. 37.
6. Ibid., p. 51. On the question of women in the public sphere, absolutist or bourgeois, see Joan B. Landes, *Women and the Public Sphere in the Age of the French Revolution* (Ithaca: Cornell University Press, 1988).
7. Keith Michael Baker, "Representation," in *The French Revolution and the Creation of Modern Political Culture*, vol. 1, *The Political Culture of the Old Regime*, ed. Keith Michael Baker (Oxford and New York: Pergamon Press, 1987), pp. 469–92; reprinted as "Representation Redefined," in Baker, *Inventing the French Revolution: Essays on French Political Culture in the Eighteenth Century* (Cambridge: Cambridge University Press, 1990), pp. 224–51.
8. Emmanuel Kant, "Beantwortung der Frage: Was Ist Aufklärung?" *Berlinische Monatsschrift* (1784), available in English as *Foundations of the Metaphysics of Morals and What Is Enlightenment*, trans. Lewis White Beck (Indianapolis: Bobbs-Merrill, 1975), pp. 85–92. On this text, see the commentaries of Ernst Cassirer, *Kants Leben und Lehre* (Berlin: Cassirer, 1918), available in English as *Kant's Life and Thought*, trans. Jame Haden (New Haven: Yale University Press, 1981), pp. 227–28, 368; Jürgen Habermas, *Structural Transformation*, pp. 104–7; Michel Foucault, "Afterword: The Subject and the Power," in *Michel Foucault: Beyond Structuralism and Hermeneutics*, ed. Hubert L. Dreyfus and Paul Rabinow (Chicago: University of Chicago Press, 1982), pp. 208–26, especially pp. 215–16; and Michel Foucault, "Un cours inédit," *Le Magazine littéraire* 207 (1984): 35–39. All quotations from Kant in this section are from the Beck translation of "What Is Enlightenment?"
9. Reference to the practices of intellectual life in the seventeenth century, founded, since the age of the learned libertines, on the exchange of correspondence, the communication of manuscripts, books lent or offered as gifts, and, after the 1750s, on learned periodicals; see Robert Mandrou, *Des humanistes aux hommes de science (XVIe et XVIIe siècles)* (Paris: Fayard, 1988), pp. 263–80, available in English as *From Humanism to Science: 1480 to 1700*, trans. Brian Pearce (Harmondsworth and New York: Penguin Books, 1978), pp. 151–53. It coexists in Kant's text with an implicit recognition of the situation in Germany, which, even more than in France, where intellectuals were more concentrated in a capital city, depended on the circulation of written matter. In 1827 Goethe noted this national trait with particular force: "All our men of talent are scattered across the country. One is in Vienna, another in Berlin, another in Königsberg, another in Bonn or Düsseldorf, all separated from each

other by fifty or a hundred miles, so that personal contact or a personal exchange of ideas is a rarity" (quoted by Norbert Elias, *Über den Prozess der Zivilisation. Soziogenetische und Psychogenetische Untersuchungen* [1939; Frankfurt-am-Main: Suhrkamp, 1969], 1:33–34, and given here from Elias, *The History of Manners: The Civilizing Process*, vol. 1, trans. Edmund Jephcott [New York: Pantheon Books, 1978], p. 28). See also Paul Dibon, "Communication in *Respublica litteraria* of the 17th Century," *Res Publica Litterarum* 1 (1978): 42–55.

10. Mona Ozouf, "L'Opinion publique," in Baker, *The French Revolution*, vol. 1, *The Political Culture of the Old Regime*, pp. 419–34. Quotations are given as per n. 24, pp. 432–33.

11. Elizabeth Fleury, "Le peuple en dictionnaires (fin XVII–XVIIIe siècle)" (Diplôme d'Etudes Approfondies, Paris, Ecole des Hautes Etudes en Sciences Sociales, 1986), typescript.

12. Pierre Corneille, *Nicomède, Oeuvres complètes* (Paris: Editions du Seuil, L'Intégrale, 1963, 1970), verses 1696–97, 1621–22, and 1779- 80, pp. 539–41, quoted from *The Chief Plays of Corneille*, trans. Lacy Lockert (Princeton: Princeton University Press, 1952), pp. 382, 380, 384.

13. *Encyclopédie, ou Dictionnaire raisonné des sciences, des arts et des métiers*, 36 vols. (Lausanne and Berne: chez les Sociétés typographiques, 1778–81), 25:543–45.

14. Ibid., 23:754–57.

15. Ibid., 27:752–53.

16. Keith Michael Baker, "Politics and Public Opinion under the Old Regime: Some Reflections," in *Press and Politics in Pre-Revolutionary France*, ed. Jack R. Censer and Jeremy D. Popkin (Berkeley: University of California Press, 1987), pp. 204–46; reprinted as "Public Opinion as Political Invention" in Baker, *Inventing the French Revolution*, pp. 167–99.

17. Quoted from Mona Ozouf, "L'Opinion publique," p. 424.

18. Jean Le Rond d'Alembert, *Discours préliminaire de l'Encyclopédie* (Paris: Editions Gonthier, Médiations, 1965), "Explication détaillée du système des connaissances humaines," pp. 155–68, quotations pp. 159–60, quoted from "Detailed Explanation of the System of Human Knowledge," in *Preliminary Discourse to the Encyclopedia of Diderot*, trans. Richard N. Schwab, with Walter E. Rex (Indianapolis: Bobbs-Merrill, Library of Liberal Arts, 1963), pp. 143–57.

19. Ibid., "Dédicace à Monseigneur le comte d'Argenson," pp. 14–15. See also Robert Darnton, "Philosophers Trim the Tree of Knowledge: The Epistemological Strategy of the *Encyclopédie*," in his *The Great Cat Massacre and Other Episodes in French Cultural History* (New York: Basic Books, 1984), pp. 190–213.

20. Malesherbes, "Remontrances relatives aux impôts, 6 mai 1775," in *Les "Remontrances" de Malesherbes 1771–1775*, ed. Elisabeth Badinter (Paris: Union Générale d'Editions, 10/18, 1978), pp. 167–284, quotation pp. 272–73.

21. Condorcet, *Esquisse d'un tableau historique des progrès de l'esprit humain* (Paris: Flammarion, GF, 1988), p. 188, quoted from *Sketch for a Historical Picture of the Progress of the Human Mind*, trans. June Barraclough (London: Weidenfeld and Nicolson, 1955), p. 100. For a discussion in another context of the connection between the circulation of printed matter and the public sphere, see Michael Warner, *The Letters of the Republic: Publication and the Public Sphere in Eighteenth-Century America* (Cambridge, Mass.: Harvard University Press, 1990).

22. Condorcet, *Esquisse d'un tableau*, p. 189; *Sketch*, p. 101.
23. Condorcet, *Esquisse d'un tableau*, p. 229; *Sketch*, p. 140.
24. Christian Jouhaud, "Propagande et action au temps de la Fronde," in *Culture et idéologie dans la genèse de l'Etat moderne*. Actes de la table ronde organisée par le Centre National de la Recherche Scientifique et l'Ecole française de Rome, Rome, 15–17 October 1984 (Rome: L'Ecole française de Rome, 1985), pp. 337–52; Christian Jouhaud, *Mazarinades. La Fronde des mots* (Paris: Aubier, 1985).
25. Malesherbes, "Remonstrances," pp. 269–70.
26. Sarah Maza, "Le tribunal de la nation: les mémoires judiciaires et l'opinion publique à la fin de l'Ancien Régime," *Annales E.S.C.* (1987): 73–90. I am indebted to this article for both quotations and ideas concerning the judicial memoirs. See also John Renwick, *Voltaire et Morangiès 1772–1773, ou, Les Lumières l'ont échappé belle*. Studies on Voltaire and the Eighteenth Century 202 (Oxford: Voltaire Foundation, 1982); Hans-Jürgen Lüsebrink, "L'affaire Cléreaux (Rouen, 1786–1790). Affrontements idéologiques et tensions institutionnelles autour de la scène judiciaire de la fin du XVIIIe siècle," *Studies on Voltaire and the Eighteenth Century* 191 (1980): 892–900.
27. Arlette Farge, "Familles: l'honneur et le secret," in *Histoire de la vie privée*, ed. Philippe Ariès and Georges Duby (Paris: Editions du Seuil, 1986), vol. 3, *De la Renaissance aux Lumières*, ed. Roger Chartier, pp. 580–617, available in English as "The Honor and Secrecy of Families," in Ariès and Duby, *A History of Private Life* (Cambridge, Mass.: Belknap Press of Harvard University Press, 1989), vol. 3, *Passions of the Renaissance*, ed. Roger Chartier, trans. Arthur Goldhammer (1989), pp. 570–607; Arlette Farge and Michel Foucault, *Le Désordre des familles. Lettres de cachet des Archives de la Bastille* (Paris: Gallimard/Julliard, Collection Archives, 1982).
28. Thomas E. Crow, *Painters and Public Life in Eighteenth-Century Paris* (New Haven: Yale University Press, 1985), p. 5.

3. THE WAY OF PRINT

1. Chrétien Guillaume de Malesherbes, *Mémoires sur la librairie et sur la liberté de la presse*, introduction and notes by Graham E. Rodmell. North Carolina Studies in the Romance Languages and Literatures (Chapel Hill: University of North Carolina Press, 1979). All quotations and page numbers from Malesherbes's memoirs refer to that text and are cited as *M*.
2. Denis Diderot, *Sur la liberté de la presse*, partial text, Jacques Proust, ed. (Paris: Editions Sociales, Les Classiques du Peuple, 1964). All quotations and page numbers cited in this text refer to this edition and are cited as *L*. Another edition of the memoir is available under the title *Lettre historique et politique sur le commerce de la librairie*, in Diderot, *Oeuvres complètes*, 15 vols. (Paris: Le Club français du Livre, 1963–1973), 5:305–81. On this memoir, see Jacques Proust, "Pour servir à une édition critique de la *Lettre sur le commerce de la librairie*," *Diderot Studies* 3 (1961): 321–45.
3. Quoted by Jacques Proust in his preface to Diderot, *Sur la liberté de la presse*, p. 7.
4. Dale K. Van Kley, *The Damiens Affair and the Unraveling of the Ancien Régime, 1750–1770* (Princeton: Princeton University Press, 1984).

5. Didier Ozanam, "La Disgrâce d'un premier commis: Tercier et l'affaire de l'Esprit (1758–1759)," *Bibliothèque de l'Ecole des Chartes* 113 (1955): 140–70; Pierre Grosclaude, *Malesherbes témoin et interprète de son temps* (Paris: Librairie Fischbacher, 1961), pp. 120–27.

6. Grosclaude, *Malesherbes*, p. 104. On the Prades affair, see John Stephenson Spink, "Un abbé philosophe: L'affaire de J.-M. de Prades," *Dix-Huitième Siècle* 3 (1971): 145–80; Jean-Claude Davis, "L'affaire de Prades en 1751–1752 d'après deux rapports de police," *Studies on Voltaire and the Eighteenth Century* 245 (1986): 359–71.

7. Grosclaude, *Malesherbes*, p. 105.

8. Ibid., pp. 127–38.

9. On Jacob-Nicolas Moreau, see Dieter Gembicki, *Histoire et politique à la fin de l'Ancien Régime: Jacob-Nicolas Moreau, 1717–1803* (Paris: A. G. Nizet, 1979); Keith Michael Baker, "Controlling French History: The Ideological Arsenal of Jacob-Nicolas Moreau," in his *Inventing the French Revolution: Essays on French Political Culture in the Eighteenth Century* (Cambridge: Cambridge University Press, 1990), pp. 59–85; Blandine Barret-Kriegel, *Les Historiens et la monarchie* (Paris: Presses Universitaires de France, 1988), vol. 1, *Jean Mabillon*, pp. 211–67, and vol. 4, *La République incertaine*, pp. 5–93.

10. Malesherbes, "Remontrances relatives aux impôts, 6 Mai 1775," in *Les "Remontrances" de Malesherbes 1771–1775*, ed. Elisabeth Badinter (Paris: Union Générale d'Editions, 10/18, 1978), p. 273.

11. Steven L. Kaplan, *Bread, Politics and Political Economy in the Reign of Louis XV* (The Hague: Martinus Nijhoff, 1976); Steven L. Kaplan, *Provisioning Paris: Merchants and Millers in the Grain and Flour Trade during the Eighteenth Century* (Ithaca: Cornell University Press, 1984).

12. Quoted in Kaplan, *Provisioning Paris*, p. 594.

13. Quoted in Diderot, *Sur la liberté de la presse*, p. 24.

14. Roger Chartier, "L'Imprimerie en France à la fin de l'Ancien Régime: l'Etat général des imprimeurs de 1777," *Revue française de l'histoire du livre* 6 (1973): 252–79.

15. Robert Darnton, *The Business of Enlightenment: A Publishing History of the Encyclopédie 1775–1800* (Cambridge, Mass.: Belknap Press of Harvard University Press, 1979), pp. 177–82.

16. Robert Darnton, "A Police Inspector Sorts His Files: The Anatomy of the Republic of Letters," in his *The Great Cat Massacre and Other Episodes in French Cultural History* (New York: Basic Books, 1984), pp. 144–89.

17. For a general view of the system of book privileges, see Raymond Birn, "Profit of Ideas: *Privilèges en librairie* in Eighteenth-Century France," *Eighteenth-Century Sudies* 4, 2 (1970–71): 131–68. On tacit permissions, see Robert Estivals, *La Statistique bibliographique de la France sous la monarchie au XVIIIe siècle* (Paris and The Hague: Mouton, 1965), pp. 107–20, 275–91.

18. Grosclaude, *Malesherbes*, pp. 92–95.

19. Alexis de Tocqueville, *L'Ancien Régime et la Révolution* (Paris: Gallimard, 1967), p. 278, quoted from *The Old Regime and the French Revolution*, trans. Stuart Gilbert (Garden City, N.Y.: Doubleday, 1955), p. 177.

20. Jacques Proust, *Diderot et l'Encyclopédie* (Paris: Armand Colin, 1967), chap. 3, "L'Encyclopédie et la fortune de Diderot," pp. 81–116.

21. Robert Darnton, "A Police Inspector Sorts His Files," pp. 147–57 and fig. 3.

22. Robert Darnton, "The Facts of Literary Life in Eighteenth-Century France," in *The French Revolution and the Creation of Modern Political Culture*, ed. Keith Michael Baker (Oxford and New York: Pergamon Press, 1987), vol. 1, *The Political Culture of the Old Regime*, pp. 261–91, especially pp. 272–76 and fig. 5.

23. Voltaire, *Oeuvres complètes*, 52 vols. (Paris: Garnier Frères, 1878–79), vols. 17–20, *Dictionnaire philosophique*. The first two quotations come from the articles "Charlatan," 2:138–41, and "Quisquis (du) de Ramus ou La Ramée. Avec quelques observations utiles sur les persécuteurs, les calomniateurs et les faiseurs de libelles," 4:318–34. The two latter quotations come from the article "Auteurs," 17:496–501, and are quoted from *The Works of Voltaire*, 42 vols., trans. William F. Fleming (Paris: E. R. DuMont, 1901), 13:175, 176.

24. John Lough, *Writer and Public in France from the Middle Ages to the Present Day* (Oxford: Clarendon Press, 1978), pp. 199–225.

25. Eric Walter, "Les auteurs et le champ littéraire," in *Histoire de l'Edition française*, 4 vols., Henri-Jean Martin and Roger Chartier, gen. eds. (Paris: Promodis, 1984–86), vol. 2, *Le Livre triomphant. 1660–1830*, pp. 382–99. For a comparatist perspective, see Mark Ross, "The Author as Proprietor: Donaldson v. Becket and the Genealogy of Modern Authorship," *Representations* 23 (1988): 51–85 (for England); Martha Woodmansee, "The Genius and the Copyright: Economic and Legal Conditions of the Emergence of the 'Author,'" *Eighteenth-Century Studies* 17, 4 (1984): 425–48 (for Germany).

26. Alain Viala, *Naissance de l'écrivain. Sociologie de la littérature à l'âge classique* (Paris: Editions de Minuit, 1985). On this work, see the criticism of Jean-Philippe Genet, "La Mesure et le champ culturel," *Histoire et Mesure* 2, 1 (1987): 137–69; Christian Jouhaud, "Littérature et société: naissance de l'écrivain," *Annales E.S.C.* (July–August 1988): 849–66.

27. Lough, *Writer and Public*, pp. 195–97.

28. John Lough, "Luneau de Boisjermain v. the Publishers of the *Encyclopédie*," *Studies on Voltaire and the Eighteenth Century* 23 (1963): 115–77. In the first suits (1768 and 1770) opposing Luneau de Boisjermain and the *syndics* of the booksellers' and printers' association in Paris (before their great dispute over the *Encyclopédie*) two points were crucial: under what conditions could an author who had received a *privilège* for a work sell it? Did the *droit d'éditer*—the right to request a *privilège* and to have the work printed and distributed—belong to any individual, even if he was not the author of the work, or only to the booksellers? The affair betrays the booksellers' fears concerning the possible emancipation of authors, who might publish not only their own works but those of others.

29. Pierre Augustin Caron de Beaumarchais, *La Folle Journée ou le Mariage de Figaro*, in his *Théâtre* (Paris: Flammarion, GF, 1965), pp. 103–242; act 5, scene 3, pp. 224–26, quoted from *Racine's Phèdre; Beaumarchais's Figaro's Marriage*, trans. Robert Lowell, Jacques Barzun (New York: Farrar, Straus and Cudahy, 1961), pp. 194–95.

30. Robert Darnton, "Trade in the Taboo: The Life of a Clandestine Book Dealer in Prerevolutionary France," in *The Widening Circle: Essays on the Circulation of Literature in Eighteenth-Century Europe*, ed. Paul J. Korshin (Philadelphia: University of Pennsylvania Press, 1976), pp. 11–83; or, in an abridged version, "A Clandestine Bookseller in the Provinces," in Darnton, *The Literary Under-*

ground of the Old Regime (Cambridge, Mass.: Harvard University Press, 1982), pp. 122–47.

31. Rolf Reichardt, "Bastille," in *Handbuch politisch-sozialer Grundbegriffe in Frankreich 1680–1820*, 10 vols., ed. Rolf Reichardt and Eberhard Schmitt (Munich: R. Oldenbourg Verlag, 1988), 9:7–74; Hans-Jürgen Lüsebrink and Rolf Reichardt, *Die Bastille. Zur Symbolgeschichte von Herrschaft und Freiheit* (Frankfurt-am-Main: Fischer Taschenbuch Verlag, 1990), available in French as "La 'Bastille' dans l'imaginaire social de la France à la fin du XVIIIe siècle (1774–1799)," *Revue d'Histoire Moderne et Contemporaine* (1983): 196–234.

32. Daniel Roche, "La Police du livre," in Martin and Chartier, *Histoire de l'Edition française*, 2:84–91.

33. On this text, see Christine Berkvens-Stevelinck, *Prosper Marchand. La vie et l'oeuvre, 1678–1756* (Leiden and New York: E. J. Brill, 1987), pp. 39–64.

34. Condorcet, *Esquisse d'un tableau historique des progrès de l'esprit humain* (Paris: Flammarion, GF, 1988), p. 190, quoted from *Sketch for a Historical Picture of the Progress of the Human Mind*, trans. June Barraclough (London: Weidenfeld and Nicolson, 1955), p. 102.

4. DO BOOKS MAKE REVOLUTIONS?

1. Alexis de Tocqueville, *L'Ancien Régime et la Révolution* (Paris: Gallimard, 1967), pp. 239–40, quoted from *The Old Regime and the French Revolution*, trans. Stuart Gilbert (Garden City, N.Y.: Doubleday, 1955), pp. 146–47.

2. Hippolyte Taine, *L'Ancien Régime* (Paris: Robert Laffont, 1966), vol. 1, *Les Origines de la France Contemporaine*, p. 205, quoted from *The Ancient Regime*, new rev. ed., trans. John Durand (New York: H. Holt, 1896), pp. 274–75.

3. Daniel Mornet, *Les Origines intellectuelles de la Révolution française 1715–1787* (Paris: Armand Colin, 1933, 1967), p. 432.

4. Roger Chartier, "Du livre au lire. Les pratiques citadines de l'imprimé 1660–1780," in his *Lectures et lecteurs dans la France d'Ancien Régime* (Paris: Editions du Seuil, 1987), pp. 165–222, available in English as "Urban Reading Practices 1660–1780," in Chartier, *The Cultural Uses of Print in Early Modern France*, trans. Lydia G. Cochrane (Princeton: Princeton University Press, 1987), pp. 183–239. For the strong rise in auction sales of private libraries after 1765, see the basic study: Friedhelm Beckmann, "Französische Privatbibliotheken. Untersuchungen zu Literatursystematik und Buchbesitz im 18 Jahrhundert," *Archiv für Geschichte des Buchwesens* 31 (1988): 1–160.

5. Jean-Louis Pailhès, "En marge des bibliothèques: l'apparition des cabinets de lecture," in *Histoire des bibliothèques françaises: Les bibliothèques sous l'Ancien Régime 1530–1789*, ed. Claude Jolly (Paris: Promodis/Editions du Cercle de la Librairie, 1988), pp. 414–21.

6. Louis-Sébastien Mercier, *Tableau de Paris. Nouvelle édition corrigée et augmentée*, 8 vols. (Amsterdam, 1782–83), "Loueurs de livres," 5:61–66, quotation pp. 61–62. On Louis-Sébastien Mercier, see Léon Béclard, *Sébastien Mercier, Sa vie son oeuvre, son temps; d'après des documents inédits . . . Avant la Révolution 1740–1789* (Paris: H. Champion, 1903); Hermann Hafer, ed., *Louis-Sébastien Mercier précurseur et sa fortune. Avec des documents inédits. Recueil d'études sur l'influence de Mercier* (Munich: Wilhelm Fink Verlag, 1977), critical biography by Geneviève Cattin, pp. 341–61.

7. François Furet, "La 'librairie' du royaume de France au 18e siècle," in *Livre et société dans la France du XVIIIe siècle*, 2 vols. (Paris and The Hague: Mouton, 1965–1970), 1:3–32; Henri-Jean Martin, "Une croissance séculaire," in *Histoire de l'Edition française*, 4 vols., Henri-Jean Martin and Roger Chartier, gen. eds. (Paris: Promodis, 1982–86), vol. 2, *Le Livre triomphant, 1660–1830*, pp. 94–103.

8. Robert Darnton, "Philosophy under the Cloak," in *Revolution in Print: The Press in France 1775–1800*, ed. Robert Darnton and Daniel Roche (Berkeley: University of California Press, in collaboration with the New York Public Library, 1989), pp. 217–49.

9. Mercier, *Tableau de Paris*, "Huissiers-priseurs," 5:337–45, quotation p. 341.

10. Jacqueline Artier, "Etude sur la production imprimée de l'année 1764," *Ecole nationale des chartes. Positions des thèses soutenues par les élèves de la promotion de 1981* (Paris: Ecole des chartes, 1981), pp. 9–18.

11. Mercier, *Tableau de Paris*, 12 vols. (Amsterdam, 1783–88), "Censeurs royaux," 11:51–52.

12. Robert Darnton, "Le livre prohibé aux frontières: Neuchâtel," in Martin and Chartier, *Histoire de l'Edition française*, 2:342–59, quotation p. 343.

13. Jeanne Veyrin-Forrer, "Livres arrêtés, livres estampillés: traces parisiennes de la contrefaçon," in *Les Presses grises. La contrefaçon du livre (XVIe–XIXe siècles)*, ed. François Moureau (Paris: Aux Amateurs de Livres, 1988), pp. 101–12; Anne Boës and Robert L. Dawson, "The Legitimation of Contrefaçons and the Police Stamp of 1777," *Studies on Voltaire and the Eighteenth Century* 230 (1985): 461–84.

14. Silvio Corsini, "La contrefaçon du livre sous l'Ancien Régime," in Moureau, *Les Presses grises*, pp. 22–38; Anne Sauvy, "Livres contrefaits et livres interdits," in Martin and Chartier, *Histoire de l'Edition française*, 2:104–19.

15. Mercier, *Tableau*, "Saisies," 7:183–88, quotation pp. 187–88.

16. Bibliothèque de l'Arsenal, MS 10 305, "Etat des Livres prohibés, saisis sur le Sr. Venant Roch Moureau, libraire à Paris, le 31 juillet 1777, et ordonnés etre mis au pilon, par le Jugement de Monsieur Lenoir du 26 aoust 1777."

17. Robert Darnton, "Un colporteur sous l'Ancien Régime," in *Censures. De la Bible aux Larmes d'Eros* (Paris: Editions du Centre Georges Pompidou, 1987), pp. 130–39.

18. Robert Darnton, "A Clandestine Bookseller in the Provinces," in his *The Literary Underground of the Old Regime* (Cambridge, Mass.: Harvard University Press, 1982), pp. 122–47; this is an abridged version of "Trade in the Taboo: The Life of a Clandestine Book Dealer in Prerevolutionary France," in *The Widening Circle: Essays on the Circulation of Literature in Eighteenth-Century France*, ed. Paul J. Korshin (Philadelphia: University of Pennsylvania Press, 1976), pp. 11–83.

19. Robert Darnton, "Livres philosophiques," in *Enlightenment Essays in Memory of Robert Shackleton*, ed. Giles Barber and C. P. Courtney (Oxford, The Voltaire Foundation, 1988), pp. 89–175.

20. Bibliothèque de l'Arsenal, MS 10 305, "Etat des Livres des pausés a St Louis de la cultur mit en ordre par ordre de m.m. les commissaires commancé le 14 juillet 1790 par Poinçot."

21. Report addressed to the mayor of Paris on 19 October 1790, quoted from Frantz Funck-Brentano, *Archives de la Bastille, la formation du dépôt* (Dole: C. Blind, 1890), p. xlv.

22. Mercier, *Tableau*, "Libelles," 7:22–28, quotation p. 22.

23. Ibid., "Trente Ecrivains en France, pas davantage," 8:106–14, quotation pp. 106–7.

24. Robert Darnton, "A Clandestine Bookseller in the Provinces," p. 147.

25. Mercier, *Tableau*, "Estampes licencieuses," 6:92–94, quotation p. 94.

26. Ibid., "Libelles," 7:22–28, quotation pp. 22–23.

27. Ibid., "Placards," 6:85–89.

28. Richard Hoggart, *The Uses of Literacy: Changing Patterns in English Mass Culture* (Fairlawn N.J.: Essential Books, 1957), pp. 197, 224, 228, 230.

29. *Journal de ma vie. Jacques-Louis Ménétra, compagnon vitrier au 18e siècle*, ed. Daniel Roche (Paris: Montalba, 1982), pp. 218–22, 300, quoted from Ménétra, *Journal of My Life*, trans. Arthur Goldhammer (New York: Columbia University Press, 1986), p. 182.

30. Daniel Roche, "Les Primitifs du rousseauisme. Une analyse sociologique et quantitative de la correspondance de J.-J. Rousseau," *Annales E.S.C.* 26 (1971): 151–72.

31. Jean Biou, "Le Rousseauisme, idéologie de substitution," in *Roman et Lumières au XVIIIe siècle* (Paris: Editions Sociales, 1970), pp. 115–28; Anna Ridehalgh, "Preromantic Attitudes and the Birth of a Legend: French Pilgrimages to Ermenonville, 1778–1789," *Studies on Voltaire and the Eighteenth Century* 215 (1982): 231–52.

32. Robert Darnton, "Readers Respond to Rousseau: The Fabrication of Romantic Sensitivity," in his *The Great Cat Massacre and Other Episodes in French Cultural History* (New York: Basic Books, 1984), pp. 214–56, quotations pp. 236 and 237.

33. Robert Darnton, *The Business of Enlightenment. A Publishing History of the Encyclopédie 1775–1800* (Cambridge, Mass.: Belknap Press of Harvard University Press, 1979), pp. 287–94.

34. Agnès Marcetteau-Paul and Dominique Varry, "Les Bibliothèques de quelques acteurs de la Révolution de Louis XVI à Robespierre," in *Mélanges de la Bibliothèque de la Sorbonne*, vol. 9, *Livre et Révolution* (Paris: Aux Amateurs de Livres, 1989), 189–207.

35. Tocqueville, *L'Ancien Régime et la Révolution*, p. 158, quoted from *The Old Régime and the French Revolution*, p. 81, emphasis added.

36. Mercier, *Tableau*, "A la Royale," 5:148–49.

37. Ibid., "Vieilles enseignes," 5:123–26, quotation p. 123.

38. Christian Jouhaud, *Mazarinades: La Fronde des mots* (Paris: Aubier, 1985), pp. 37–39.

39. Jacques Revel, "Marie-Antoinette," in *Dictionnaire critique de la Révolution française*, ed. François Furet and Mona Ozouf (Paris: Flammarion, 1988), pp. 286–98, available in English as *A Critical Dictionary of the French Revolution*, trans. Arthur Goldhammer (Cambridge, Mass.: Belknap Press of Harvard University Press, 1989), pp. 252–64.

40. Mona Ozouf, "Le Panthéon. L'Ecole normale des morts," in *Les Lieux de mémoire*, 2 vols., ed. Pierre Nora (Paris: Gallimard, 1984), vol. 1, *La République*, pp. 139–66; Roger Barny, *Rousseau dans la Révolution: Le personnage de Jean-Jacques et les débuts du culte révolutionnaire (1787–1791)*. Studies on Voltaire and the Eighteenth Century 246 (Oxford: Voltaire Foundation, 1986).

41. James Leith, "Les trois apothéoses de Voltaire," *Annales Historiques de la Révolution Française* 34 (1979): 161–209, quotation p. 200.

42. Robespierre, "Sur les rapports des idées religieuses et morales avec les principes républicains et sur les fêtes nationales," in his *Textes choisis*, 3 vols. (Paris: Editions Sociales, 1958; 1974), vol. 3 *(Novembre 1793–juillet 1794)*, pp. 155–80, quotation pp. 171–72.

43. Lise Andriès, "Les florilèges littéraires pendant la Révolution," *Littérature* 69, "Intertextualité et Révolution" (1988): 5–18.

44. Hans-Jürgen Lüsebrink, "L' 'Histoire des Deux Indes' et ses 'extraits.' Un Mode de dispersion textuelle au XVIIIe siècle," *Littérature* 69, "Intertextualité et Révolution" (1988): 28–41.

45. Leith, "Les trois apothéoses de Voltaire," p. 207.

46. Quoted from Hans Ulrich Gumbrecht and Rolf Reichardt, "Philosophe, Philosophie," in *Handbuch politisch-sozialer Grundbegriffe in Frankreich 1680–1820*, 10 vols., ed. Rolf Reichardt and Eberhard Schmitt (Munich: R. Oldenbourg Verlag, 1985–), 3:7–88, quotation p. 64.

47. Rolf Engelsing, "Die Perioden der Lesergeschichte in der Neuzeit. Das statistische Ausmass und die soziokulturelle Bedeutung der Lektüre," *Archiv für Geschichte des Buchwesens* 10 (1970): 946–1002.

48. Roger Chartier, "Représentations et pratiques: lectures paysannes au XVIIIe siècle," in his *Lectures et lecteurs dans la France d'Ancien Régime*, pp. 223–46, available in English as "Figures of the 'Other': Peasant Reading in the Age of the Enlightenment," in Chartier, *Cultural History: Between Practices and Representations*, trans. Lydia G. Cochrane (Ithaca: Cornell University Press, 1988), pp. 151–71.

49. Mercier, *Tableau*, "Bouquiniste," 2:128–32, quotation pp. 131–32.

50. Ibid., "Petits formats," 4:80–84, quotation pp. 80–81.

51. Immanuel Kant, "Beantwortung der Frage: Was Ist Aufklärung?" in his *Berlinische Monatsschrift* (1784), quoted from "What Is Enlightenment?" in *Foundations of the Metaphysics of Morals and What Is Enlightenment*, trans. Lewis W. Beck (Indianapolis: Bobbs-Merrill, 1959, 1975), p. 87.

5. DECHRISTIANIZATION AND SECULARIZATION

1. Alexis de Tocqueville, *L'Ancien Régime et la Révolution* (Paris: Gallimard, 1967), quoted from *The Old Régime and the French Revolution*, trans. Stuart Gilbert (Garden City, N.Y.: Doubleday, 1955). The quotations are from *L'Ancien Régime*, book 1, chap. 3, pp. 68–72 (*The Old Régime*, "How though its objectives were political, the French Revolution followed the lines of a religious revolution and why this was so," pp. 10–13), and book 3, chap. 2, pp. 242–53 (*The Old Régime*, "How vehement and widespread anti-religious feeling had become in eighteenth-century France and its influence on the nature of the Revolution," pp. 148–57).

2. *L'Ancien Régime*, p. 251; *The Old Régime*, p. 156.

3. Jean Delumeau, *Le Catholicisme entre Luther et Voltaire* (Paris: Presses Universitaires de France, Nouvelle Clio 30 bis, 1971), p. 330, quoted from *Catholicism between Luther and Voltaire: A New View of the Counter-Reformation*, trans. Jeremy Moiser (London: Burns and Oats, Philadelphia: Westminster Press, 1977), p. 231.

4. Jacques Toussaert, *Le Sentiment religieux en Flandre à la fin du Moyen-Age* (Paris: Plon, 1963), especially pp. 122–204. For an overview of Sunday and Easter

practices in the fourteenth and fifteenth centuries, see Jacques Chiffoleau, "Les 'banalités' paroissiales," in *Histoire de la France religieuse*, 2 vols., ed. Jacques Le Goff and René Rémond (Paris: Editions du Seuil, 1988), vol. 2, *Du christianisme flamboyant à l'aube des Lumières*, ed. François Lebrun, pp. 62–79.

5. Dominique Julia, "La Réforme posttrindentine en France d'après les procès-verbaux des visites pastorales: ordre et résistances," in *La società religiosa nell'età moderna* (Naples: Guida Editori, 1973), pp. 311–433, especially pp. 351–53. See also Robert Sauzet, "L'Acculturation des masses populaires," in Le Goff and Rémond, *Histoire de la France religieuse*, 2:434–43.

6. Marie-Hélène and Michel Froeschlé-Chopard, *Atlas de la Réforme pastorale en France de 1550 à 1790* (Paris: Editions du CNRS, 1986), pp. 64–69 and map 65, pp. 192–93.

7. Alphonse Dupront, *Du sacré. Croisades et pèlerinages, images et langage* (Paris: Gallimard, 1987), p. 422.

8. Louis Perouas, *Le diocèse de La Rochelle de 1648 à 1724. Sociologie et pastorale* (Paris: SEVPEN, 1964).

9. Michel Vovelle, *Piété baroque et déchristianisation en Provence au XVIIIe siècle. Les attitudes devant la mort d'après les clauses des testaments* (Paris: Plon, 1973); Pierre Chaunu, *La mort à Paris, XVIe, XVIIe et XVIIIe siècles* (Paris: Fayard, 1978).

10. Vovelle, *Piété baroque et déchristianisation en Provence*, pp. 128–29.

11. Jean-Paul Poisson and Joannès Chetail, "Foi et au-delà dans les clauses religieuses des testaments déposés au Sénat de Savoie au XVIIIe siècle," *The Gnomon: Revue Internationale d'Histoire du Notariat* 54 (March 1987): 30–46.

12. Alain Bideau and Jean-Pierre Bardet, "Fluctuations chronologiques ou début de la révolution contraceptive?" in Jacques Dupâquier et al., *Histoire de la population française*, 2 vols. (Paris: Presses Universitaires de France, 1988), vol. 2, *De la Renaissance à 1789*, pp. 373–98.

13. Pierre Chaunu, "Malthusianisme démographique et malthusianisme économique. Réflexions sur l'échec industriel de la Normandie à l'époque du démarrage," *Annales E.S.C.* 27 (1972). 1 -19; and Chaunu, "Postface," in Dupâquier et al., *Histoire de la population française*, 2:553–63.

14. Jean-Louis Flandrin, *Familles, parenté, maison, sexualité dans l'ancienne société*, rev. ed. (Paris: Editions du Seuil, 1984), pp. 204–33, available in English as *Families in Former Times: Kinship, Household, and Sexuality* (New York: Cambridge University Press, 1979), pp. 212–42.

15. Jean-Louis Flandrin, *Les Amours paysannes. Amour et sexualité dans les campagnes de l'ancienne France XVIe–XIXe siècle)* (Paris: Editions Gallimard/Julliard, Collection Archives, 1975), pp. 177–79, 233–35.

16. Peter Laslett, Karla Oosterveen, and Richard M. Smith, eds., *Bastardy and Its Comparative History: Studies in the History of Illegitimacy and Marital Nonconformism in Britain, France, Germany, Sweden, North America, Jamaica and Japan* (London: Edward Arnold, and Cambridge, Mass.: Harvard University Press, 1980).

17. Timothy Tackett, "L'Histoire sociale du clergé diocésain dans la France du XVIIIe siècle," *Revue d'Histoire Moderne et Contemporaine* (1979): 198–234.

18. Maurice Agulhon, *Pénitents et Francs-Maçons dans l'ancienne Provence* (Paris: Fayard, 1968), pp. 189–211.

19. Louis Châtellier, *L'Europe des dévots* (Paris: Flammarion, 1987), pp. 195–232, available in English as *The Europe of the Devout: The Catholic Reformation and the*

Formation of a New Society, trans. Jean Birrell (Cambridge: Cambridge University Press, Paris: Editions de la Maison des Sciences de l'homme, 1989), pp. 177–93.

20. Alphonse Dupront, "Livre et culture dans la société française du 18e siècle: Réflexions sur une enquête," in *Livre et société dans la France du XVIIIe siècle* (Paris and The Hague: Mouton, 1965), pp. 185–238, quotation p. 225.

21. Michel Vovelle, "La Sensibilité pré-révolutionnaire," in *Vom ancien régime zur französischen Revolution. Forschungen und Perspektiven*, ed. Ernst Hinrichs, Eberhard Schmitt, and Rudolf Vierhaus (Göttingen: Vandenhoeck and Ruprecht 1978), pp. 516–38.

22. Michel de Certeau, "La Formalité des pratiques. Du système religieux à l'éthique des Lumières (XVIIe–XVIIIe)," in *La società religiosa nell'età moderna*, pp. 447–509; reprinted in his *L'Ecriture de l'histoire* (Paris: Gallimard, 1975), pp. 153–212, and available in English in Certeau, *The Writing of History*, trans. Tom Conley (New York: Columbia University Press, 1988), pp. 153–212; Dominique Julia, "Déchristianisation ou mutation culturelle? L'exemple du Bassin parisien au XVIIIe siècle," in *Croyances, pouvoirs et société. Des limousins aux français. Etudes offertes à Louis Perouas*, ed. Michel Cassan, Jean Boutier, and Nicole Lemaître (Treignac: Editions Les Monédières, 1988), pp. 185–239.

23. Dale K. Van Kley, *The Damiens Affair and the Unraveling of the Ancien Régime, 1750–1770* (Princeton: Princeton University Press, 1984), especially pp. 163–65.

24. Quoted from Julia, "Déchristianisation ou mutation culturelle?" p. 222.

25. Dupront, *Du sacré*, p. 424.

26. See, for example, Timothy Tackett, *Priest and Parish in Eighteenth-Century France. A Social and Political Study of the Curés of Dauphiné* (Princeton: Princeton University Press, 1977), pp. 194–215.

27. Michel de Certeau, "La Formalité des pratiques," cited from *L'Ecriture de l'histoire*, p. 165; *The Writing of History*, pp. 156–57.

28. Timothy Tackett, *Religion, Revolution and Regional Culture in Eighteenth-Century France: The Ecclesiastical Oath of 1791* (Princeton: Princeton University Press, 1985); Dominique Julia, "La Révolution, l'Eglise et la France (note critique)," *Annales E.S.C.* 43 (1988): 761–70.

29. Michel Vovelle, *Religion et Révolution. La déchristianisation de l'an II* (Paris: Hachette, 1976); Vovelle, *La Révolution contre l'Eglise. De la Raison à l'Etre Suprême* (Brussels: Editions Complexe, 1988).

30. Dupront, *Du sacré*, p. 466.

31. Roger Dupuy, *De la Révolution à la Chouannerie. Paysans en Bretagne 1788–1794* (Paris: Flammarion, 1988), p. 328.

32. Mona Ozouf, *La fête révolutionnaire 1789–1799* (Paris: Gallimard, 1976), pp. 317–40, available in English as *Festivals and the French Revolution*, trans. Alan Sheridan (Cambridge, Mass.: Harvard University Press, 1988), pp. 262–82.

6. A DESACRALIZED KING

1. Alphonse Dupront, *Les Lettres, les sciences, la religion et les arts dans la société française de la deuxième moitié du dix-huitième siècle* (Paris: Centre de Documentation Universitaire, 1963), p. 52.

2. The extracts from *cahiers de doléance* given in this and the preceding paragraph

are quoted from Pierre Goubert and Michel Denis, *1789 les Français ont la parole . . . Cahiers de doléances des Etats Généraux* (Paris: Julliard, Collection Archives, 1964), pp. 39–49 (for Saint-Jean de Cauquessac, Lauris, and Sèvres); Dupront, *Les Lettres, les sciences, la religion et les arts*, p. 53 (for Barcelonette); Régine Robin, *La Société française en 1789: Semur-en-Auxois* (Paris: Plon, 1970), pp. 298–308 (for Toutry).

3. John Markoff, "Images du Roi au début de la Révolution," in *L'Image de la Révolution française: Communications présentées lors du Congrès Mondial pour le Bicentenaire de la Révolution, Sorbonne, Paris, 6–12 juillet 1989*, 4 vols., Michel Vovelle, gen. ed. (Paris and Oxford: Pergamon Press, 1989–1990), 1:237–45.

4. Michael Walzer, ed., *Regicide and Revolution: Speeches at the Trial of Louis XVI*, trans. Marian Rothstein (Cambridge: Cambridge University Press, 1974); Jeffrey W. Merrick, *The Desacralization of the French Monarchy in the Eighteenth Century* (Baton Rouge: Louisiana State University Press, 1990).

5. Yves-Marie Bercé, *Histoire des Croquants. Etudes des soulèvements populaires au XVIIe siècle dans le Sud-Ouest de la France*, 2 vols. (Geneva: Librairie Droz, 1974), 2:608–11.

6. Arlette Farge and Jacques Revel, *Logiques de la foule. L'affaire des enlèvements d'enfants Paris 1750* (Paris: Hachette, 1988), quotations pp. 112, 133.

7. Pierre Rétat, ed., *L'Attentat de Damiens. Discours sur l'événement au XVIIIe siècle* (Paris: Editions du CNRS, Lyons: Presses Universitaires de Lyon, 1979).

8. Michel Foucault, *Surveiller et punir. Naissance de la prison* (Paris: Gallimard, 1975), chap. 2, "L'éclat des supplices," pp. 36–72, quotation p. 52, quoted from *Discipline and Punish: The Birth of the Prison*, trans. Alan Sheridan (New York: Random House Vintage Books, 1979), chap. 2, "The Spectacle of the Scaffold," pp. 32–69, quotation p. 48.

9. Dale K. Van Kley, *The Damiens Affair and the Unraveling of the Ancien Régime 1750–1770* (Princeton: Princeton University Press, 1984), chap. 5, "Damiens' Peers," pp. 226–65.

10. Edmund Jean François Barbier, *Journal d'un bourgeois de Paris sous le règne de Louis XV* (Paris: Union Générale d'Editions, 1963), pp. 279–80.

11. Arlette Farge, *La Vie fragile. Violence, pouvoirs et solidarités à Paris au XVIIIe siècle* (Paris: Hachette, 1986), pp. 206–34, shows the increasing criticism of public executions, expressed by means of requests for pardon issuing from the crowd and, on occasion, by the sabotage of the means for carrying out the king's punishment.

12. Van Kley, *The Damiens Affair*, p. 232.

13. Ibid., p. 255.

14. The quotations in this paragraph and the two following paragraphs (with the exception of the one from the *Dictionnaire de Trévoux*) are taken from Steven L. Kaplan, *Bread, Politics and Political Economy in the Reign of Louis XV*, 2 vols. (The Hague: Martinus Nijhoff, 1976), 1:309, 320, 321; and Kaplan, *The Famine Plot Persuasion in Eighteenth-Century France.* Transactions of the American Philosophical Society, vol. 72, pt. 3 (Philadelphia: American Philosophical Society, 1982), p. 54.

15. *Dictionnaire Universel françois et latin, vulgairement appelé Dictionnaire de Trévoux*, new ed. (Paris, 1771), s.v. "Peuple."

16. This quotation from Hardy's journal and the next are taken from Farge, *La vie fragile*, pp. 204–5.

17. Van Kley, *The Damiens Affair*, pp. 253–54.

18. Ibid., pp. 247–48, and n. 86, pp. 347–48.

19. As in *Les Fastes de Louis XV*, the title most in demand among Mauvelain's customers in Troyes, where he sold prohibited books between 1782 and 1784. See Robert Darnton, "A Clandestine Bookseller in the Provinces," in his *The Literary Underground of the Old Regime* (Cambridge, Mass.: Harvard University Press, 1982), pp. 122–47, especially pp. 145–46.

20. Marc Bloch, *Les Rois thaumaturges. Etude sur le caractère surnaturel attribué à la puissance royale particulièrement en France et en Angleterre* (1924; Paris: Gallimard, 1983), chap. 5, "Le miracle royal au temps des luttes religieuses et de l'absolutisme," pp. 309–79, quotation p. 347, quoted from *The Royal Touch: Sacred Monarchy and Scrofula in England and France*, trans. J. E. Anderson (London: Routledge and Kegan Paul, Montreal: McGill–Queen's University Press, 1973), chap. 5, "The Royal Miracle during the Wars of Religion and the Absolute Monarchy," pp. 177–213, quotation p. 197.

21. Given in Bloch, *Les Rois thaumaturges*, p. 351; *The Royal Touch*, p. 199.

22. Alain Boureau, *Le Simple corps du roi. L'impossible sacralité des souverains français XVe–XVIIIe siècle* (Paris: Les Editions de Paris, 1988), p. 23.

23. Jean-François Courtine, "L'héritage scolastique dans la problématique théo-ogo-politique de l'âge classique," in *L'Etat baroque. Regards sur la pensée politique de la France du premier XVIIe siècle*, ed. Henry Méchoulan (Paris: Librairie Philosophique J. Vrin, 1985), pp. 89–118.

24. Jacques-Louis Ménétra, *Journal de ma vie. Jacques-Louis Ménétra, compagnon vitrier au 18e siècle*, presented by Daniel Roche (Paris: Montalba, 1982), pp. 161, 212, and n. 18, p. 402, quoted from Ménétra, *Journal of My Life*, ed. Daniel Roche, trans. Arthur Goldhammer (New York: Columbia University Press, 1986), pp. 131, 176, n. 18, p. 366.

25. Barbier, *Journal d'un bourgeois de Paris*, pp. 301–2.

26. Ménétra, *Journal de ma vie*, pp. 389–94, quoted from *Journal of My Life*, p. 329.

27. Ralph E. Giesey, "The King Imagined," in *The French Revolution and the Creation of Modern Political Culture*, 2 vols., ed. Keith Michael Baker (Oxford and New York: Pergamon Press, 1987), vol. 1, *The Political Culture of the Old Regime*, pp. 41–59; Giesey, "Modèles de pouvoir dans les rites royaux français," *Annales E.S.C.* 41 (1986): 579–99.

28. On the overturning of constitutional symbolism and the theory of royalty in 1610, see Sarah Hanley, *The Lit de Justice of the Kings of France: Constitutional Ideology in Legend, Ritual, and Discourse* (Princeton: Princeton University Press, 1983), chaps. 10 and 11, pp. 231–80; Ralph E. Giesey, *The Royal Funeral Ceremony in Renaissance France* (Geneva: Librairie Droz, 1960).

29. Ralph E. Giesey, *Cérémonial et puissance souveraine. France, XVe–XVIIe siècles*, trans. Jeannie Carlier. Cahiers des Annales 41 (Paris: Armand Colin, 1987), especially chap. 3, "La crise du cérémonial en 1610," pp. 33–47.

30. Hélène Himelfarb, "Versailles, functions et légendes," in *Les Lieux de mémoire*, 2 vols., ed. Pierre Nora, vol. 2, *La Nation* (Paris: Gallimard, 1984–86), pt. 2, pp. 235–92, quotation, p. 246.

31. Edouard Pommier, "Versailles, l'image du souverain," in Nora, *Les Lieux de mémoire*, 2:193–234 (the 1685 medal, illustrated on p. 227, is taken from *Médailles sur les principaux événements du Règne de Louis-le-Grand* [1702]).

32. Marianne Grivel, *Le Commerce de l'estampe à Paris au XVIIe siècle.* Histoire et civilisation du livre 16 (Geneva: Librairie Droz, 1986), pp. 157–60.

33. Michèle Fogel, *Les Cérémonies de l'information dans la France du XVIe au milieu du XVIIIe siècle* (Paris: Fayard, 1989), pp. 133–245.

34. Ibid., p. 243.

35. Michèle Fogel, "Propagande, communication, publication: points de vue et demande d'enquête pour la France des XVIe–XVIIe siècle," in *La Culture et l'idéologie dans la genèse de l'Etat moderne.* Actes de la table ronde organisée par le Centre de la recherche scientifique et L'Ecole française de Rome, Rome, 15–17 October 1984 (Rome: Ecole française de Rome, 1985), pp. 325–36, statistics pp. 328–29.

36. Jacques Le Goff, "Reims, ville du sacre," in Nora, *Les Lieux de mémoire*, vol. 2, *La Nation*, pt. 1, pp. 89–184.

37. Giesey, *Cérémonial et puissance souveraine*, p. 85.

38. Louis Marin, *Le Portrait du roi* (Paris: Les Editions de Minuit, 1982), introduction, "Les trois formules," pp. 7–22, quotation p. 10, quoted from *Portrait of the King*, trans. Martha M. Houle (Minneapolis: University of Minnesota Press, 1988), p. 5.

39. Ibid.: *Le Portrait du roi*, p. 19; *Portrait of the King*, p. 13.

40. Anne-Marie Lecoq, "La Symbolique de l'Etat. Les images de la monarchie des premiers Valois à Louis XIV," in Nora, *Lieux de mémoire*, vol. 2, pt. 2, pp. 145–92.

41. Louis XIV, *Mémoires*, ed. Jean Longnon (Paris: Tallandier, 1978), p. 35.

42. André Félibien, *Description sommaire du château de Versailles* (Paris: G. Desprez, 1674), quoted from Pommier, "Versailles, l'image du souverain," n. 25, p. 229.

43. Bernard Teyssèdre, *L'Art au siècle de Louis XIV* (Paris: Le Livre de Poche, 1967), chap. 5, "Versailles, vivante folie, 1666–1678," pp. 128–202.

44. Pommier, "Versailles, l'image du souverain," p. 213.

45. Himelfarb, "Versailles, fonctions et légendes," pp. 252–57.

46. Pierre Bourdieu, *Le Sens pratique* (Paris: Les Editions de Minuit, 1980), p. 226.

47. Marin, *Le Portrait du roi*, p. 11; *Portrait of the King*, p. 6.

48. Blaise Pascal, *Pensées*, in Pascal, *Oeuvres complètes*, ed. Louis Lafuma (Paris: Editions du Seuil, L'Intégrale, 1963), no. 25, p. 503, quoted from *Pascal's Pensées*, trans. H. F. Stewart (London: Routledge and Kegan Paul, 1950), pp. 483–85.

49. Pascal, *Pensées*, no. 44, p. 504; *Pascal's Pensées*, p. 41.

50. Roger Chartier, "Du rituel au for privé: les chartes de mariage lyonnaises au XVIIe siècle," in *Les Usages de l'imprimé (XVe–XIXe siècle)*, ed. R. Chartier (Paris: Fayard, 1987), pp. 229–51, available in English as "From Ritual to the Hearth: Marriage Charters in Seventeenth-Century Lyons," in *The Culture of Print: Power and the Uses of Print in Early Modern Europe*, ed. R. Chartier, trans. Lydia G. Cochrane (Princeton: Princeton University Press, 1989), pp. 174–90.

51. Pascal, *Pensées*, no. 124, p. 514; *Pascal's Pensées*, p. 91.

7. A NEW POLITICAL CULTURE

1. Peter Burke, *Popular Culture in Early Modern Europe* (New York: Harper and Row, 1978), "Politics and the People," pp. 259–70, quotations, p. 259.

2. Roger Chartier, "Pamphlets et gazettes," in *Histoire de l'Edition française*, 4 vols., ed. Henri-Jean Martin and Roger Chartier (Paris: Promodis, 1982–86), vol. 1, *Le livre conquérant*. *Du Moyen Age au milieu du XVIIe siècle* (1982), pp. 405–25, especially table, p. 423, which makes use of Henri-Jean Martin, M. Lecocq, et al., *Livres et lecteurs à Grenoble*. *Les registres du libraire Nicolas (1645–1668)*, 2 vols., (Geneva: Librairie Droz, 1977).

3. Alfred Morin, *Catalogue descriptif de la Bibliothèque bleue de Troyes (Almanachs exclus)* (Geneva: Librairie Droz, 1974). On the Bibliothèque bleue, see Jean-Paul Oddos, "Simples notes sur les origines de la Bibliothèque bleue," in Giovanni Dotoli, *La 'Bibliothèque bleue' nel Seicento o della letteratura per il popolo* (Bari: Adriatica, Paris: Nizet, 1981), pp. 159–68; Roger Chartier, "Stratégies éditoriales et lectures populaires, 1530–1660," and "Livres bleus et lectures populaires," in his *Lectures et lecteurs dans la France d'Ancien Régime* (Paris: Editions du Seuil, 1987), pp. 87–124, 247–70, available in English as "Publishing Strategies and What the People Read, 1530–1660," and "The *Bibliothèque bleue* and Popular Reading," in Chartier, *The Cultural Uses of Print in Early Modern France*, trans. Lydia G. Cochrane (Princeton: Princeton University Press, 1987), pp. 145–82, 240–64.

4. Frédéric Deloffre, ed., *Agréables conférences de deux paysans de Saint-Ouen et de Montmorency sur les affaires du temps (1649–1651)*. *Edition critique* (Lyons: Annales de l'Université de Lyon, 1962); Christian Jouhaud, *Mazarinades. La Fronde des mots* (Paris: Aubier, 1985), pp. 223–25.

5. Hans-Jürgen Lüsebrink, ed., *Histoires curieuses et véritables de Cartouche et de Mandrin* (Paris: Montalba, Bibliothèque bleue, 1984), pp. 11–76, quotation p. 66; Roger Chartier, "Figures littéraires et expériences sociales: la littérature de la gueuserie dans la Bibliothèque bleue," in his *Lectures et lecteurs dans la France d'Ancien Régime*, pp. 271–351, available in English as "The Literature of Roguery in the *Bibliothèque bleue*," in Chartier, *The Cultural Uses of Print*, pp. 265–342.

6. Roger Chartier, "Représentations et pratiques: lectures paysannes au XVIIIe siècle," in his *Lectures et lecteurs dans la France d'Ancien Régime*, pp. 223–46, available in English as "Figures of the 'Other': Peasant Reading in the Age of the Enlightenment," in Chartier, *Cultural History: Between Practices and Representations*, trans. Lydia G. Cochrane (Ithaca: Cornell University Press, 1988), pp. 151–71.

7. Norbert Elias, *Über den Prozess der Zivilisation. Soziogenetische und psychogenetische Untersuchungen* (1939; Frankfurt-am-Main: Suhrkamp, 1969; reprint edition, Suhrkamp Taschenbusch Wissenschaft, 1978–1979), "Zur Soziogenese des Staates," pp. 123–311, available in English as *Power and Civility: The Civilizing Process Volume 2*, trans. Edmund Jephcott (New York: Pantheon Books, 1982), "On the Sociogenesis of the State," pp. 91–225.

8. Yves-Marie Bercé, *Histoire des Croquants, Etudes des soulèvements populaires au XVIIe siècle dans le Sud-Ouest de la France*, 2 vols. (Geneva: Librairie Droz, 1974).

9. Boris Porchnev, *Les soulèvements populaires en France de 1632 à 1648* (Paris: SEVPEN, 1963), maps of the locations of revolts, pp. 665–76.

10. Joël Cornette, "Fiction et réalité de l'Etat baroque (1610–1652)," in *L'Etat baroque. Regards sur la pensée politique de la France du premier XVIIe siècle*, ed. Henry Méchoulan (Paris: J. Vrin, 1985), pp. 7–87, especially pp. 14–27.

11. Emmanuel Le Roy Ladurie, "Révoltes et contestations rurales en France de
     1675 à 1788," *Annales E.S.C.* 29 (1974): 6–22.
12. Hilton L. Root, *Peasants and King in Burgundy: Agrarian Foundations of French
     Absolutism* (Berkeley: University of California Press, 1987), chap. 5, "Chal-
     lenging the Seigneurie: Community and Contentions on the Eve of the Revolu-
     tion," pp. 155–204.
13. Yves Durand, ed., *Cahiers de doléances des paroisses du bailliage de Troyes pour les
     Etats généraux de 1614* (Paris: Presses Universitaires de France, 1966); Jean-
     Jacques Vernier, ed., *Cahiers de doléances du bailliage de Troyes (principal et
     secondaire) et du bailliage de Bar-sur-Seine pour les Etats généraux de 1789* (Troyes,
     1909–11).
14. See Roger Chartier and Jean Nagle, "Doléances rurales: le bailliage de Troyes,"
     in *Représentation et vouloir politiques. Autour des Etats généraux de 1614*, ed. Roger
     Chartier and Denis Richet (Paris: Editions de l'Ecole des Hautes Etudes en
     Sciences Sociales, 1982), pp. 89–111; Roger Chartier, "Culture, Lumières,
     doléances: les cahiers de 1789," *Revue d'Histoire Moderne et Contemporaine* 28
     (1981): 68–93, available in English as "From Words to Texts. The *Cahiers de
     doléances*," in Chartier, *The Cultural Uses of Print*, pp. 110–44.
15. A. N. Galpern, *The Religions of the People in Sixteenth-Century Champagne*
     (Cambridge, Mass.: Harvard University Press, 1976).
16. Dominique Julia, "Le clergé paroissial du diocèse de Reims à la fin de l'Ancien
     Régime," *Etudes Ardennaises* 49 (1967): 19–35, and 55 (1968): 41–66.
17. Alexis de Tocqueville, *L'Ancien Régime et la Révolution*, 2 vols. (Paris: Gal-
     limard, 1958), vol. 2, *Fragments et notes inédites sur la Révolution*, p. 126.
18. Porchnev, *Les soulèvements populaires in France*, pp. 132–35.
19. Cynthia M. Truant, "Independent and Insolent: Journeymen and Their 'Rites'
     in the Old Regime Workplace," in *Work in France: Representations, Meaning,
     Organization, and Practice*, ed. Steven Laurence Kaplan and Cynthia J. Koepp
     (Ithaca: Cornell University Press, 1986), pp. 131–75, summaries of journey-
     men's labor activity in Nantes and Lyons, pp. 174–75.
20. Steven Kaplan, "Réflexions sur la police du monde du travail, 1700–1815,"
     Revue Historique 261 (1979): 17–77.
21. Michael Sonenscher, "Journeymen, the Courts and the French Trades 1781–
     1791," *Past and Present* 114 (February 1987): 77–109; Sonenscher, *Work and
     Wages: Natural Law, Politics, and Eighteenth-Century French Trades* (Cambridge:
     Cambridge University Press, 1989), chap. 8, "Conflict and the Courts," pp.
     244–94.
22. Steven Laurence Kaplan, "Social Classification and Representation in the
     Corporate World of Eighteenth-Century France: Turgot's 'Carnival,'" in Kap-
     lan and Koepp, *Work in France*, pp. 176–228.
23. Sonenscher, "Journeymen," pp. 108–9.
24. Steven Kaplan, "Les corporations, les 'faux ouvriers' et le faubourg Saint-
     Antoine au XVIIIe siècle," *Annales E.S.C.* 43 (1988): 353–78.
25. Michael Sonenscher, "Les sans-culottes de l'an II: Repenser le langage du
     travail dans la France révolutionnaire," *Annales E.S.C.* 40 (1985): 1087–1108,
     quotation pp. 1094–95.
26. Jürgen Habermas, *Strukturwandel der Öffentlichkeit, Untersuchungen zu einer Kate-
     gorie der bürgerlichen Gesellschaft* (Neuwied: Hermann Luchterhand Verlag,
     1962), available in English as *The Structural Transformation of the Public Sphere: An*

Inquiry into a Category of Bourgeois Society, trans. Thomas Burger and Frederick Lawrence (Cambridge: Polity Press, Cambridge, Mass.: MIT Press, 1989).

27. Benedetta Craveri, *Madame du Deffand e il suo mondo* (Milan: Adelphi Editori, 1982); for an overall view of the salons, see Dena Goodman, "Enlightened Salons: The Convergence of Female and Philosophic Ambitions," *Eighteenth-Century Studies* 22, 3 (1989): 329–50.

28. Alan Charles Kors, *D'Holbach's Coterie: An Enlightenment in Paris* (Princeton: Princeton University Press, 1976); Daniel Roche, "Lumières et engagement politique: la coterie d'Holbach dévoilée," *Annales E.S.C.* 33 (1978): 720–28, also available in his *Les Républicains des Lettres. Gens de culture et Lumières au XVIIIe siècle* (Paris: Fayard, 1988), pp. 242–53.

29. Voltaire, *Lettre à M. Lefèvre sur les inconvénients attachés à la littérature* (1732), quoted from Craveri, *Madame du Deffand e il suo mondo*, p. 137.

30. Craveri, *Madame du Deffand e il suo mondo*, pp. 136–42.

31. Jean Sgard, "La multiplication des périodiques," in Martin and Chartier, *L'Histoire de l'Edition française*, 2:198–205.

32. Jean Sgard, *Bibliographie de la presse classique (1600–1789)* (Geneva: Editions Slatkine, 1984).

33. Claude Labrosse and Pierre Rétat, with Henri Duranton, *L'instrument périodique. La fonction de la presse au XVIIIe siècle* (Lyons: Presses Universitaires de Lyon, 1985), especially pp. 71–86.

34. According to the comparison of data furnished by Henri Duranton, Robert Favre, Claude Labrosse, and Pierre Rétat, "Etude quantitative des périodiques de 1734," in *Presse et histoire au XVIIIe siècle. L'année 1734*, ed. Pierre Rétat and Jean Sgard (Paris: Editions du CNRS, 1978), pp. 63–126; François Furet, "La 'librairie' du royaume de France au 18e siècle, in *Livre et société dans la France du XVIIIe siècle*, 2 vols. (Paris and The Hague: Mouton, 1965, 1970), 1:3–32.

35. Jean Ehrard and Jacques Roger, "Deux périodiques français du XVIIIe siècle: Le *Journal des Savants* et les *Mémoires de Trévoux*," in *Livre et société dans la France du XVIIIe siècle*, 2:33–59.

36. Claude Labrosse, *Lire au XVIIIe siècle. La Nouvelle Héloïse et ses lecteurs* (Lyons: Presses Universitaires de Lyon, 1985), pp. 119–74.

37. Thomas E. Crow, *Painters and Public Life in Eighteenth-Century Paris* (New Haven: Yale University Press, 1985).

38. William Weber, "Learned and General Musical Taste in Eighteenth-Century France," *Past and Present* 89 (1980): 58–85.

39. Udolpho van de Sandt, "Le Salon de l'Académie de 1759 à 1781," in *Diderot et l'Art de Boucher à David. Les Salons: 1759–1781* (Paris: Editions de la Réunion des Musées Nationaux, 1984), pp. 79–84; Bernadette Fort, "Voice of the Public: Carnivalization of Salon Art in Prerevolutionary France," *Eighteenth-Century Studies* 22, 3 (1989): 368–94.

40. François Furet, *Penser la Révolution française* (Paris: Gallimard, 1978), p. 59, quoted from *Interpreting the French Revolution*, trans. Elborg Forster (Cambridge: Cambridge University Press, Paris: Editions de la Maison des Sciences de l'homme, 1981), p. 38.

41. Immanuel Kant, *The Critique of Pure Reason*, trans. Norman Kemp Smith (New York: The Humanities Press, 1950), p. 9.

42. Gérard Gayot, *La Franc-Maçonnerie française. Textes et pratiques (XVIIIe–XIXe siècles)* (Paris: Editions Gallimard/Julliard, Collection Archives, 1980), p. 32.

43. Ran Halévi, *Les loges maçonniques dans la France d'Ancien Régime. Aux origines de la sociabilité démocratique.* Cahiers des Annales 40 (Paris: Librairie Armand Colin, 1984).

44. Daniel Roche, *Le siècle des Lumières en province. Académies et académiciens provinciaux, 1680–1789*, 2 vols. (Paris and The Hague: Mouton, 1978), vol. 2, table 38, p. 419; table 13, p. 382; table 41, pp. 423–24.

45. Quoted in Gayot, *La Franc-Maçonnerie française*, pp. 170–71; Halévi, *Les loges maçonniques*, pp. 79, 80.

46. Quoted in Roche, *Le siècle des Lumières en province*, 1:273.

47. Denis Richet, "Autour des origines idéologiques lointaines de la Révolution: Elites et despotisme," *Annales E.S.C.* 24 (1969): 1–23.

48. Reinhart Koselleck, *Kritik und Krise. Eine Studie zur Pathogenese der bürgerlichen Welt* (Fribourg and Munich: Verlag Karl Albert, 1959), quoted from *Critique and Crisis: Enlightenment and the Pathogenesis of Modern Society* (Cambridge, Mass.: MIT Press, 1988), p. 75.

49. Keith Michael Baker, "Politics and Public Opinion under the Old Regime: Some Reflections," in *Press and Politics in Pre-Revolutionary France*, ed. Jack R. Censer and Jeremy D. Popkin (Berkeley: University of California Press, 1987), pp. 204–46; reprinted as "Public Opinion as Political Invention," in Baker, *Inventing the French Revolution: Essays on French Political Culture in the Eighteenth Century* (Cambridge: Cambridge University Press, 1990), pp. 167–99.

50. Pierre Bourdieu, *La distinction. Critique social et jugement* (Paris: Les Editions du Minuit, 1979), chap. 8, "Culture et politique," pp. 463–541, available in English as *Distinction: A Social Critique of the Judgment of Taste*, trans. Richard Nice (Cambridge, Mass.: Harvard University Press, 1984), chap. 8, "Culture and Politics," pp. 397–465.

51. Bronislaw Baczko, *Comment sortir de la Terreur. Thermidor et la Révolution* (Paris: Gallimard, 1989), p. 346.

8. DO REVOLUTIONS HAVE CULTURAL ORIGINS?

1. Lawrence Stone, *The Causes of the English Revolution 1529–1642* (New York: Harper Torchbook, 1972), p. 98.

2. Ibid., p. 113.

3. Ibid., p. 103.

4. Dale Van Kley, "The Jansenist Constitutional Legacy in the French Prerevolution," in *The French Revolution and the Creation of Modern Political Culture*, 2 vols., ed. Keith Michael Baker (Oxford and New York: Pergamon Press, 1987), vol. 1, *The Political Culture of the Old Regime*, pp. 169–201, quotation p. 179; Van Kley, "The Estates General as Ecumenical Council: The Constitutionalism of Corporate Consensus and the *Parlement*'s Ruling of September 25, 1788," *Journal of Modern History* 61, 1 (1989): 1–52.

5. Michael Fried, *Absorption and Theatricality: Painting and Beholder in the Age of Diderot* (Berkeley: University of California Press, 1980), pp. 136–38, 145–60, Diderot quotation, pp. 147–48.

6. Thomas E. Crow, *Painters and Public Life in Eighteenth-Century Paris* (New Haven: Yale University Press, 1985), chap. 7, "David and the Salon," pp. 210–54.

7. Stone, *Causes of the English Revolution*, p. 104.

8. Roger Chartier, "Culture, Lumières, doléances: les cahiers de 1789," *Revue d'Histoire Moderne et Contemporaine* 28 (1981): 68–93, available in English as "From Words to Texts: The Cahiers de doléances of 1789," in Chartier, *The Cultural Uses of Print in Early Modern France*, trans. Lydia G. Cochrane (Princeton: Princeton University Press, 1987), pp. 110–44.

9. Edna-Hindie Lemay, "La composition de l'Assemblée Nationale Constituante: les hommes de la continuité?" *Revue d'Histoire Moderne et Contemporaine* 24 (1977): 341–63.

10. Regine Robin, *La société française en 1789: Semur-en-Auxois* (Paris: Plon, 1970), pp. 294–98.

11. André Burguière, "Société et culture à Reims à la fin du XVIIIe siècle: la diffusion des 'Lumières' analysée à travers les cahiers de doléance," *Annales E.S.C.* 22 (1967): 303–39.

12. Alphonse Dupront, "Formes de la culture de masses: de la doléance politique au pélerinage panique (XVIIIe–XXe siècle)," in *Niveaux de culture et groupes sociaux*. Actes du colloque réuni du 7 au 9 mai 1966 à l'Ecole Normale Supérieure, Paris (Paris and The Hague: Mouton, 1967), pp. 149–67, quotation p. 158.

13. Ibid.

14. Daniel Mornet, *Les origines intellectuelles de la Révolution française 1715–1789* (1933; Paris: Armand Colin, 1967), p. 454.

15. Jean Hébrard, "Les catéchismes de la première Révolution," in *Colporter la Révolution*, ed. Lise Andriès (Ville de Montreuil: Bibliothèque Robert-Desnos, 1989), pp. 52–81.

16. Stone, *Causes of the English Revolution*, p. 105.

17. Jean-François Solnon, *La Cour de France* (Paris: Fayard, 1987), pp. 421–46.

18. Hélène Himelfarb, "Versailles, functions et légendes," in *Les lieux de mémoire*, 2 vols., ed. Pierre Nora (Paris: Gallimard, 1984–86), vol. 2, pt. 2, pp. 235–92, especially pp. 261–69.

19. Louis-Sébastien Mercier, *Tableau de Paris. Nouvelle édition corrigée et augmentée*, 8 vols. (Amsterdam, 1782–1783), "De la Cour," 4:261–64.

20. Robert Darnton, "Trade in the Taboo: The Life of a Clandestine Book Dealer in Prerevolutionary France," in *The Widening Circle: Essays on the Circulation of Literature in Eighteenth-Century Europe*, ed. Paul J. Korshin (Philadelphia: University of Pennsylvania Press, 1976), pp. 11–83.

21. Ibid., p. 62.

22. Jean-Claude Perrot, "Nouveautés: l'économie politique et ses livres," in *Histoire de l'Edition Française*, 4 vols., Henri-Jean Martin and Roger Chartier, gen. eds. (Paris: Promodis, 1982–1986), vol. 2, *Le livre triomphant. 1660–1830*, pp. 240–57, especially p. 254.

23. Robert Darnton, "Ideology on the Bourse," in *Image de la Révolution française*. Communications présentées lors du Congrès Mondial pour le Bicentenaire de la Révolution, Sorbonne, Paris, 6–12 July 1989, 4 vols., ed. Michel Vovelle (Paris and Oxford: Pergamon Press, 1989–1990), 1:124–39; Darnton, "Trends in Radical Propaganda on the Eve of the French Revolution (1782–1788)" (Ph.D. diss., Oxford University, 1964), chap. 9, "The Final Assault on the Government," which quotes, among other works, the journal of the bookseller Hardy in 1788: "One could not read this piece [the *Histoire du siège de Paris*] without shedding a torrent of tears, so truthful it was found to be,

touching, and well done. One felt moved, simultaneously, by sorrow, indignation, and terror for what was to come." See also Jeremy Popkin, "Pamphlet Journalism at the End of the Old Regime," *Eighteenth-Century Studies* 22, 3 (1989): 368–94.

24. Sarah Maza, "The Diamond Necklace Affair Revisited (1785–1786): The Case of the Missing Queen," in *Eroticism and the Body Politic in France*, ed. Lynn Hunt (Baltimore: Johns Hopkins University Press, 1990).

25. Alexis de Tocqueville, *L'Ancien Régime et la Révolution* (Paris: Gallimard, 1967), quoted from *The Old Régime and the French Revolution*, trans. Stuart Gilbert (Garden City, N.Y.: Doubleday, 1955), p. 32.

26. Ibid.: *L'Ancien Régime*, book 2, chap. 7, pp. 146–52; *Old Régime*, p. 72.

27. Ibid.: *L'Ancien Régime*, pp. 148, 150; *Old Régime*, pp. 74, 75.

28. Jean-Claude Perrot, *Genèse d'une ville moderne. Caen au XVIIIe siècle*, 2 vols. (Paris and The Hague Mouton, 1975), 2:app. 28, "Le couple culturel Paris-province," p. 1026 (which lists twenty-one titles published between 1737 and 1793). See also Simon Davies, *Paris and the Provinces in Eighteenth-Century Prose Fiction*. Studies on Voltaire and the Eighteenth Century 214 (Oxford: Voltaire Foundation, 1982); Jean Mohsen Fahmy, *Voltaire et Paris*. Studies on Voltaire and the Eighteenth Century 195 (Oxford: Voltaire Foundation, 1981).

29. Fougeret de Monbron, *Le Cosmopolite ou le Citoyen du Monde suivi de La Capitale des Gaules ou la Nouvelle Babylone* (Bordeaux: Editions Ducros, 1970), pp. 145–56.

30. Mercier, *Tableau*, "De l'influence de la capitale sur les provinces," 4:296–99.

31. Ibid., "Le Parisien en province," 1:87–88.

32. Ibid., "Auteurs nés à Paris," 4:21–29, quotations pp. 21, 27.

33. Roger Chartier, "Les deux France. Histoire d'une géographie," *Cahiers d'Histoire* (1978): 393–415, especially pp. 412–14, available in English as "The Two Frances: The History of a Geographical Idea," in Chartier, *Cultural History: Between Practices and Representation*, trans. Lydia G. Cochrane (Ithaca: Cornell University Press, 1988), pp. 172–200.

34. Norbert Elias, *Die höfische Gesellschaft. Untersuchungen zur Soziologie des Königtums und der höfischen Aristokratie mit einer Einleitung· Soziologie und Geschichtwissenschaft* (Neuwied: Hermann Luchterhand Verlag, 1969), available in English as *The Court Society*, trans. Edmund Jephcott (Oxford: Blackwell, 1983).

35. Norbert Elias, *Über den Prozess der Zivilisation. Soziogenetische und Psychogenetische Untersuchungen*, 2 vols. (1939; Frankfurt-am-Main: Suhrkamp, 1969), 2:274, quoted from *Power and Civility: The Civilizing Process Volume 2*, trans. Edmund Jephcott (New York: Pantheon Books, 1982), p. 198.

36. Elias, *Die höfische Gesellschaft*, p. 401; *The Court Society*, p. 273.

37. Stone, *Causes of the English Revolution*, pp. 108–10.

38. Ibid., pp. 113–14.

39. Mark H. Curtis, "The Alienated Intellectuals of Early Stuart England," *Past and Present* 23 (1962): 25–43. On the topic of "alienated intellectuals," see also Roger Chartier, "Espace social et imaginaire social. Les intellectuels frustrés au XVIIe siècle," *Annales E.S.C.* 37 (1982): 389–400, available in English as "Time to Understand: The 'Frustrated Intellectuals,'" in Chartier, *Cultural History*, pp. 127–50.

40. Dominique Julia and Jacques Revel, "Les étudiants et leurs études dans la France moderne," in *Les universités européennes du XVIe au XVIIIe siècle. Histoire*

sociale des populations étudiantes, 2 vols., ed. Dominique Julia, Jacques Revel, and Roger Chartier (Paris: Editions de l'Ecole des Hautes Etudes en Sciences Sociales, 1986–89), 2:25–486. All data on French universities used here are taken from this study.

41. Lenard R. Berlanstein, *The Barristers of Toulouse in the Eighteenth Century (1740– 1793)* (Baltimore: Johns Hopkins University Press, 1975).

42. Maurice Gresset, *Gens de justice à Besançon: de la conquête par Louis XIV à la Révolution française, 1674–1789*, 2 vols. (Paris: Bibliothèque Nationale, 1978); Gresset, "L'état d'esprit des avocats comtois à la veille de la révolution," in *Actes du 102e Congrès national des Sociétés Savantes (Limoges, 1977), Section d'Histoire Moderne et Contemporaine* (Paris: Bibliothèque Nationale, 1978), vol. 1, *Contributions à l'histoire des mentalités de 1610 à nos jours*, pp. 85–93.

43. Robert Darnton, "The High Enlightenment and the Low-Life of Literature in Pre-Revolutionary France," *Past and Present* 51 (1971): 81–115; reprinted in Darnton, *The Literary Underground of the Old Regime* (Cambridge, Mass.: Harvard University Press, 1982), pp. 1–40.

CONCLUSION

1. Alphonse Dupront, *Les lettres, les sciences, la religion et les arts dans la société française de la deuxième moitié du dix-huitième siècle* (Paris: Centre de Documentation Universitaire, 1963), p. 21.

FOR FURTHER READING

All reflection on the cultural origins of the French Revolution must begin with a rereading of the "classics": Alexis de Tocqueville, *L'Ancien Régime et la Révolution* (1856; Paris: Gallimard, 1967), available in English as *The Old Régime and the French Revolution*, trans. Stuart Gilbert (Garden City, N.Y.: Doubleday, 1955); Hippolyte Taine, *L'Ancien Régime* (1875; Paris: Robert Laffont, 1986), available in English as *The Ancient Regime*, new rev. ed., trans. John Durand (New York: H. Holt, 1896); and Daniel Mornet, *Les origines intellectuelles de la Révolution française 1715–1787* (1933; reprint, Paris: Armand Colin, 1967).

Two guides provide an entry into the culture of the Enlightenment: Jean Starobinski, *L'invention de la liberté. 1700–1789* (Geneva: Skira, 1964), available in English as *The Invention of Liberty, 1700–1789*, trans. Bernard C. Swift (Geneva: Skira, 1964); Alphonse Dupront, *Les lettres, les sciences, la religion et les arts dans la société française de la deuxième moitié du dix-huitième siècle* (Paris: Centre de Documentation Universitaire, 1963).

For a series of definitions, complementary or contradictory, of French political culture of the eighteenth century, see Jürgen Habermas, *Strukturwandel der Öffentlichkeit. Untersuchungen zu einer Kategorie der bürgerlichen Gesellschaft* (Neuwied: Hermann Luchterhand Verlag, 1962), available in English as *The Structural Transformation of the Public Sphere: An Inquiry into a Category of Bourgeois Society*, trans. Thomas Burger in association with Frederick Lawrence (Cambridge, Mass.: MIT Press, 1989); François Furet, *Penser la Révolution française* (Paris: Gallimard, 1978, revised and corrected 1983), available in English as *Interpreting the French Revolution*, trans. Elborg Forster (Cambridge: Cambridge University Press, Paris: Editions de la Maison des Sciences de l'homme, 1981); Mona Ozouf, *L'homme régénéré. Essais sur la Révolution française* (Paris: Gallimard, 1989); Keith Michael Baker, *Inventing the French Revolution: Essays on French Political Culture in the Eighteenth Century* (New York: Cambridge University Press, 1990). One might add the collaborative work: Keith Michael Baker, ed., *The French Revolution and the Creation of Modern Political Culture*, 2 vols. (Oxford and New York: Pergamon Press, 1987), vol. 1, *The Political Culture of the Old Regime*. On the place of women in the new political culture, see Joan B. Landes, *Women and the Public Sphere in the Age of the French Revolution* (Ithaca: Cornell University Press, 1988).

A fundamental reference, published in German, greatly aids the understanding of commonly held or conflicting meanings in the principal notions of the political vocabulary of the Old Regime: Rolf Reichardt and Eberhard Schmitt, *Handbuch politisch-sozialer Grundbegriffe in Frankreich, 1680–1820,* 10 vols. to date (Munich: R. Oldenbourg Verlag, 1985–).

The long-term evolution of the monarchy as it moved from public ceremonials to the court society can be grasped from two works by Ralph E. Giesey: *The Royal Funeral Ceremony in Renaissance France* (Geneva: Librairie Droz, 1960), and *Cérémonials et puissance souveraine. France, XVe-XVIIe siècles,* trans. Jeannie Carlier. Cahier des Annales 41 (Paris: Armand Colin, 1987); and from the fundamental work of Norbert Elias, *Die Höfische Gesellschaft. Untersuchungen zur Soziologie des Königtums und her höfischen Aristokratie mit einer Enleitung: Soziologie und Geschichtwissenschaft* (Darmstadt and Neuwied: Hermann Luchterhand Verlag, 1969), available in English as *The Court Society,* trans. Edmund Jephcott (Oxford: Blackwell, 1983).

On the theme of the "desacralization" of the king and the monarchy, see Michael Walzer, *Regicide and Revolution: Speeches at the Trial of Louis XVI,* trans. Marian Rothstein (Cambridge: Cambridge University Press, 1974); Dale K. Van Kley, *The Damiens Affair and the Unraveling of the Ancien Régime, 1750–1770* (Princeton: Princeton University Press, 1984); Arlette Farge and Jacques Revel, *Logiques de la foule. L'affaire des enlèvements d'enfants, Paris, 1750* (Paris: Hachette, 1988); Jeffrey W. Merrick, *The Desacralization of the French Monarchy in the Eighteenth Century* (Baton Rouge: Louisiana State University Press, 1990).

For an overall view of the movement that led from the Catholic Reformation to the dechristianization of the Enlightenment, see Jean Delumeau, *Le Catholicisme entre Luther et Voltaire* (Paris: Presses Universitaires de France, Nouvelle Clio 30 bis, 1971), available in English as *Catholicism between Luther and Voltaire: A New View of the Counter-Reformation,* trans. Jeremy Moiser (Philadelphia: Westminster Press, and London: Burns and Oats, 1977); Jacques Le Goff and René Rémond, eds., *Histoire de la France religieuse,* 4 vols. (Paris: Editions du Seuil, 1988), vol. 2, *Du christianisme flamboyant à l'aube des Lumières,* ed. François Lebrun (1988), and vol. 3, *Du roi Très Chrétien à la laïcité républicaine,* ed. Philippe Joutard (forthcoming). Various aspects of the process of dechristianization are elucidated in Michel Vovell, *Piété baroque et déchristianisation en Provence au XVIIIe siècle. Les attitudes devant la mort d'après les clauses des testaments* (Paris: Plon, 1973); Pierre Chaunu, *La mort à Paris. XVIe, XVIIe, XVIIIe siècles* (Paris: Fayard, 1978); and Timothy Tackett, *Religion, Revolution and Regional Culture in Eighteenth-Century France: The Ecclesiastical Oath of 1791* (Princeton: Princeton University Press, 1986). For a broad view, an article that merits consideration is Michel de Certeau, "La formalité des pratiques. Du système religieux à l'éthique des Lumières (XVIIe-XVIIIe)," reprinted in Certeau, *L'Ecriture de l'histoire* (Paris: Gallimard, 1975), pp. 153–212, available in English as *The Writing of History,* trans. Tom Conley (New York: Columbia University Press, 1988).

Advances in literacy are measured in François Furet and Jacques Ozouf, *Lire et écrire. L'alphabétisation des français de Calvin à Jules Ferry* (Paris: Editions du Minuit, 1977), available in English as *Reading and Writing: Literacy in France from Calvin to Jules Ferry* (Cambridge: Cambridge University Press, 1982). For the changes in elementary and secondary education, see Roger Chartier, Marie-Madeleine Compère, and Dominique Julia, *L'éducation en France du XVIe au XVIIIe siècle* (Paris: SEDES, 1976); Willem Frijhoff and Dominique Julia, *Ecole et société dans la France d'Ancien Régime. Quatre exemples: Auch, Avallon, Condom, Gisors* (Paris: Armand Colin, 1975); Marie-Madeleine Compère, *Du collège au lycée (1500–1850). Gé-*

néalogie de l'enseignement secondaire français (Paris: Gallimard, 1985). On university recruitment, see Dominique Julia and Jacques Revel, eds., *Les universités europénnes du XVIe au XVIIIe siècle*. *Histoire sociale des populations étudiantes*, 2 vols. (Paris: Editions de l'Ecole des Hautes Etudes en Sciences Sociales, 1986–1989), vol. 2, *France* (1989). On female education, see Martine Sonnet, *L'éducation des filles au temps des Lumières* (Paris: Cerf, 1987). Harvey Chisick, *The Limits of the Reform in the French Enlightenment: Attitudes toward the Education of the Lower Classes in Eighteenth-Century France* (Princeton: Princeton University Press, 1981), describes Enlightenment resistance to popular education. A general view of work in the historical sociology of education is furnished by Serge Bonin and Claude Langlois, eds., *Atlas de la Révolution française*, 4 vols. (Paris: Editions de l'Ecole des Hautes Etudes en Sciences Sociales, 1987–), vol. 2, *L'enseignement 1760–1815*, ed. Dominique Julia (1987).

The importance and impact of the circulation of prohibited books and pamphlets are studied in the various works of Robert Darnton: *The Business of Enlightenment: A Publishing History of the Encyclopédie, 1775–1800* (Cambridge, Mass.: Belknap Press of Harvard University Press, 1979); *The Literary Underground of the Old Regime* (Cambridge, Mass.: Harvard University Press, 1982); *The Great Cat Massacre and Other Episodes in French Cultural History* (New York: Basic Books, 1984). These works complete and rectify the perspectives proposed in the two volumes of *Livre et société dans la France du XVIIIe siècle*, 2 vols. (Paris and The Hague: Mouton, 1965–1970).

On the periodical press, see Jack R. Censer and Jeremy D. Popkin, eds., *Press and Politics in Pre-Revolutionary France* (Berkeley: University of California Press, 1987); Claude Labrosse and Pierre Rétat, with Henri Duranton, *L'instrument périodique. La fonction de la presse au XVIIIe siècle* (Lyons: Presses Universitaires de Lyon, 1985). A fundamental reference is Jean Sgard, *Bibliographie de la presse classique (1600–1789)* (Geneva: Editions Slatkine, 1984).

For a long-term history of book production and reading practices between the sixteenth and the eighteenth centuries, see Roger Chartier, *Lectures et lecteurs dans la France d'Ancien Régime* (Paris: Le Seuil, 1987), available in English as *The Cultural Uses of Print in Early Modern France*, trans. Lydia G. Cochrane (Princeton: Princeton University Press, 1987); Robert Darnton and Daniel Roche, eds., *Revolution in Print: The Press in France, 1775–1800* (Berkeley: University of California Press, in collaboration with the New York Public Library, 1989). A first survey of studies bearing on publishing in the Old Regime can be found in Henri-Jean Martin and Roger Chartier, gen. eds., *Histoire de l'Edition française*, 4 vols. (Paris: Promodis, 1982–86), vol. 1, *Le livre conquérant. Du Moyen Age au milieu du XVIIe siècle* (1982; reprinted 1989), and vol. 2, *Le livre triomphant. 1660–1830* (1984; reprinted 1990).

Changes affecting the condition of the writer between the seventeenth and the eighteenth centuries are outlined in John Lough, *Writer and Public in France: From the Middle Ages to the Present Day* (Oxford: Clarendon Press, 1978). For more on the same topic, see Alain Viala, *Naissance de l'écrivain. Sociologie de la littérature à l'âge classique* (Paris: Les Editions de Minuit, 1985); the various studies of Robert Darnton in the works already cited; Eric Walter, "Les auteurs et le champ littéraire," *Histoire de l'Edition Française* 2:382–99.

The fundamental study on intellectual sociability in the eighteenth century is Daniel Roche, *Le Siècle des Lumières en province. Académies et académiciens provinciaux, 1680–1789*, 2 vols. (Paris and The Hague: Mouton, 1978). For Freemasonry, see two works that reach contradictory conclusions: Gérard Gayot, *La Franc-Maçonnerie française. Textes et pratiques (XVIIIe–XIXe siècles)* (Paris: Gallimard/Julliard, Collection Archives, 1980); Ran Halévi, *Les loges maçonniques dans la France d'Ancien Régime. Aux origines de la sociabilité démocratique.* Cahier des Annales 40 (Paris: Armand Colin, 1984). On the salons, Carolyn C. Lougee, *Le Paradis des Femmes: Women, Salons, and Social Stratification in Seventeenth-Century France* (Princeton: Princeton University Press, 1976), can be completed, chronologically, by Alan Charles Kors, *D'Holbach's Coterie: An Enlightenment in Paris* (Princeton: Princeton University Press, 1976); Benedetta Craveri, *Madame du Deffand e il suo mondo* (Milan: Adelphi Editori, 1982); and Dena Goodman, "Enlightened Salons: The Convergence of Female and Philosophic Ambitions," *Eighteenth-Century Studies* 22, 3 (1989): 329–50. On the milieux and the practices that founded the Republic of Letters, see Daniel Roche, *Les Républicains des Lettres. Gens de culture et Lumières au XVIIIe siècle* (Paris: Fayard, 1988).

The constitution of a public that was both a social reality and a tribunal of judgment is at the heart of Thomas Crow, *Painters and Public Life in Eighteenth-Century Paris* (New Haven: Yale University Press, 1985); Michael Fried, *Absorption and Theatricality: Painting and Beholder in the Age of Diderot* (Berkeley: University of California Press, 1980); William Weber, "Learned and General Musical Taste in Eighteenth-Century France," *Past and Present* 89 (1980): 58–85.

On Parisian culture, focusing on popular practices, see Daniel Roche, *Le Peuple de Paris. Essai sur la culture populaire* (Paris: Aubier Montaigne, 1981), available in English as *The People of Paris: An Essay in Popular Culture in the Eighteenth Century*, trans. Mark Evans and Gwynne Lewis (Berkeley: University of California Press, 1987); Jacques-Louis Ménétra, *Journal de ma vie. Jacques-Louis Ménétra, compagnon vitrier au 18e siècle*, presented by Daniel Roche (Paris: Montalba, 1982), available in English as *Journal of My Life*, ed. Daniel Roche, trans. Arthur Goldhammer (New York: Columbia University Press, 1986); Robert Isherwood, *Farce and Fantasy, Popular Entertainment in Eighteenth-Century Paris* (New York: Oxford University Press, 1986); Arlette Farge, *La vie fragile. Violence, pouvoirs et solidarités à Paris au XVIIIe siècle* (Paris: Hachette, 1986).

On changes in sensibility during the last decade of the Old Regime, see Robert Darnton's unpublished dissertation, "Trends in Radical Propaganda on the Eve of the French Revolution (1782–1788)" (Oxford University, 1964); Darnton, *Mesmerism and the End of the Enlightenment in France* (1968; reprint, Cambridge, Mass.: Harvard University Press, 1970). On two of the myths most strongly present in the mentality of the French of the eighteenth century, see Steven L. Kaplan, *The Famine Plot Persuasion in Eighteenth-Century France.* Transactions of the American Philosophical Society, n.s. vol. 72, pt. 3 (Philadelphia: American Philosophical Society, 1982); Hans-Jürgen Lüsebrink and Rolf Reichardt, *Die Bastille. Zur Symbolgeschichte von Herrschaft und Freiheit* (Frankfurt-am-Main: Fischer Taschenbuch Verlag, 1990).

There is a wide range of works on the *cahiers de doléances* of 1789. One might read George V. Taylor, "Revolutionary and Nonrevolutionary Content in the *Cahiers* of 1789: An Interim Report," *French Historical Studies* (1972): 479–502; Gilbert Shapiro and Philip Dawson, "Social Mobility and Political Radicalism: The Case of the French Revolution of 1789," in *The Dimensions of Quantitative Research in History*, ed. William O. Aydelotte, Allan G. Bogue, and Robert William Fogel (Princeton: Princeton University Press, 1972), pp. 159–91; Roger Chartier, "Culture, Lumières, doléances: les cahiers de 1789," *Revue d'Histoire Moderne et Contemporaine* 28 (1981): 63–93, available in English as "From Words to Texts. The *Cahiers de doléances* of 1789," in Chartier, *The Cultural Uses of Print in Early Modern France*, pp. 110–44; John Markoff, "Some Effects of Literacy in Eighteenth-Century France," *Journal of Interdisciplinary History* 17, 2 (1986): 311–33.

Relations between the private sphere of existence and public space are approached, in various ways, by Reinhart Koselleck, *Kritik und Krise. Eine Studie zur Pathogenese der bürgerlichen Welt* (Fribourg: Verlag Karl Albert, 1959; Frankfurt-am-Main: Suhrkamp, 1976), available in English as *Critique and Crisis: Enlightenment and the Pathogenesis of Modern Society* (Cambridge: MIT Press, 1988); Arlette Farge and Michel Foucault, *Le désordre des familles. Lettres de cachet des Archives de la Bastille* (Paris: Gallimard/Julliard, Collection Archives, 1982); Philippe Ariès and Georges Duby, eds., *Histoire de la vie privée*, 4 vols. (Paris: Editions du Seuil, 1986), vol. 3, *De la Renaissance aux Lumières*, ed. Roger Chartier (1986), available in English as *A History of Private Life* (Cambridge, Mass.: Belknap Press of Harvard University Press, 1987–1988), vol. 3, *Passions of the Renaissance*, trans. Arthur Goldhammer; Sarah Maza, "Le tribunal de la nation: les mémoires judiciaires à la fin de l'Ancien Régime," *Annales E.S.C.* 42 (1987): 73–90; Maza, "Domestic Melodrama as Political Ideology: The Case of the Comte de Sanois," *American Historical Review* 94, 5 (1989): 1249–65.

INDEX

ABOUT THE AUTHOR
Roger Chartier is Director of Studies at the Center for Historical
Research, Ecole des Hautes Etudes en Sciences Sociales, Paris.
He is the author of *Cultural History: Between Practices and
Representations*, *The Cultural Uses of Print in Early Modern France*,
and *The Culture of Print*, and the editor of volume 3 of *The
History of Private Life*.

Library of Congress Cataloging-in-Publication Data
Chartier, Roger, 1945–
The cultural origins of the French Revolution / Roger Chartier ;
translated by Lydia G. Cochrane.
p.   cm. — (Bicentennial reflections on the French Revolution)
Includes bibliographical references and index.
ISBN 0-8223-0981-5. — ISBN 0-8223-0993-9 (pbk.)
1. France—History—Revolution, 1789–1799—Causes.
2. Politics and culture—France—History—18th century.
3. Enlightenment—France.   4. Violence—France—History—
18th century.   I. Title.   II. Series.
DC138.C48   1991
944.04—dc20   90-24404 CIP